RENA'S PROMISE

RENA'S PROMISE

A Story of Sisters in Auschwitz

Rena Kornreich Gelissen

WITH

Heather Dune Macadam

BEACON PRESS

BOSTON

Beacon Press
25 Beacon Street
Boston, Massachusetts 02108-2892

Beacon Press books
are published under the auspices of
the Unitarian Universalist Association of Congregations.

"The Story (for Rena)" appears by permission
of its author, Annette Allen.

99   8 7 6 5 4

Text design by Boskydell Studio
Composition by Wilsted & Taylor

Library of Congress Cataloging-in-Publication Data
Gelissen, Rena Kornreich, 1920–
Rena's promise : a story of sisters in Auschwitz / Rena Kornreich
Gelissen with Heather Dune Macadam.
        p.   cm.
Includes bibliographical references.
ISBN 0-8070-7070-X (cloth)
ISBN 0-8070-7071-8 (paper)
1. Auschwitz (Poland : Concentration camp)   2. Holocaust, Jewish
(1939–1945)—Personal narratives.   3. Gelissen, Rena Kornreich,
1920– .   I. Macadam, Heather Dune.   II. Title.
D805.P7G45   1995
940.53'18'094386—dc20   95-10359
CIP

Dear Mama and Papa:
This book is for you. For fifty years
I've been telling you this story in my mind.
Now it's finally written down
and I won't have to tell it anymore.
Love, Rena

And for Danka:
Without you there would
be no story.

It goes on burning in the bones,
in the brain, years after, smoke
still rising behind the walls, even on
May second, a birthday to liberate
all others. In Poland, though the stone
well-water near Tylicz never ceases,
it never soothes the smoldering,
nor the fearful dreams fueling sleep.

For months a redwood tree can flame
the fire that consumes it, burning
a black scar to its core. Within the
burnt sepulchre, as if a miracle, seeds
bearing a young tree begin to green. Let
us sift the ashes for new life, for the story
forged in suffering; where the birth into
language is as terrifying as fire or love.

Annette Allen
The Story (for Rena)

CONTENTS

PROLOGUE

I touch the scar on my left forearm, just below the elbow. I had the tattoo surgically removed. There were so many people who didn't know and so many questions: "What do those numbers mean?" "Is that your address?" "Is that your phone number?"

What was I supposed to say—"That was my name for three years and forty-one days"?

One day a kind doctor offered to remove it for me. "This is not charity," he assured me. "It is the least I can do as an American Jew. You were there, I was not."

So I chose to have the questions excised from my arm, but not my mind—that can never be erased. The piece of skin the doctor surgically removed rests in a jar of formaldehyde which has turned the flesh to an eerie green. The tattoo has probably faded by now, I haven't checked. I need no reminders. I know who I am. I know what I was.

I was on the first Jewish transport to Auschwitz. I was number 1716.

—*Rena Gelissen*
January 1994

Rena's Passage through Wartime Europe

TYLICZ

I drive steadily uphill into the North Carolina mountains on a Saturday morning in January to meet a woman I have only spoken to twice—Rena. We've been putting off this meeting for two months now, but with the holidays finally over we have no more excuses.

My thoughts tumble across one another; I'm uneasy about the task I'm about to undertake. I hope that I can help Rena tell her story without either of us drowning in the undertow of painful memories, but I'm concerned. Since I was a child I've read stories and biographies of Holocaust survivors. I've worked as a volunteer in a hospice grief counseling center, and I've been personally involved with people who suffer from post-traumatic stress disorder, but I'm no psychologist. I'm afraid that I'll come up wanting in her eyes because I am not Jewish, because I am not Polish, because I am American, because I am young. Maybe I'm not the best person for this job.

The first time we spoke on the phone I was cooking pierogies and kielbasa for dinner.

"Are you Polish?" she asked excitedly.

"No," I told her, "I just love pierogi. We used to eat them at an all-night diner called the Kiev, on the Lower East Side in New York."

"I think I'd like that place."

I laughed. "I'm sure you would."

Rena's house lies in a small valley, with a pasture full of grazing cows behind it; trussed across the horizon, hemming us in on all sides, are the voluptuous rolling hills of the Blue Ridge Mountains. I try to organize my thoughts and my book bag before stepping out of the car. It is a glorious day. The air is cooler up here, but the sun is shining and the wind, although it has a nip of winter, has none of its cruelty.

Inside, I'm greeted warmly by her husband, John. We shake hands and he calls Rena.

"You're so tall!" She smiles as we greet each other for the first time.

"I am?" I laugh. "I'm the short one in my family."

"I'm the tall one in mine." Her eyes twinkle.

"Heather, come see Rena's linen closets!" John waves to me.

"Jan, no!" She starts to reprimand him in Dutch, then, for my benefit, adds in English, "You're embarrassing me."

"You spent all day yesterday straightening them, at least let Heather see your hard work. How else will she know?"

"That's not true," she says, aside. "They're always this neat." Showing me the beautiful linens she's collected over the years, she says quietly, "I didn't have any linens or heirlooms from my family. So I collected my own. I've stayed up til three in the morning scrubbing a stain out that somebody else thought was impossible to remove."

"There. Now Heather knows how neat and clean you are. Heather, are you going to clean out your linen closets when we come to visit?" John teases.

"I don't have linen closets." I laugh again. "You'll be lucky if I dust."

Rena takes my arm. "Don't you dare clean for me! I clean too much. When I get nervous I can't stop."

In the basement, where we will spend many hours over the next year exhuming the past and embracing ghosts, there is a gas fire flickering. The room has a rosy glow from the pink sheers she has hung over the windows.

I'm led from the pink room with its fire into an adjoining room where the family photos are on display. The wall is divided into two sections: the Gelissen family, from Holland, is on the left; the Korn-reich family, from Poland, is on the right. In the middle are Rena and John's wedding photo and pictures of their children.

Rena tells me that she wouldn't have any prewar photos if her el-dest sister, Gertrude, hadn't emigrated to America before the war. She shows me her mother's wedding portrait. A Victorian lace collar wraps high up her neck and her hair is piled so gracefully on top of her head that one cannot tell she's wearing a wig.

"What was her name?" I ask.

"Sara." Rena kisses her hand, touches the face in the photo. "You know, when we moved here I thought to myself, I've had my num-ber removed, no one here knows me, I can leave it all behind. That's when I decided I'm not going to talk about it ever again. It's not worth it."

"Why did you tell Corrine?" I ask her, naming our only mutual friend.

"I don't know!" She laughs. "It was the strangest thing." Her eyes are wide as she recounts the story that has led to this meeting.

"I dialed a wrong number but the voice on the other end of the line sounded familiar. 'Is this Corrine from the tennis club?' I say. 'Is this Rena?' she asks."

Rena does the voices, acting out their conversation as if it were occurring in front of me.

"I was calling somebody else but got her instead. We both thought it was so funny, because she'd been out of town for several weeks. 'How're you doing?' I say. 'I haven't seen you in a while.' 'I've been going through a tough time,' she tells me.

"She said something about her past being painful and the next thing I know I'm saying, 'I know about that. I had bad things happen to me, too. I was in Auschwitz.' I told her I'd been writing my story for fifty years in my head but I couldn't get it on paper. 'I need someone with kind eyes to sit across from me, listen to the whole thing, and write it down for me.' And she says, 'I know just the person.'

"And here you are! All because of a wrong number." She pats my knee. "Did I tell you what I thought the very first time we spoke on the phone?" I shake my head. "That you eating pierogi was a sign that you're the right person for my story." She laughs and I join her.

We settle on the couch in front of the fire. Quietly, I click on my tape recorder; it's time to start.

My original approach to interviewing Rena about her story was to get her to start at the beginning and go to the end, from point A to point B. I thought it was a good plan; I would listen with my eyes, my ears, and the prickling of my skin—she would talk, I would write. But the mind does not move linearly, it plays hopscotch and jump rope with our memories. Point A was not as simple as I thought, and somewhere during our year of excavating, sharing, and writing, point B became Z.

"I have a lot of books on the Holocaust." She jumps up. "You want to see them?"

"Not now. Let's talk first."

"Okay," She looks at me warily, resignedly, before sitting down. I feel like a dentist about to extract a tooth.

"Where do you want me to start?"

"Auschwitz?" I ask.

She looks disappointed. "Wouldn't you rather hear about my childhood first? I had a wonderful childhood. I could tell you about my sister, Danka, and Mama and Papa." She looks hopeful and, realizing my mistake, I nod willingly.

She launches into her family history with relish, making sure that I understand the lifestyle of Orthodox Jews and diagraming the family dynamics for me. She speaks quickly; animated and alive, her hands gesture, her eyes smile.

Rena's father, Chaim, believed that a woman's place was to bear the children, keep a kosher kitchen, and know how to pray. But Rena's mother was determined that her girls know Hebrew. "I'm not going to have my girls embarrassed like I was, when they get married in temple, because they can't read from the prayer book." She made such a fuss that in order to placate her, the elders of the synagogue decided that in this one instance they would allow Sara Kornreich's daughter to attend the cheder, the Hebrew school for boys, after her regular school day. Her mother paid the melamed, the teacher, with eggs, butter, and milk so that Rena could sit on one side of the room (the boys sat on the other side) and learn Hebrew. After class Rena would take the lessons home to teach Danka.

"What am I doing?" Rena exclaims. "I'm starting in the middle without the beginning!" We backtrack.

Rena was born in Tylicz, Poland, in 1920, when Sara was in her late thirties and Chaim in his late forties. The family was split between the two children of their youth and the two children of their later years. Gertrude, the oldest, was sixteen years older than Rena. Then there was Zosia, who was two years younger than Gertrude. Danka, the youngest, was born when Rena was just two years old.

I remember looking in Danka's cradle with Mama. She was so delicate, so small. When she was just a few months old she got the croup. It was awful. She coughed and coughed all day and all night, then there was no more coughing. The silence was terrible.

Mama began to lament. I had never seen her so distraught. Slowly, she covered Danka's head with a white sheet and her baby blanket.

The stillness in our house was so sad . . . I was only three, but I remember wanting to wipe away Mama's tears and I prayed to God in heaven to bring my baby sister back to Mama.

Then there was a wail from beneath the blanket. First there was terror—a ghost, an apparition, something unknowable had entered our house. But the wailing did not stop. Mama ran to

Danka's side, threw back the blanket, and there she was, red-faced and breathing and not at all happy about being covered up.

Our baby was alive!

From that time on, even though I was just two years older than Danka, I was the big one and Danka was the little one. She was always more fragile and Mama fussed over her because she had come back from death's portal. "Watch the little one," Mama would say. "Take care of the baby." It was my favorite job.

Rena could speak all day about Tylicz and her childhood. It wasn't just the memories she treasured, but the closeness of the community, her Jewish and Gentile friends, and the simplicity of their life.

The underlying question in my mind when we first started talking was, How did Rena keep her mind, heart, and spirit intact for three years and forty-one days of virtual slavery in Nazi concentration camps? At first she seemed to want to avoid talking about it, preferring to describe her childhood, her family, and the friends she grew up with. After our first weekend together we had barely touched on Auschwitz, skirting the issue like nervous thoroughbreds. Still I waited and listened, looking for the pattern, and perhaps the purpose, behind it all—there was a reason she was telling me her whole story and gradually I realized that in her own way she was answering my question.

When we were growing up I had a crush on Andrzej Garbera and he had a crush on me. I was just five years old when Andrzej pushed a wagon over the mud pies we'd made. Needless to say all our hard work was ruined and, being a boy, he didn't care in the least, preferring instead to laugh at our misfortune. His sole purpose, as a boy, seemed to be to torment us girls. He used to throw snowballs at us on our way to school, but then one day he was not throwing snowballs or being a general irritation anymore, instead he just said, "Hi."

So I said "Hi" back and that was the beginning of Andrzej and me. . .

She pauses, looking across the room as if someone were standing there in front of her, someone I cannot see. Leaning forward, she smooths the cloth on the coffee table, making sure that the edges lie perfectly flat and at right angles to the table.

She switches topics and begins to speak tenderly of the holidays.

Frania was one of my best friends. She'd come over to our house to celebrate Sukkot, the harvest festival. We'd build an open-air shelter which we hung with little baskets with chestnuts or apples in them, colorful rings of paper, and nuts from the roof, which was made of tree branches. Then at Christmastime, Mama would let us go over to Frania's house and help her family decorate the Christmas tree.

My favorite holiday was Yom Kippur, because on that day everyone forgave each other and would hug and make up. I loved the whole idea of wiping the slate clean and beginning new and fresh. Being hungry was all in my mind. I would dawdle on the way home just to stretch out my fast as long as possible, eating my dinner slowly and thinking about how my hunger was already gone. There was a sense of accomplishment in fasting all day, and a sense of peace after the Day of Atonement.

When Zosia, Rena's second-oldest sister, got married, she begged their father to let her keep a little bit of her hair. Rena questioned the reason married women shaved their heads. It was a promise not to be attractive to other men, Mama explained, an acknowledgment of commitment to one's husband.

Every few weeks Mama would take off her wig and I would shave her head, as is customary in Orthodox homes. With the washbasin and Papa's clippers I guided the teeth across her scalp, careful not to catch the delicate skin with the sharp teeth of the clippers. Mama would close her eyes as if in meditation, and I'd take that moment to study the serenity in her face. Then I'd wipe her scalp as if it were porcelain china. It was so clean and shiny, soft as a baby.

She would let her eyes remain shut for just a few seconds after

I was done, then she'd call out to Papa so I could shave his head. As they changed places their eyes would lock together for an instant and Mama would smile affectionately.

I dreamt of the day that I would have my head shaved as a solemn vow to my husband. It was a rite of passage that we feared yet anticipated. Still, like Zosia, I worried about being ugly. To lose one's hair was not such a wonderful thing, but to be married, that was what we yearned for, to be married like Mama and Papa.

Every time Papa passed Mama he reached out and touched her. This is how it was with them—silent greetings and sweet hellos, a hand patting her gently between the shoulder blades.

The room is bright as the sun strikes its noonday pose. Hoping Rena won't notice, I glance at my watch quickly. We've been working for less than an hour.

"Am I confusing you?" she asks. "I don't think I'm doing this right. I should've written everything down for you so it would be clear. I'm jumping around so much—I keep thinking you know everything already, but you don't."

"You're doing fine, Rena," I assure her while scanning my notes for names I've jotted down through her discourse. There is one name that stands out from the rest, but I'm not sure why. Maybe it was the way her eyes shifted into space that caused my elbow to tingle. I've scratched a star beside his name. "Tell me about Andrzej. Who was he?"

"Andrzej Garbera was the first boy I ever . . . I have his picture in one of my books. You want to see it?" She darts into the storage area, returning with an armful of books and notepads. "I've been writing everything down for years. Anytime I remember a date or a name I write it down. It's in Polish, but maybe it'll help us as we go along."

I scan her notes and the titles of the books she's placed on the table: The Holocaust Encyclopedia, The Abandonment of the Jews,

Anus Mundi. *I have a lot of research to do and I know I will read these and many other books in the course of this project, but not today.*

"Now I've gone and made a mess." She starts to rearrange the books according to size as I open one of them and look at a photograph of people in a forest clearing. A small girl, squeezing her little hands in front of her chest, stares into the camera. I try to read the caption, but my eyes keep blurring—I know what it says: the child is dead, all of the people in the clearing are dead. I feel completely overwhelmed.

"This is Andrzej . . ." She shows me his photograph in a book of Polish World War II heroes. "It doesn't do him justice." She sighs.

"The marketplace in Tylicz was the center of our world and from there everything was downhill," Rena tells me.

The kosher butcher and the Gentiles' butcher stood on the avenue, as well as the cheese shop and the city hall. Here the Garbera family lived, next door to Rena's close friends Erna and Fela Drenger. Danka and Rena spent many evenings at Erna and Fela's house. Dina, Erna and Fela's cousin, was also there. Playing dominoes and acting grown up, the girls would sit in the parlor confiding their dreams to each other.

One cold winter evening as Danka and Rena stepped outside to go home, Andrzej greeted them. "I've been waiting to bring you both home. The hill is very icy and I wouldn't want you to fall and hurt yourselves."

After that night it became a habit for Andrzej to wait outside of Erna and Fela's and walk Rena home. She was never completely sure, though, whether or not she would hear Andrzej's voice from the shadows saying, "Servus, Rena. Can I walk you home tonight?"

One spring night as they ambled home, for no reason at all he took her hand. Rena does the voices for me again.

"There's no ice on the road tonight, Andrzej," I told him.

"No, there isn't." But he didn't let go. The sound of water dripping, unceasing, into the stone well drew us toward the side of the lane. He slowed down as if he were looking at something and then he murmured my name very softly. "Rena?"

"Yes?" I looked up into his face, and there, beside the village well, Andrzej Garbera stole a kiss from my lips. There was no walking from that point on; I ran the whole way home.

Mama was waiting for me at the door of our farmhouse with her lantern lit and bobbing in the dark.

"Rena!" I hear her calling my name.

"I'm coming, Mama."

"Where have you been? It's late. Come inside."

"I was studying at Erna and Fela's," I answer, wiping my feet.

"Studying, eh?" She pushed my hair back from my face, looking into my eyes. I wonder if she can read the truth in them. "Go get ready for bed."

"Yes, Mama." I kiss her cheek. She smells so good.

I notice, as Rena speaks, that she dissolves from past into present tense and then back again, wavering between the worlds of "was" and "is" as if there were no definitive separation between the two.

"Her skin was so soft." She inhales. "I can still smell her as if she were standing right next to me. A blend of challah and vanilla extract, that is how Mama smelled." Her eyes wince shut as if the breath itself were cutting her deep inside.

Admiring myself in front of the mirror, I brush my hair for one hundred strokes while imagining that Andrzej is stooping for a kiss. Again and again I remember how his lips felt on mine. My heart races.

"I have been kissed." I confide this enormous secret to my reflection. We blush.

With my nightdress on I crawl between cool, clean, cotton sheets and wait for Mama to come tuck me in. "Rena, you are practically glowing. What have you been up to?"

"Nothing, Mama. It's just such a beautiful night." I smile in the darkness.

"Sweet sleep." She kisses me good-night.

A tiny pit of sadness that my secret can never be shared overcomes me. I have grown up going to public school with Gentiles and being taught by Catholic teachers despite the fact that we are strict Orthodox Jews. Andrzej and I have played together since we were children, but he is still a Gentile. Nothing can come of his kiss, I know that.

I knew that.

Through their preteen years Rena and Andrzej flirted quietly. As time went on, though, Andrzej, who was three years older than Rena, started attending high school in Krynica, a larger town about seven kilometers away, and they saw each other rarely. Rena was thirteen when she met him in the marketplace again. Happy to see each other, they talked about their favorite books and subjects in school. Rena made sure she maintained the proper distance away from him at all times, as she'd been instructed, but she forgot to watch the time. It was almost dark when a member of the synagogue passed by on his way to temple and saw her. It was prohibited for Rena to speak with a Gentile boy, or any boy for that matter, without a chaperone, and the man reminded her of that before going to inform her father of her conduct.

Rena hurried down the hill alone to face the wrath of her father. Her mother wept and her father sternly forbade her to have anything to do with Andrzej ever again.

She rarely saw and didn't speak with Andrzej for several years. Then, one night when she was fifteen, he walked her home and told her he was leaving for Krakow to join the military. Rena would miss their chance meetings, but he promised to think of a way to write to her without her parents knowing.

A few weeks later Andrzej's sister, Hania, met Rena in the mar-

ketplace and when no one was watching, slipped her a letter from Krakow. It took Rena quite a few days to get up the courage to write him back, but finally she answered, and from that time on, either Hania or Andrzej's mother would post her letters, so that no one in the village would know they were corresponding.

Rena worked for two summers in Krynica as an apprentice to a seamstress, dating a few boys and going to picture shows. At seventeen, she was feeling very grown up and was starting to think about her future when Andrzej wrote:

Dear Rena,

I just got my officer's stripes and am no longer living in the barracks on the base. I am now entitled to an apartment in the city. I've enclosed enough money for the train to Krakow. Would you come to marry me? You can do anything you want to with the Jewish religion. You can bring up the children in the Jewish faith. I will buy you a silver candelabra so that you may light the candles on Friday night in our home just like your mother. If this is not acceptable to your parents, I will have myself circumcised and accept the Jewish religion. I have loved you since the first day I saw you when we were children. If you love me as well, why should we not be happy? If you would come to be my wife I would be the happiest man in the whole of Poland.

Rena longed to marry and raise a family. In one way, Andrzej's proposal was a dream come true, but she knew marriage with him was an impossibility. She wrote back:

Dear Andrzej,

My parents do not want you to convert to Judaism, even that would not be enough. You must be born Jewish. I thought you understood the strict rules of our faith and our people. I'm sorry if I have led you on in any way. For me to marry a Gentile would destroy my parents. They would mourn for me as if I had died and then treat me as if I were no longer their daughter. It is impossible for you and me to be together. Despite my feelings

for you, I could not bear never seeing my family again. Here is
your money back. I am sorry, but I cannot marry you.

Love, Rena

"To tell you the truth, I didn't even discuss Andrzej's letter with
my parents," Rena tells me.

"Why not?" I ask.

"It would have been devastating to them. I had to marry a Jewish
man, preferably Orthodox, and I would never have done anything
to upset them."

I wonder—if Rena had married Andrzej, would she have been
spared Auschwitz? I find that I cannot help trying to rewrite history.
The more I read and study about Auschwitz and about the Holocaust, the more she weaves her tale for me, pulling me into the warp
of her childhood, the more I find myself wanting to save her from
the inevitable. I want her to see the dangers lurking in the neighboring country of Slovakia; I want her and her family to join Gertrude in America before the war breaks out; I want someone—anyone—to save Rena and her sister Danka.

"Are you tired?" she asks. "You look tired."

"A little. How are you?"

"Oh, I could go on forever." I believe her when she says this, but
I also wonder if it's wise to continue. I decide we should take a
break and start again in the morning. We eat pierogies and kielbasa
for dinner and talk late into the night. The couch we've been sitting
on all day pulls out into a bed. Looking at the other photos from Peter Hellman's book The Auschwitz Album and reading the narrative
of the survivor, I drift off in front of the fire to a deep but dreamless
sleep.

The next morning, with the sun shining in through her rose-col-
ored curtains and coffee steaming in front of me, Rena confesses, "I
didn't sleep at all last night."

Over time our relationship has transformed. We've become
closer and often call one another just to chat, because we miss each

*other. One night she says, "You don't have to bear me by yourself,
Heather. I can share your burdens, too, you know. I just want you to
know that—you're not alone."*

*I have tried to foster a sense of trust between us, but we pro-
gressed beyond that phase quickly. It's as if we've known from the
beginning that we are friends. She still tries to protect me at times,
but I am insistent that she does not have to endure Auschwitz alone
anymore. It's not that she hasn't had her family and friends to support her, but I believe she tries to insulate us from her truth—as if
she's afraid that she's too heavy, too painful. There are times when
I know there's more she's not telling me. Then there are times when
her words collapse under the weight of her tears, and I know that
only silence can speak for Rena.*

*"Did I ever tell you about my dream?" she asks me on the phone
one day.*

"No." I grab a pen and a pencil.

I used to have this dream in Holland, after the war, every night
. . . Danka is in danger. Sometimes they order her to jump, sometimes they are pushing her into the pit. Always I am standing
there watching.

"Danka!" I scream, running past them, grabbing her hand just
before she plummets out of reach. Standing on the edge of an
abyss, her fate completely dependent upon what strength I have
left, I stare into the void below us that they forced us to dig. How
did we ever dig a hole so deep that there is no bottom?

"Rena, help me." Her voice is muted by our palpitating hearts.
"Please, don't let go of me."

"I won't," I assure her. My muscles quiver. Every twitch and
spasm threatens to betray my promise. My body tenses. This is no
dream. "Don't give up, Danka." Shuddering, my nails dig into her
flesh, determined to cling onto life.

From behind us Andrzej appears. He takes our hands in his
powerful grip and lifts her effortlessly out of the pit. I am so relieved to see him that I cannot speak. He smiles at me, vanishing

before my eyes. "Andrzej!" I call out his name. There is no answer. He is gone.

"If you die before me"—I hear Danka's voice—"no one is going to cry more than me. But if I die before you, even if there's no one left in the world to mourn for me, I know that you will weep over my grave."

Panting like a wild animal trapped by hunters, I wake. Chilled by internal night fears, uncertain of where I am or who I am, I struggle against the sheets entangling my arms and legs. I search the night table for a candle to light, but the room remains dark. My name has been erased from my mind. I am a number once more.

Rena shows me the scar on her forearm where her number used to be; there's a small dot of grey-blue ink still imbedded in her skin. "That was the bottom part of the one," she tells me.

It is the color of faded black.

SLOVAKIA

Only one family had a radio in Tylicz. In the afternoon they would open the window and everyone would gather outside to hear the news of the world and listen while Adolf Hitler made strange and fervored speeches threatening the Poles, the Jews and anyone not Aryan. The Kornreichs were concerned about the sudden annexation of Slovakia with Germany, in 1938, because Sara and Chaim both had brothers who lived just across the border, in Bardejov. But the anguish of Andrzej's secret proposal made the rest of the world seem far less significant to Rena.

Germany and Russia made a pact between them; with trepidation the Kornreich family listened to the news and Poland itself trembled with fear. While Europe held its breath to see if appeasement would work, Poland called up its young men to join the army and defend their country; it had been divided too many times not to take the threat of Stalin and Hitler seriously.

On September 1, 1939, Germany invaded Poland. "And there was no more innocence in our lives," Rena tells me. Lulled into the belief that the world would help them, Poland was plundered. Tylicz was immediately transformed from a sleepy little border town into a strategic position within occupied Poland; German border guards, watchdogs, and guns were everywhere, and the Nuremberg Laws were put into effect. A man named Joseph, from the synagogue, was appointed as head of a new organization, the Judenrat, or Jewish Council, and was ordered to deliver the names of all the young Jewish people living in Tylicz. Within the first week of the Nazi invasion, Jews were forced to wear armbands at all times, with the star of David embroidered on them in blue. They could no longer buy food from Gentiles, hire Gentiles to work for them, or cross the Polish border (they were still allowed to trade goods with Gentiles). Any Jew or Gentile disobeying German law, it was proclaimed, would be considered a traitor and punished by death.

Danka and Rena, along with other young Jewish men and women, were assigned to clean the army quarters, polish shoes, scrub floors, and do anything else the Germans ordered them to do. For years a poor Gentile woman had come to the Kornreichs' house every Sabbath morning to light the fire and reheat the meal Mama had prepared the day before. Under these new regulations she was no longer allowed into their house or to do any work for the Kornreichs. She cried when she came to say good-bye, and the Kornreichs, along with the other Jews in Tylicz, in order not to break Orthodox law, refused to light a fire on the Sabbath. Papa and the other Jewish farmers, unable to hire anyone to help, resorted to working overtime to harvest their crops. Danka and Rena worked from first light to late in the night, dividing their chores between the Germans and their own farm.

Since there was no law against trading services for goods, Zosia's sewing was used to trade for butter, cheese, and flour. There were still Gentile farmers who would do business with their Jewish neighbors because Tylicz was a close-knit community and the Germans were not respected, they were only feared.

The Kornreichs hadn't heard anything from Zosia's husband, Nathan, since the start of the German occupation, when he had joined the Polish army along with the rest of the able-bodied men in the country. Then, in October, a card came in the mail with a Russian postmark. Zosia handed it to Mama, folded her hands in front of her

face, as if she were saying the Sabbath prayer, and waited for the
news.

Mama cleared her throat. "Dear Family. It is very cold where I
am. I love you all. Nathan."

They stared at the floor as Zosia sobbed, "He must be in Siberia."

Herschel, Zosia's young son, became very ill and needed an operation, but the new regulations did not allow Jews to see doctors.
The Slovakian Jews were being treated far less harshly than the Polish Jews, probably because of the annexation of Slovakia by Germany; they were allowed to work and earn money, they weren't being forced to wear stars, and most importantly for Herschel, they
could be treated by doctors.

"If we can get across the border it shouldn't be too difficult to get
to Uncle Jacob Schützer's in Bardejov. At least Herschel can get
treatment there," Zosia explained. "Who knows where Nathan is
now or if he will ever be able to return home? In Slovakia I can work
in Uncle Jacob's dress shop until I find work of my own, and when
I'm settled I'll send for little Ester."

"I will send a note to my brother that you are coming," Mama
said, "and pray for your safety and joy."

From the Schützer's home in Slovakia Zosia wrote every week,
sending her letters with Gentile friends from Tylicz, who could still
cross the border and trade in the marketplace in Bardejov. Herschel's operation went well, one letter said. The family's prayers
had been answered.

A few weeks later she wrote that she had been offered a position
as a housekeeper in Bratislava. Bratislava was all the way across
Slovakia, on the border with Austria. Zosia moved, and her letters
became less frequent.

Meanwhile, Danka and Rena worked long, hard days and often
stayed up as late as four-thirty in the morning because they'd taken
over Zosia's sewing business. Rena was becoming well known as
the local seamstress, and one Sunday while she was busy working
at her sewing machine she heard a knock at the window.

She was shocked to see an Austrian officer waiting outside. He asked her if she could make two pillowcases for him. It was a question and not a command, which seemed strange in and of itself. Rena told him that she could make the pillowcases, and a week later Officer Joksch came to pick them up, complimented her on her craftsmanship, ordered two more, and handed her a few coins for her work.

Rena ran through the house to show her mother the coins. "An Austrian officer paid me for the pillowcases!" she exclaimed.

Mama stared at the money in wonderment. "You are a miracle, Rena. Even in all this hardship, you are able to inspire kindness in those who would normally treat us with cruelty." She hugged her daughter and hid the coins in the teapot where all of their valuables were stored.

In early November it was ordered that the Torah, the Talmud, and all the holy books must be burned, and all the men were forced to come to the temple with their tomes. To a people who are not only deeply religious but scholarly as well, this command was unimaginable. The temple was closed for good and all the books harbored within its walls were tossed into the street. The women and children waited at home as the Jewish men of Tylicz gathered outside their synagogue. Rena, Danka, and Mama sat on the steps of their farmhouse waiting and praying that Papa would return.

"Line up!" A tall German officer barked his orders. In a daze, Chaim Kornreich and the other men moved alongside one another before the mound of kindling and manuscripts.

"It is against our policy for any Jew to grow these ridiculous curls or beards. Every man in this line must be shaved or shot!" Brandishing scissors like street-hardened youths carrying switchblades, the soldiers ordered the men to remove their hats and then systematically began to sever their earlocks and beards.

A German SS man lit a torch, and in moments angry sparks began *to burn the pages of their heritage. "You are no longer allowed to pray or to enter the temple for any reason whatsoever!" The latest list of proclamations was read over the raging pyre. "It is against the law to worship on the Jewish Sabbath, and to light candles on Friday night." Helpless, Chaim Kornreich and the others watched their history devoured by flames.*

A few days later, Rena heard Officer Hans Joksch's familiar voice at her window. She handed him the pillowcases he'd requested, careful to keep her eyes lowered in respect; she nodded politely to another officer standing next to him.

"Rena, invite us into your home," Officer Joksch said.

His request turned everything upside down. Who was I to say no? He seemed like a nice man, but he was endangering our lives by entering under our roof. I could not help but suspect him of some other motive, but who would have thought what his true reason would be?

Rena ran through the house to warn her parents. Clasping her hands over her eyes, Mama prayed, "Good Lord, my Lord, protect us." Then, taking her place in the parlor, she composed herself with unnerving stillness.

Officer Joksch and his friend acted casually and asked if there were a gramophone in the house.

"No." Rena spoke quickly, too quickly.

"I bet you are a good dancer, Rena."

"So-so." She stared at the floor.

"Well, if my friend whistles something would you dance with me?"

She glanced at her parents' ashen faces. His friend started to whistle a tango as Officer Joksch took Rena's hands and they began shuffle awkwardly around the parlor.

I was so nervous, wondering what he would do if I missed even a step, but I tried to look as if I were having a good time.

His friend whistled until he ran out of breath and spittle, and Officer Joksch said, "You dance beautifully, Rena."

I could barely get the words *Danke schön* out of my mouth, it was so dry.

"Nein, nein, Fraulein. Thank *you*. You have made this day truly memorable to me and I will never forget your good faith." He bade us good evening—without shaking hands, of course, but still very nicely—paid for the pillowcases, and left.

Mama wept quietly, wringing her hands. Papa did not speak.

Oh, my God, how I was shaking. I don't know why I didn't stumble or how my knees didn't just buckle completely under me. Then it occurred to me that maybe I was a good dancer.

It was Sabbath, and standing in front of the mirror with her dirndl on, Rena began to plait her long hair into a single braid down her back. Even if they couldn't go to temple they tried to carry on as if everything were normal because in their hearts they could still worship. Despite what had been decreed, some of the elders of the synagogue had decided to meet anyway, but no sooner had the prayers begun than soldiers barged in.

"You people are disobeying orders and for this you will be punished." One of the officers barked commands, pushing the men against a wall. *"Today we will teach you a lesson! And today's lesson shall be that every time you meet, one of you will be taken down to the river and shot. Take him!"*

Two soldiers dragged a man out the door with them, and that man was my father.

"Rena! Rena!" Joseph, the head of the Judenrat, yelled as he ran toward our house. Running to the window, my hands tangled in my braid, I leaned out to ask what was wrong.

"They have your father and they're going to kill him!" Joseph's voice quaked. "Run to the river and stop them before it's too late!"

My feet flew down the steps before he could breathe another word. "Fly, Rena!" His voice chased me down the road.

I was barefoot. My hair was not braided. I didn't even have on my white armband with the blue star of David, which I was always supposed to wear. This was how I ran down the dirt road toward the river—my hair heavy against my back, falling in my face, clinging to my neck—racing across the Carpathian Hills, every step a prayer to our Lord to save my father. I did not feel the stones cutting into my flesh. I did not see the trail of blood in the dirt as I ran.

There were many bodies found along the river in the mornings, because to kill a Jew was no crime, so I knew exactly where to run. What had Joseph been thinking, though, sending me to save Papa? I don't care to admit this, but the truth is, at that moment all I could think about was having to tell Mama, I stood right there and watched them kill Papa—there was nothing I could do. The thought of her pain-stricken face was more than I could bear, so while I ran I tried to come up with a plan that would save me from having to tell Mama that Papa was dead.

I could see them across the field as soon as I broke free of the trees lining the path to the river. Papa was standing against the fence as two soldiers raised their rifles level with his heart.

"Stop!" I screamed, jumping in front of him. "This is my father. If you're going to kill him, you're going to have to kill me, too." I was thinking to myself, They won't kill me, I'm a young girl. I was so naive.

"*Scheiss-Jude!* Filthy dog!" they hissed.

I dared not look in Papa's face, so instead I chose to look in the eyes of his would-be assassins. "I'm not leaving my father," I told them firmly.

"Look at this girl!" they laughed in my face. "She thinks we won't kill her and her dirty Jew of a father."

I turned around and pointed to Papa's white shirt. "Look how white the collar of his shirt is. He's not dirty. How dare you tell my father he's filthy!" I didn't understand what they meant. "My mother cleaned and ironed this shirt herself." I showed them his clean collar.

"You are too funny!" they laughed, cocking their guns. "You want to say a prayer, little Jew girl, before you die?" I blinked into the barrel of their shotgun. It was strange to think that such a small, dark hole could be the last thing I looked at in life.

My hands squeezed wrinkles across my freshly pressed skirt. For a second I imagined that there was laughter coming from the river road. It sounded so good-hearted, so jovial, that I wondered if I had suddenly gone mad while waiting to die.

"What are you boys doing there?" a familiar voice shouted from the road. Behind the soldiers, two men were laughing and riding their bikes.

Our death squad answered, "Heil Hitler, Officer Joksch! We're just about to kill this Jew and his daughter." They saluted him. "Would you like to do the honors instead?"

I could barely believe my watering eyes. I was not mad. I was not dreaming. There, just a few feet away, stood Hans Joksch.

"I would rather have a beer." He slapped them on the back. They laughed. "Come, hop on our bikes and I'll buy you a round!"

"Let's kill them first—then we'll be really thirsty!"

"Why bother with them? Besides, I don't want to wait any longer." He got on his bike, indicating he wouldn't take no for an answer. "Come on, hurry up. I haven't got all day. I'm sure you'll find other Jews to kill tomorrow." The soldiers looked angrily at us but did as they were told because Officer Joksch was higher-ranking.

Their voices seemed to carry across the field forever, making it impossible for either of us to move. It was as if my feet had taken root in the ground. I did not dare to look at Papa. He did not dare to look at me. Tears of shock smarted our eyes. Slowly we started walking toward home, but in the middle of the road we sank down clutching the dirt beneath our hands. Our legs weren't going to carry us any farther.

According to the Nuremberg Laws, any Aryan having sex with a non-Aryan could be punished by death, and many of the Jewish families thought their daughters were safe because of this concept of Rassenschamde, or "race disgrace." Not long after the incident at the river, though, a German soldier saw Rena walking to work and asked Joseph's son, Alex, who she was.

It was the middle of the night when the soldier staggered drunkenly up to Alex's house. "Open up this door!" he shouted. "Alex, I insist you open up this door and take me to Rena's house!"

Joseph quickly woke up his son, sending him out the window to run and warn the Kornreichs. Then he stalled the SS man until Alex could return.

"Chaim! Sarah!" Alex shouted outside. "Hide Rena quickly! There is a German soldier looking for her." My eyes shot open.

"Papa, you keep a lookout while I hide Rena. Yell when you see them." I could hear Mama's voice downstairs and was out of bed before she could reach my room. "Follow me." She took my hand, leading me into the attic.

"Lie down on your stomach." Her voice did not waver, her hands did not tremble. I lay down as she covered me with straw. "Do not move until you hear me telling you it's all right." She smoothed the straw out over my body, making it even so it would not look as if anyone was hiding.

"Mama, they're near!" Papa's voice warned us.

"*Ribono shel olam*, Lord of the universe, protect my child," Mama prayed before hurrying downstairs. Lying very flat, my stomach pulsating against the floorboards, I turned my face sideways and tried very hard not to breathe. I could hear the rifle butt denting our front door and the officer yelling, "Where's Rena? Bring me Rena!"

"She's not at home." Father pretended that he'd been rudely awakened.

"I do not believe you! *Scheiss-Jude!* You would not let your precious daughter stay out this late at night."

"She is visiting family in another town."

"We'll see about that! I know where you cursed dogs hide your favorite things!" He pushed Papa aside, barging into our home, walking immediately up the stairs to our attic. This was the only place to hide in farmhouses, besides the potato cellars, so it was the first place he looked.

"Is she here?" I heard him poking through the straw. "Perhaps you want to tell me before I stab her through her pretty eye!" The boards creaked beneath the weight of his feet; every movement he made shuddered the floor beneath me.

He dared Mama and Papa to make a move that would betray my hiding place. They were stone, solid and silent.

"So she isn't hiding under that pile—but maybe here?" He stabbed the straw repeatedly, as if it were alive and he were killing it. My heart thumped against the wood flooring. I tried not to panic, but I was sure he could hear every skip and beat of the throbbing river of blood racing through my head. A flash of steel found its mark four inches from my nose.

I did not move.

"I know you're lying to me, Jew. You'd better make sure she's here the next time a German officer comes to call or I'll cut your throat!" He slammed the door of our house so hard that the china tinkled in the cabinets.

Mama came back to the loft. "Rena, are you okay?" I held her, trying not to cry, trying to be brave. But I was shaken beyond all bravery.

"You will have to sleep up here tonight"—she smoothed my hair back across my head—"in case he returns. Try to rest. We will see about this in the morning. You're not going back to those barracks to work, though, that's for sure." She kissed my forehead, squeezing me tight against her breasts while I dampened her nightdress with my tears.

That night changed everything. It had become dangerous for Rena to live in Tylicz. The village was distraught over the incident and almost everyone rallied to help. A Gentile friend took a letter to Rena's uncle in Slovakia, saying that she would be coming to live with them just as Zosia had done, and Papa deliberated long and hard over whom to contact about smuggling her across the border. Andrzej had been fighting the Germans when Poland had first been invaded, but he'd been fortunate enough to escape capture; returning secretly to Tylicz, he was now working for the Polish resistance.

Who knew the border better than Andrzej?

My father had never met Andrzej, yet that morning he sent for the boy he had forbidden me to see to come into our house. Not a word had been spoken to me about these arrangements. This was my father, and of course I was not consulted.

I was standing in the kitchen when I heard Andrzej's voice at our door. My knees sank. Mama scrutinized me, but I did not even look at his face.

"Welcome, Andrzej. Please have a seat." Papa offered him a chair. "Would you like a cigarette?" Mama and I watched them from the other room.

"Thank you, Mr. Kornreich." Andrzej took the cigarette with a grateful nod.

"I have a favor to ask of you, Andrzej . . . This is very difficult for me, but I must ask. It is no longer safe in Tylicz for Rena. Her mother and I are worried for her safety every day."

"I heard what happened last night, Mr. Kornreich. I understand your concern."

"I have no money to pay you for this favor."

"Sir, I would not take any money from you. She is my friend since childhood. I will do whatever you ask to help your daughter."

"Thank you." Papa paused, stroking his chin where his beard should have been. "You seem like a man of your word. If you would bring Rena across the border to Slovakia, her mother and I might find sleep at night."

"I will see to it," Andrzej answered gallantly. "And I swear that with my life I'm going to guard her and not one hair is going to fall from her head. I give you my word of honor that I will bring her safely to Slovakia according to your wishes. I will hold only her hand because it is rough terrain, but I will not touch her, sir. You may trust me."

My father concluded their business with a handshake, but there was a look in his eyes I had never seen before, the appearance of complete humiliation and defeat.

That evening my mother kissed my brow, weeping. "Rena, be brave, be careful, be well."

I promised to write and send them food. "I'll come home as soon as things get better."

"Safe journey," Papa said solemnly. "Bless you." I kissed him good-bye and hugged Danka. Then I walked into the dark winter night, unchaperoned, to join Andrzej.

"We will have to walk all night. We cannot as much as whisper—not a word—because the dogs can pick up sounds for a long distance and once they begin to bark there is no stopping them," Andrzej instructed me. "The search teams will be out looking for us and the chance of slipping through their net is very slim. If I motion down, lie flat on the ground. Do not raise your head or move in the slightest until I motion you to get up." He took my hand. "I am going to hold your hand the whole way so you won't fall. It will be just like when we were children and I brought you and Danka down the hill."

It was rainy, cold, and just beginning to sleet. Whenever searchlights cascaded across the landscape we fell face down so as not to create a shadow. It would have been hard enough walking in that slippery slush in daylight while laughing and singing winter sledding songs, but silent, under threat of death, trying not to crunch through the new crust of snow, it was nearly impossible. Along a ravine, we threaded our way between trees, using the underbrush to hide our tracks.

Andrzej stumbled, losing his grasp on my hand for a second. Thrown off balance, struggling to keep from falling into the abyss below, I plummeted out of reach. Rolling down the steep incline, I grabbed at tree branches to break my fall as they ripped the mittens from my hands. Biting my tongue, I splashed into a stream with no cushion but ice-covered boulders. The silence of the night shrank. Icy water crept into my clothes. Our ears pricked up for the sound of rudely woken dogs in the nearby kennels. There was the sound of water dripping off my elbows. Neither of us dared move or breathe. No dogs barked.

Finally, Andrzej signaled for me to stand up. Slowly, bracing my hands against the river rocks, I stood. My legs were barely able to stand my weight, they were shaking so badly with cold and fear. Grabbing hold of a tree for an anchor, Andrzej reached toward me. My nails dug into his flesh. My muscles shuddered, but he didn't weaken as I forced myself up the embankment. Finally I stood on level ground. His hands rubbed mine, trying to warm them as I clamped my mouth shut to muffle the chattering of my teeth. He smiled, knowing how wet and cold I was, then, taking my hand more firmly than before, he led me toward our destination.

The light from the farmhouse seemed at first to be a mirage. I was sure I was dreaming; it was late, one or two in the morning, but there were these gorgeous lights shimmering out across the snow. Andrzej motioned me toward the stable. There, snuggling between the horses and cows, we waited.

"This is the connecting point between the Slovakian and Polish undergrounds," he whispered into my ear. I nodded, knowing we were now safe.

They were greeted by a farmer who boasted about his poker game with the border guards, and his wife, who served them hot cocoa and gave Rena some dry clothes. The farmer, Karl, assumed that Rena and Andrzej would sleep together, but Andrzej assured him that that wouldn't be proper, so Rena was given the couple's bed while Andrzej slept in the attic. The next morning, dressed like Slovakian farmers, Karl, Andrzej, and Rena climbed into a wagon and headed for the city of Bardejov.

Outside of Uncle Jacob's, Andrzej took my hand. "I kept my promise to your father, didn't I?"

"Yes you did, Andrzej."

"I only held your hand." I wanted him to hold it forever and never let go. I was so frightened of this big city and this strange country.

"I love you, Rena."

"Thank you for delivering me to my Uncle Jacob Schützer's house." I blushed, darting inside.

Rena hid in the Schützers' house until she could speak Slovakian fluently, and had her long braids cut off so she would look more like a city girl. She tried to tell her aunt and uncle about the horrors the Jews in Poland were experiencing, but they thought she was being far too serious and didn't believe her. Cili and Gizzy, her cousins, tried to get Rena to go out and have fun. As hard as Rena tried, they just didn't seem to understand the severity of the situation.

Two weeks after my arrival in Bardejov, I saw Andrzej standing outside the house. He'd smuggled in a package from Mama with some clothes in it for me. I got nervous and tried to cut our conversation short, but he asked if we could speak privately. We stepped behind my uncle's house.

"I've just heard that they're going to start taking young Jewish people to camps for forced labor unless they are a mixed couple," Andrzej began. "If you were married to a Gentile there'd be a good chance they wouldn't take you." I wanted to stop his words before he spoke them. "I want to marry you—tomorrow. I have it all arranged. My brother is living about fifteen kilometers away and has a room we can stay in. I would not have to go back and forth to Poland anymore, except for the important people, and we could live here in Slovakia, where it's safe."

I was all alone. I had no one to talk with about this idea. I did not know what to do but I knew I could not betray my family or my faith. Finally I said, "I'm not actually happy in Slovakia, Andrzej. My parents are still in Poland and I'm dying for them. I am young and strong, more assertive than they are, yet they are the ones exposed to the Germans. I don't really want to stay here. I want to go home to Tylicz, but I can't and I don't know what else to do." My heart ached to tell him just once that I loved him, too, and if it were not for the rest of the world I would happily marry him. "There is still the matter of our religions, too," I said instead. "I'm sorry. I cannot be your wife." I couldn't look into his face any longer. "I can't talk to you anymore. My aunt and uncle might get suspicious."

"If you change your mind, Rena, send word." He grabbed my hand in his for one tender moment. "I will never change mine." How I wanted to tell him the truth of my heart! But I remained silent and dutiful to my family, stepping back into the house bewildered and confused.

Jacob Schützer and his wife, Regina, gave Rena a weekly allowance and asked Gizzy and Cili to lend Rena some nice clothes to wear to the dances and the movies. Rena spent her allowance on food for her parents, though. Going to the marketplace to meet their Gentile friends from Tylicz was the closest she could get to home, and she waited eagerly for those days.

Most of the Jewish youths of Bardejov were involved with the Zionist organization. They would meet and talk about forming a new state of Israel, and held dances. Gizzy and Cili dragged Rena to these soirees. "We're going to find you a nice Jewish boy!" they teased her gently.

Uncle Jacob approved of her socializing and informed her that he would like her to go out with Schani Gottlobb, a tailor. "I want to be able to tell your father that you've found a suitable escort." He gave her a little extra for a new outfit. Obediently, Rena bought just enough fabric for one dress, then went straight to the market with the rest of the money to send home more flour, sugar, and cheese.

Schani was mad about me. He flattered me, thinking me both daring and smart for escaping from Poland, and didn't mind that I spent money on my parents rather than clothes. We went to socials together, and a few movies; I put a good face on for everyone, but inside I was not happy. There was nothing to be happy about.

After we'd been dating for about two months, Schani got it into his head that I was the one for him and proposed.

"Schani, you're crazy . . . I can't marry you!" I didn't know how to get out of this mess.

"Why not? Your uncle approves of me and he's your guardian while you're away from home."

"Schani, you're real nice . . . I like you very much . . ." I tried to be as kind and honest as possible without hurting his feelings. "I like your company very much, but my heart isn't with you."

"There's someone else, isn't there?"

I nodded, biting my lip for admitting even that much. "I didn't mean to lead you on. Anyway, it doesn't matter because nothing can come of it, but I'm not over him yet, so I cannot love you. I'm sorry."

"I can wait. You'll see. I'm going to love you so much that I will have enough love for both of us. And to prove it, I'm going to make you a beautiful coat for an engagement gift, so when you're over him in your heart I can step into his place."

That week Rena received a letter from her parents saying they were very happy about her relationship with Schani and she knew Uncle Jacob had informed them of their courtship. "Schani will make a good husband," Gizzy told her, "and he cares for you very much." In a state of confusion, Rena accepted the beautiful gray coat which Schani made for her and they were officially engaged.

It was a lovely Saturday morning in early spring. The air was still crisp and snow clung to the ground, unwilling to release its winter hold on the land. Schani and Rena were walking to the marketplace when she saw Andrzej heading toward them on the opposite side of the street.

"Hi, Rena." He tipped his hat, his eyes latching onto her soul. Her heart began predictably pounding and her face turned red.

I wanted to do something to show him how I really felt, but I couldn't acknowledge him without embarrassing Schani, my future husband. There was nothing in the Orthodox rules or traditions about proper conduct in this kind of situation. I knew what I wanted to do—I wanted to go over and hug him and tell him how much I missed him, I wanted to tell him all that was in my heart—but I heard my father's voice forbidding me to speak to "that boy." My desires were against my parents and my faith, and for all my courage I did not have enough to say, Hi, Andrzej. I never said a word. He passed us unacknowledged but not ignored.

"Isn't that the Gentile who risked his life to bring you here?" Schani interrupted my thoughts.

"Yes." I turned away.

"That's the boy you love, isn't it?"

"Why do you say that?" I said angrily.

"Rena, look at yourself. You're flushed." He defended himself.

Suddenly I realized that this man bore me no malice. "I'm sorry, Schani . . . Yes, that is Andrzej." My eyes fell to the ground. Normally I would have stood up proudly and spoken those words, but I was embarrassed by my own inaction.

"Why didn't you go over to him? Why didn't you greet him? He saved your life."

"I didn't know how you were going to take it!" I snapped.

"What do you mean, how I'm going to take it? Like a man, like a human being, that's how I'm going to take it! I will shake his hand and thank him for bringing you to Bardejov where you are safe."

"You would do that for me?"

"Rena, I would do anything for you."

Hurriedly I looked around so I could say something, anything, to Andrzej, but he was gone. The street was empty.

"Next time you will introduce us." Schani took my arm.

"Yes, next time I would like you to meet," I answered. And for the first time I felt a tenderness toward Schani that I knew might someday turn to love.

Passover came and went; winter's defeat was final and spring blossoms decorated the city streets. Looking for goods to send home, Rena heard one of the neighbors greeting her.

"Good morning, Rena. Have you heard the rumor that they are going to move all the Jews in Tylicz forty kilometers from the border?"

"No, I hadn't heard that. What about my parents? How will I send them food if they aren't in Tylicz?"

"Don't worry, Rena. It's just a rumor."

Another woman patted my arm. "You remember Andrzej Garbera, don't you?"

"Of course, she remembers Andrzej, you silly cow," the other woman quipped at her friend.

"We grew up together." I tried to act nonchalant.

"He died a few weeks ago."

The words fell on my head. The earth shattered from beneath my feet. I collapsed without a word at the feet of my neighbors.

Above me, I could hear a man saying, "You dummy, didn't you know they were in love? They used to write to each other secretly." From beneath a haze of unconsciousness I wondered how these people could know something we'd kept so well hidden.

Their voices hovered above me as if they were miles away. I reached toward them, trying to bring myself around, shaking my head, covering my eyes—I couldn't cry here in the middle of the marketplace with half of Tylicz and Bardejov watching. There was no place to show my grief, no place for me to run. From that day on I didn't care to be in Slovakia anymore. I didn't care about anything but my mother's arms, my father's voice.

I said farewell to Schani and contacted Tolek, a new family friend of ours who worked in the underground. "Take me home," I told him. "I cannot bear to be here anymore. I am tired of being safe." So Tolek took my hand and brought me home to my mother's arms.

It was not a happy, carefree homecoming but it was what I wanted. "Mama! Papa!" I never thought I would say those precious words again. I hugged them as if I would never let go, as if their arms could chase my pain away. Arm in arm, we entered our house.

"You heard about Andrzej?" Mama whispered.

I nodded, biting back more tears, "Yes, Mama. I would like to go pay my respects to his mother and sisters, if you and Papa don't mind."

"It is only proper that you honor him so, Rena. Let me send a loaf of challah with you."

The streets were muddy from rain. Accompanied by the smell of warm bread in my arms, I walked the same path Andrzej and I had trod together so many times. Passing the village well, I tried not to think of his laughing face, his sweet tender kiss. Swallowing hard, I knocked on the door, forcing a smile upon my lips.

His mother answered quickly, as if she had been standing at the door waiting for me.

"Sit down, Rena. Make yourself at home." His mother motioned for me to take a chair. "Andrzej will be here any minute." She ran to the window, looking for him. "He'll be so happy to see you." Wringing her hands, she checked the road outside. "I think he likes you, Rena. I shouldn't be surprised if he asked you to marry him some day."

Tears cascaded down my face as Hania pulled me into the kitchen. Hania explained that it was better for her mother not to remember. She told me that there had been a search by the border guard, with dogs. Andrzej had to climb a tree and had hidden there all night. It was so cold he froze and fell out. "Fortunately, some of our people found him and carried him home, so the Nazis, thank the Lord, never captured him," Hania explained." He got pneumonia, though. We tried to nurse him back to health, but his lungs gave out."

I was lost in my heart for Andrzej. Wandering the streets of Tyl-icz, I found my way to the village graveyard. I could not place anything on his headstone because it was against German law for a Jew to put flowers on a Gentile's grave—that would be considered desecration; I would be shot. I could only water the flowers which had already been placed there with my tears, thinking of the boy I used to say 'Hi' to on my way to school, thinking how there was no one in the world to hold my hand or greet me on that hill anymore.

❖   ❖   ❖

After Andrzej died, the law was passed expelling all Jews from towns within thirty kilometers of the Polish border. They were allowed to take with them only one loaf of bread and one change of clothes per person. The Kornreichs lost all of their belongings, their house, and their land. Forced out along with the other Jews of Tyl-icz, they moved to Florynka and forfeited what Gentile allies they had left. They rented one room from a local farmer and slept on the floor, on straw mattresses. Rena had gotten special permission to bring their cow, but if she was late for milking, the farmer would steal the milk and pretend that their cow was dry. There was not as much sewing to do in this new town because very few people knew the Kornreichs, but every few weeks Tolek would show up at their door with almonds from Slovakia. Rena and Danka would take the almonds to the town of Grybōw, where they could sell them to the local Jews and make a meager sum which Tolek insisted they keep for themselves. In spite of all of these troubles and hardships, Rena was simply grateful that they were together. She felt useful and knew that her parents depended on Danka and her to take care of those things they were no longer able to do for themselves.

News spread rapidly through the neighboring communities that several Jewish girls had been raped by German soldiers in a nearby town. The memory of the soldier who had stormed into their attic looking for Rena surged back into their lives.

Late into the night Danka and Rena listened to their parents' hushed voices discussing their fate. In the morning they woke to see Mama's tear-streaked face.

"Uncle Jacob cannot take you, so both of you must go to Zosia, in Bratislava. Things are still good in Slovakia and she knows many wealthy Jewish families there who are aware of the situation here. They will take you in and give you a place to work where you can be safe."

"I'm not going to leave you again." I hope to weaken her resolve.

"Yes you will, Rena, because if you don't I am going to go some-where and just die. I never want to see my girls raped." My arguments dry up in my throat. I have never seen such defeat or dismay in Mama's eyes. "And I need you to take care of Danka, Rena."

"We will go, Mama."

In the morning Tolek arrives with a sleigh. "We will have to camp off the border tonight because of the full moon, but we should be close enough that the walk won't be too strenuous to-morrow night."

His friendly face is a comfort amid so much strangeness. It occurs to me that he does not think of us as Jewish, but as friends. I wonder why the rest of the world cannot see things the way he does, the way I do.

Danka and I hold Mama very close to us. She seems so small, as if she is shrinking under the weight of the world. My parents have always seemed ageless, but overnight they have aged visibly. I am struck by Mama's frailness and Papa's white hair.

"Maybe you and Schani will be getting married after all." Mama tries to lighten our mood, allowing her eyes to twinkle for just a moment. "You are good girls. We are so proud of you."

Folding blankets around our feet and shoulders as if we are still young children she is tucking into bed, she speaks softly of faith and hope and taking care of each other. Her eyes are sad and soft. Papa kisses both of our foreheads. He speaks a Hebrew prayer, blessing the daughters he cannot protect.

Tolek clucks to the ponies to begin their trek toward the border, and once again we depart for Slovakia, leaving our parents behind. They stumble through the deep December snow, waving good-bye. Mama's babushka falls from her head. She places one hand on her wig, holding it securely to her head, while the other chases the air frantically, as if she is trying to hold onto one last glimpse of us.

"Good-bye, Papa!"

"Good-bye, Mama!"

Our voices yell repeatedly in unison until all we have left are hoarse whispers.

Long after they have become tiny specks on the horizon we wave, hoping they can still see us. I know that they are waving, too, hoping the same thing. Mama's and Papa's black shapes etched against the snow are engraved in my mind as if they are still there waiting for us to return, as if they always will be there, waiting.

Tears usually taste salty but mine are bitter, frozen to the sides of my cheeks, frozen in time.

❖   ❖   ❖

I write slowly, lingering over each word as if the very act of pen on paper will bring my youngest sister closer to me.

March 18, 1942
Hummene, Slovakia

Dear Danka,

I miss you very much. I wish I could speak with you in person, but that is not possible. I know how excited you were about Schani and I getting married, but there is not going to be a wedding after all. With Slovakia under this martial law now, I don't see that there is any way out of this situation but to turn myself in to the authorities and go to a labor camp. The Silbers think I'm overreacting too strongly when I tell them they'll be shot for harboring me, but you and I know differently. And they have been so kind to me these past few months I cannot bear to put them in danger.

I'm afraid this is going to be just like leaving Poland all over again, and my heart won't stand breaking one more time. Will the Germans ever stop ruining our lives? I don't want to leave you alone, but I cannot risk anyone's life and I don't think the Slovakian Jews understand that the Germans mean business. Please, be careful. I will pray that things are safe for you in Bratislava. Give my love to Zosia and tell Herschel and Ester their Auntie Rena sends them a big kiss and a hug. I miss you.

Your loving sister, Rena

I tuck the letter into its envelope, wishing there was something else I could send to protect Danka, but she's all the way across Slovakia and beyond my reach. The forces that are taking control of all our lives have accelerated like an avalanche through a mountain pass and everything we know and love has been swept up into its path. There's nothing more I can do, I must trust God to take care of those I leave behind.

There is another letter to write. This one I truly wish to avoid but there is no way around it:

Dear Schani,

I'm sorry to be telling you this with the wedding just two weeks away, but I don't know what else to do. I am obeying the recent order and turning myself in to the authorities for a German labor camp. Please understand why I must do this and try to forgive me. I've told you what Poland was like before I escaped to Slovakia, so believe me when I write, Don't Take Anything The Germans Say For Granted. Maybe I won't have to work for more than a few months. I don't know anything yet about where I'm going or for how long. I pray you will respect my decision. I'll write you and Danka as soon as I arrive in camp and know more.

We are young enough that when I'm released from this work camp we can begin again; I'm only twenty-one years old after all—that's not too old for you is it? (That is supposed to be funny, Schani. I don't want you to cry about this.) Someday we will have a good life and you will make a fine husband for me, but not right now. I hope you can wait for me one last time. I do not know what to expect, but I know that the work camp will be hard. Pray that I will not have to be there for very long. Thank you for loving me through all my trials and troubles. Give my best to Aunt Regina, Uncle Jacob, Cili, and Gizzy.

Bless you.
Love, Rena

Folding my wedding nightgown and placing it in a chest with no hope, I wonder how my fiance will take this news. The new shoes the cobbler made for my wedding, the robe that the tailor has sewed, everything I own has been packed and, with my dreams, put away.

Leaving the letters on the table, I turn toward the wardrobe already knowing what I will wear. My green-and-white checkered suit is both warm and attractive. I want to look my best even if I am going to a work camp, and this is my nicest outfit. Danka has a suit just like it which a kind tailor bought for us when we arrived last year in Slovakia. I smile fondly, remembering how he took us to a real department store, purchasing each of us a brand new suit and gorgeous white felt boots with red trim. With a warm pair of socks on, I slip the boots onto my feet. They are snug and comfortable; I know they will travel well.

I wonder about Mama and Papa. Where are they now? What are they doing? They don't even know that Schani and I are getting married. Why couldn't I reach them on Rosh Hashanah?

Danka and I sent them raisins, matzos, and some money for Passover, but the border to Poland is now completely closed. The tailor who bought the suit I'm wearing knew how worried I was, so he asked one of his customers, a German officer, to make the call to Poland for me in exchange for a leather coat.

At the post office, the officer placed my call and handed me the receiver.

"I am calling for Sara and Chaim Kornreich." I told the postmaster in Florynka.

"There's no one in this town by that name."

"Are you sure?" I pleaded. "Is this Florynka?"

"I'm sure. There's no one in this town by the name of Kornreich." I hung up the phone, stunned.

"Maybe they've been moved," the officer suggested.

"Where?"

He shrugged.

Where are Mama and Papa? How I long to tell them everything that's happened.

Checking my appearance casually in the mirror, I give myself an approving nod before picking up the letters and the coat Schani has given me as an engagement gift.

Mrs. Silber has gone to the market, so my departure will go unnoticed. I do not want her to know I'm going to the army barracks, even though she and her husband have said they will hide me despite the consequences. I cannot risk their lives, nor the life of their young daughter, who has been my charge. I do what I have to do. There is no question in my mind that this is the right thing; my only desire is to protect these kind people who have taken me into their home and treated me like a member of their family. A work camp is not going to be so bad, especially if it means saving their lives. I'm not afraid of work. I know what the Germans expect: cleanliness, promptness, order, everything must be spotless. It will be just like working in the barracks in Tylicz.

I leave the Silbers' house, looking back one last time to seal it in my memory. I'll return, I tell myself; this won't last forever.

"Good morning," I greet our good Christian neighbor.

"Good morning, Rena. Are you all right, dear?"

"I must go away and have a favor to ask of you."

Her eyes narrow quickly. "What is it?" Everyone seems to be on their guard. I slip the diamond ring Mama gave me off my finger and place it into her palm, folding her hand around it. "I would like you to take care of this ring. It was my mother's . . . Would you take this coat for me, too, please?"

Her eyes shift between disbelief and desire for these beautiful things. "These are valuable. Won't you need them?"

Suddenly it occurs to me that I will never see these things again. I cannot speak. Placing the coat in her arms quickly, before I can change my mind, I try to turn away before she can see me cry.

"Whoever made this for you must love you very much." She touches the beaver trim admiringly.

"I am afraid that is true. I must go." I do not want to say goodbye to our neighbors, to my friends, my sister, or anyone ever again. Saying good-bye to my mother's diamond ring is painful enough. If I never wave farewell to another person in this lifetime, it will be a blessing. I keep my head to the ground, refusing to look back, hurrying towards town.

Standing for a moment in the center of Hummene, I think about what a nice place this is and how kind the people have been to me. Slovakia has not been a bad place to live; although the past year has been wrought with trials and homesickness, there has been happiness here. I will accept what the Nazis fork out, but

I am afraid of the future. Taking a deep breath, I post my letters and walk resolutely toward the barracks. A line is already forming.

"Name?"

"Rena Kornreich."

"Nationality?"

"Polish."

He smirks as if sharing a secret joke with the officer next to him. "Do you have other family hiding here in Slovakia?"

"I am engaged to a Slovakian citizen, does that change my status?"

"Not unless you want him to join you." Their eyes narrow dangerously.

I shake off a sudden chill. "I don't want him to join me."

"Wait outside tonight." I am dismissed.

"What about my things?"

"Tomorrow someone will take you for your things."

For a moment I wish I had my coat. Its warm fur would chase the chill from my neck. I wonder if my ring and coat are safe. I wonder if I am. What does it feel like to be safe? I can't recall.

There are other Jews next to me. Shivering against the barrack walls with nothing but my wool jacket on, I use my arms to hug myself. The lights around the barracks are cruelly bright, shedding no warmth on those of us in line. It is going to be a hostile night.

The events which have abandoned me to this place tease my mind. Everything moves faster than usual, as if I am inventorying what should be preserved in memory and what should be discarded. I tuck my knees up under my skirt for warmth. My stomach growls—how I would love a piece of challah. The rich smell of egg penetrates my perception. There is something so comforting about the aroma of fresh-baked bread. I sniff the air but cannot tell if the impression is real or imagined and do not care. Rolling an imaginary morsel over my tongue, smelling it from within my mouth, I slowly allow its goodness to warm me from the inside out. I recall Mama kneading the dough, preparing our Sabbath meal on Friday. Tomorrow is Friday; I wonder if Mama is kneading dough somewhere in Poland.

Searching for a place to rest my weary mind, I shut my eyes tightly, willing myself to see Mama's face in our kitchen. Like benevolent spirits, I conjure up the smells, the sounds of home. Mama asking me to bring in more wood for the fire; Papa's pipe smoke wafting in from the parlor where he studies the texts. Like fingers, the mountain peaks surrounding Tylicz pull me into their embrace. I drift between the realms of sleep and waking until I am running barefoot across the field beckoned by the voices of my past. When everything else has changed, one's sole comfort lies in what is, what was, familiar.

Rena!

Escaping into the world of dreams, I imagine that I can see Mama standing at the door of our farmhouse with her lantern lit, watching out for me, calling my name.

Rena!

The grass is wet and cool, springing between my toes. I run down the hill toward home.

I'm coming, Mama, I answer her bobbing light. But the soft, flickering flame of her lantern mutates into a searing glare that burns my eyes.

Disoriented and cold, I shake myself out of a stupor. Searchlights pass over our restless bodies. It was a dream, nothing but a waking dream. I feel tired, depressed, and overcome in these foreign surroundings. My mind takes the mental images of my past and begins weaving them through my subconscious.

I fidget with my plaid skirt. Like a wave receding from the shore, the past leaves me lonely and forlorn.

Rena!

I swear I hear Mama's voice calling. Cautiously I drift off once more, only to be startled repeatedly by the obtrusive glare of the searchlights swaying across the compound. It is a sleepless night. My eyes may shut, my breathing may slow, my mind may shimmer like a movie picture, I may drowse, but I do not escape into sweet sleep. I have been snared.

There is something in the chill at dawn that cuts to the bone. It's almost as if all the warmth from the earth is being sucked into a vacuum and dragged from the land. My jaw aches into a yawn. I wonder when Danka will receive my note.

The soldiers rouse those who aren't up yet. I stand alert, shivering in protest to this rude awakening, then smooth my skirt against my legs. I want to look my best today. It is important to make a good first impression.

"Line up! Those of you who need to go back to your residences will be taken to get your things. Line up!" I rush to the line to retrieve what few belongings I have at the Silbers' house. Like prisoners we walk through town with an officer on each side of our pitiful group. My head is down, hoping to avoid recognition. I do not know why I feel such shame, but I do.

Mrs. Silber is in the kitchen baking challah for the Sabbath meal when the guards pound on her door. "This Jew has turned herself in and has come for her things." They enter her kitchen uninvited; I run upstairs, unable to look in my hostess's eyes. The aroma from the kitchen is so pungent that I stagger under a sudden burst of hunger. In seconds I have my suitcase and am downstairs again.

Mrs. Silber slips a loaf of challah and a few oranges in my bag. "For Sabbath," she whispers. "You'll need it." There is no time for gracious farewells. We barely kiss good-bye.

At the railway station there are hundreds of men, women, and children standing in line. There are many girls about my age. What is going on? Why are children being sent to work? What am I doing here? I am supposed to be getting married, not going to a labor camp. I have to remind myself that I am doing the right thing, but reality is not a comfort.

Word has spread quickly through the town of Hummene that there are Jews being shipped off to work camps today. Our people shout encouragement while standing by the station gates throwing oranges to those of us being loaded onto the train. I catch a few, sticking them in my handbag. For a moment I scan the crowd, looking for a familiar face; I do not know if I should be sad or happy that there is no one waving to me.

When one thinks of a train ride, one imagines benches, or at least seats, or, if one has a little money, perhaps a berth. It is obvious, however, that the cars they are loading everyone into are for animals—cattle cars, to be exact.

"Where are we supposed to sit?" The people around me voice their outrage. "This is not a train for people!" No one is listening as eighty of us are piled into the car. It is standing room only. We step on each others toes, apologize, then step on someone else's.

There's a steady buzz of dismay over our plight. The lady next to me is nursing her baby. She is not a Jew, she is a communist.

"Would you like an orange?" I ask.

"I didn't know I needed to bring food or clothing," she says in Slovakian. I tear off a piece of challah and place a piece of precious chocolate into her hands.

"Bless you, bless you." Her voice breaks from dryness; I wish I had water to quench our thirst. The train starts with a lurch. There is nothing to lean against but the next person.

"Where's the toilet?" someone asks. There is a bucket which is supposed to be a toilet. Hours go by before an embarrassed elder woman has to use "the facilities." Her daughter holds up her coat as a screen while the lady tries to squat on her shaky legs.

"I'm sorry," she apologizes, "I could not hold myself any longer." Some people are shocked, hiding their eyes in shame, but sooner or later everyone must follow suit or mess themselves. It has become apparent that this will not be a short journey, and before the day is out excrement slops freely over the edge.

We expect someone to come dump our refuse for us. Every time the train stops, the ones closest to the door pound against its indifference, yelling, "Open the door! The smell is killing us!"

No one answers our cries. The train moves again. There is no relief.

Somebody dies. We try to move away from the corpse, but there's no place to go. I have never been so close to death. I pray for his eyes to blink and flicker once more. A thin wail rises up out of the belly of the woman whose husband has passed. Lamentations. My bones resonate with her voice. Staring at her mouth, I am amazed at how such sounds of pain and sorrow can emanate from such a small place. She begins to panic. "What will happen to me?" she asks us in Yiddish. "Why has my husband died?" No one can answer her questions. She cradles his head against her bosom, speaking to him as if he can hear her.

Another person dies. There is sobbing, then shocked silence. I stare at the bodies. They can't be dead. They are sleeping and will wake up. I wait for the nightmare to end. If they're not going to wake, surely I will. It is a chant in my head: they can't be dead. It's impossible. This is just supposed to be a train ride to a work camp, not an ordeal. The bodies never move.

Someone pounds against the door. "Please help us!" Others join him. "Someone has died! Please, let us remove the dead." There is no sitting shiva, no one to say the Kaddish. There is a prayer, but we have no rabbi with us. Our faith dangles before us. We cannot prepare the bodies properly. We cannot honor their passing. We are too afraid for our own lives. The train stops again and again. We pound and plead for mercy, but the voices outside ignore us.

Is it days or is it hours?

The door opens. For just a split second, daggers of light blind us. Like wild animals caught by a farmer's lantern, we freeze immobile and in shock. The air saturates our lungs. We have forgotten what fresh smells like—gentle and sweet, not acrid, as the car has become.

"Throw out your dead!" The orders are immune to our pain.

Bodies are tossed out as unceremoniously as the bucket, which is also dumped. The door slams shut too quickly, severing the outside world from our senses. Now that we have something to compare it to, the closeness is more suffocating than before. The train continues its endless trek.

This journey is a blur in my mind. I have no idea if it is three days or five days since I wrote my letters to Danka and Schani. I begin to wish I could change my mind and go into hiding. I wish I could send a letter to Danka warning her. I have made a terrible mistake. I cannot think about that—there is no turning back.

There is no more food to nosh on. There never has been any water to drink. Nothing is left to relieve the growing ulcers in our stomachs.

They are not expert at shipping human cargo yet. The stops are so many I give up trying to count them, reserving my energy for more important things. My mind is as heavy as wet sand sifted through a net of unconscious daze. I think about nothing.

The woman feeds her baby. The voices around me share stories. I have nothing to share. Somewhere in the lapse of time I hear somebody say, "Is anyone here Polish?"

I do not answer at first. It takes time to register what my ears have heard. Looking across the dingy compartment of strangers, I remember. "I'm Polish!"

"Can you read the signs we're passing?" The men in our car lift me up so I can see the signs along the tracks through the barred window high above our heads.

The wind whips across my eyes. I blink back the pain as I recognize my native tongue, my native land. "We're in Poland," I say from high above their heads.

"Where are they bringing us?" Speculation and theories are discussed, but mostly there are just more questions.

"What are they doing?" Our voices ice the air.

Then there is nothing but the sound of wheels against tracks, tracks against wheels; even the baby has stopped crying.

It is as if I am in a tunnel with no light at the end and nothing to stop the onslaught of darkness. The faces around me have changed over the days until no one is far from losing control of their minds. It is as if the world has been shorn of all color, the only hues in the spectrum being black, gray, and the white of my boots. In this dank and fetid car I determine what I must do to survive. Everything that reminds me of what once was—my childhood, my past, my life—must be locked away in the recesses of the unconscious, where it can remain safe and unmolested. The only reality is now. Nothing else can matter.

AUSCHWITZ

Was I born from a stone?
Did a mother not bear me?
If you cut me don't I bleed?

From a Yiddish song sung by Mama

The brakes squeal with such finality that we know instinctively that our journey has ended. The doors are pushed open to a dull gray haze. We blink at the light stinging our eyes. The sign reads AUSCHWITZ.

"Get out of the car," the Germans order. We shift from blank stares to the business of collecting our belongings.

"Go quick!" Men in striped caps and uniforms prod us with sticks, whispering under their breath, "Move quickly. We don't want to hurt you." The SS aim their guns, forcing these poor prisoners to hit us so that we jump from the car. And we jump, half dead, with our luggage, if we have luggage.

It is four feet to the ground. My knees, cramped from being stationary for so long, feel as if they will snap as I land. I turn to help the woman with her baby. A stick taps my shoulder, "Go quick." I look for the eyes belonging to the voice, but there are only hollow black holes staring into my face.

"Get in line!" Orders are sharp, punctuated by whips against shining leather boots.

"Throw your suitcases over there," the SS shout.

I place mine upright, neatly, next to the growing pile, then turn to ask one of the SS guards, "How are we going to find our suitcases later?" I figure I am a human being, I have a right to ask.

"Get in line and shut up!" he yells in my face, pointing his gun at me. The hair on my skin bristles. He doesn't see that I am human.

There is an odor I cannot identify. It is not from human waste or people who have not bathed in days, although those smells are also prevalent. It is the scent of fear permeating the air around me. It is everywhere, in the eyes of the men and women around me, in our clothing and our sweat.

The baby isn't alive anymore, but its mother does not notice the limpness of the form in her arms. Her desperate grasp on its corpse spooks me. There is too much happening. Everything is so hurried, so haphazard, that there is no way to make sense of the situation. I look through the crowd for some direction, for someone to tell me why we are here and what will befall us. I see him. He stands before us, superior and seraphic, taking control, directing us to go this way or that. He is so neat and refined in his gray uniform; he is gorgeous. I smile into his blue eyes, hoping he will see me for who I am.

"Do you want to give up the child?" he asks the woman with the dead baby.

"No." Her head shakes frantically.

"Go over there," he says.

How kind of him not to point out to her that her infant is dead, I think to myself. How kind of him to send her over to the group who is obviously weaker. The elderly and the very young are gathered apart from those of us who are stronger, able to work long, hard hours. I have no idea how many men, women, and children are on the platform, but each of us is told to go either to the left or the right. The direction has no meaning to us. I wonder which way the man in gray will tell me to go.[1]

Parents try to hug their children before they are taken away.

1. It has been thought that there were no selections on the train platform prior to July 1942 (source: Czech, 148), but a survivor—Lenka, No. 1735—from Proprad, the town where the first transport originated, states that she was taken from her home because she was over the age of fifteen, while her younger sister was left behind. For some reason this system of selecting only young women was not practiced in Hummene, where

"We have to go work." They try to comfort each other. "You are young enough not to have to come work with us. Grandmama will take care of you, . . ." they assure their flesh and blood. "Everything will be okay, you'll see. You'll be happier if you're not with Mommy and Daddy." Then Mommy and Daddy are separated.

I cannot bear the sound of children crying. This is madness. My mind begins to whirl. Struggling to focus on something, anything, to keep me from screaming, I stare at the man in gray. He is so stunning I am sure he must be considerate too. His orders are always obeyed. The SS around us defer to him quickly, answering, "Heil Hitler!"

His finger points. I answer by walking to the side of the other able-bodied young women. On the other end of the compound, we envy the group that will not have to work. They will go someplace warm, somewhere where they will be taken care of. It is natural to think this way—we are human beings, we assume we will all be treated humanely. I watch the proceedings with semi-fascination before lapsing into the fog where nothing needs to make sense. This is not daydreaming, this is electric shock.

Trucks come and load up the old, the sick, and the babies. There is nothing nice or caring about the way they rush them. These feeble souls are herded onto the flatbeds like so many sacks of potatoes piled on top of one another. My stomach somersaults. For one sick moment it occurs to me that maybe they're not going to be treated as well as I've been thinking, but I chase that thought away. They're in a hurry, I chide myself. There are so many of us; they have only momentarily forgotten to treat them gently.

Many of the girls next to me wave good-bye to those being taken away. I watch their stricken faces realizing that my prayer has been temporarily answered. There is no one for me to wave to, and for one brief moment I feel a tiny shred of gratitude. At least

men, women, and children were put on this same transport. It would follow that because of this oversight there was indeed a selection on the train platform in Auschwitz of the first transport of Jews and that Rena was witness to that first selection.

when I said good-bye to my family it was not in this place. The tears around me are too plentiful, the pain too raw, as mothers and daughters are driven apart. I shut my eyes but I cannot shut my ears.

"Good-bye, Papa!"

"Good-bye, Mama!"

There is a smudge on my left boot. Spitting into my palm, I stoop to wipe it away. It is white again.

"Line up! Get into rows of five! *Raus! Raus!*" The prisoners poke us with sticks. The SS aim their guns at us. We are civilians unfamiliar with military drill. We line up clumsily. "March! Stay in your rows! If you step out of line you will be shot! March!" One thousand girl-women step in semi-perfect time, in semi-perfect rows of five, through the iron gates of Auschwitz. Above our heads, welded in iron, are the words ARBEIT MACHT FREI, and we believe what the sign says: "Work Will Make You Free."

"We are young," we remind ourselves. "We will work hard and be set free. We will see what happens." But on the outside we are walking as if we are doomed. It is raining, chilled like March rain. We are lost in thought but it is too cold to do much thinking. Everywhere it is gray. My heart is turning gray.

There are men along barbed-wire fences, in striped jackets, caps, and pants, watching us.[2] Their eyes reflect nothing. I think to myself, This must be an insane asylum, but why would they make the mentally ill work? That's not fair.

I do not comprehend my surroundings. I keep thinking, I am well brought up, well educated, well dressed. I was looking very nice when I went to the barracks in Slovakia wearing my beautiful suit, though it does not look so good now. Still, my white boots look pretty and spotless because I've been careful not to step in any mud. Walking through these gates, I forget my resolve and think

2. Prior to March 26, 1942, the only prisoners in Auschwitz were men, mostly Polish Gentiles serving time for their political or religious beliefs and Russian prisoners of war.

for one moment about who I was at home. I'm a neat person. I should not be here. I am different. I come from a good family. The desire to curl up in a warm blanket of past memories permeates my effort to keep in step. Forget about that *now,* Rena, I reprimand my weakness, that's history. I stare at the acres of barbed wire around us. This is reality.

"Halt!" We freeze, complacent and obedient under the rifles and watchtowers around us. There are rows of brick buildings going down the side of the camp road, the Lagerstrasse, and a high wall with barbed wire. We are forced to line up so as to be going in the door of the first block. Time passes. Is it hours or is it days? I am somewhere toward the end of this line when people start coming out of the other side with no hair on their heads.

Leaning toward the girl next to me, I whisper, "There are more crazy people. We must be in an institution for the insane." She nods in agreement.

"Sophie! It's me!" some crazy bald person shouts to one of the girls nearby.

"Freida? Is that you? What happened to your hair?" Sophie yells back.

"Don't ask questions." Her bald head checks around her to see if anyone is listening. "If you have jewelry, step it into the mud."

I look at the watch I am wearing. *I can hear the children of Tylicz laughing with me as I run through the streets toward the post office, where I have just received my first phone call all the way from Krynica. "Rena has a boyfriend!" they chant. "Rena has a boyfriend!" "Do you like the watch I gave you?" my current beau asked on the crackling wire. "I love it," I flirted, "I will never take it off." "Well, you better if you go swimming or bathe," he flirted back.*

I break my foolish promise, ripping the band from my wrist. You cannot have my memories! You cannot have anything of mine! Driving it into the mud with my heel, dirtying my precious white felt boots, I smash it into a thousand pieces.

The door to Block One looms before us. Inside, the unknown is happening. We can hear screams. We can see the girl-women coming out, but we tell ourselves we will not look different when we exit this place. Digging my fingernails into my palms, I pray I will be the one girl to exit with my hair. Then I am inside the block.

In a daze I walk up to the first table, as I have just seen the girl in front of me do. "What are you?" a German woman asks.

"Polish," I answer. She grunts, writing down my information. She does not ask me what race I am, and I do not offer the fact that I am also Jewish. I am puzzled by her clothes. She is not SS, she is definitely Reichdeutsche, but she is wearing a triangle with a number over it. It occurs to me that she may be a prisoner.[3]

"Two gold crowns," she announces.

My mind races. Why would they make a note about my teeth? Oh, my God, they're going to take my crowns and then I'll look ugly. I go to the second table pulling my upper lip over my teeth, tilting my head down just slightly so no one notices the money in my mouth.

"Get those earrings off," the next German woman barks at me. I look around wondering who is being spoken to in such a tone of voice. "You there! Take those earrings off or I'll rip them out!"

"Me?" I am stunned. Touching my lobes gingerly, I realize my mistake. The earrings my Grandpa Zayde gave me when I was six years old are glistening from beneath my curls. I have worn them for so long that they are not jewelry but a part of me.

"I forgot about them," I tell her quickly, placing the last remnant of my life on a cold table, to be tossed into a box with everyone else's past.

"Take your clothes off and leave them here." They grab my

3. March 26 [1942]. . . . 999 German women prisoners classified as asocial, criminal, and a few as political prisoners . . . receive Nos. 1–999 and are lodged in the part of the main camp separated by the wall along Blocks 1 to 10. . . . 999 Jewish women from Proprad [near Humenne] in Slovakia are [also] sent to the women's section of Auschwitz. This is the first registered transport sent to the camp" (Czech, 148).

clothes from me before I have a chance to fold them neatly or place them in a safe corner to be retrieved later.

"*Raus! Raus!*" We hurry forward. We have never stood naked in front of strangers before. Trying to cover ourselves with our hands, we look at the floor, hoping this will protect our modesty. Insensitive to our nudity, they prod us into a tub of disinfectant.

"They are filthy. Don't touch them." Their voices sting as badly as the solution against our bare skin. We stand for several minutes embarrassed to look at each other, staring into a green liquid that feels as if it will eat the flesh off our bodies.

"Get out! Get out!" Orders, more orders. The guards' words jump into our brains, dislodging free thought, exiling it to the nether regions of sanity. There are no towels to dry our shivering frames. Our clothes are not waiting for us, but the line is. Our lives have become one long line moving slowly from one horror to another.

I am held by the head and pushed abruptly into a chair. The cuss of electric shears moves closer to my ears as a tough hand pushes my head forward. "Don't move!" I am spoken to roughly, handled as if my skin were sandpaper. Running from the nape of my neck to my forehead, the clippers cut and scrape against my skin, tearing the hair from my head. Digging my fingernails deeper into my arm, I try to prevent tears from falling down my disinfected cheeks. Only married women shave their heads. Our traditions, our beliefs, are scorned and ridiculed by the acts they commit. They shear our heads, arms; even our pubic hair is discarded just as quickly and cruelly as the rest of the hair on our bodies. We are shorn like sheep and then ordered back into the vat of disinfectant. My flesh burns like fire. I wonder if I will get my jacket and skirt back now that the ordeal is over. They can't possibly do anything more—what else is there?

A girl screams.

There is a long table where an officer is standing. He has rubber gloves on and there are other men holding the girl down. I hear her scream again. I have no idea what he is doing but I know I don't want him doing it to me. There are two lines, the one I am in, going to the table with the man and his gloves, and the line facing in the opposite direction. Blood drips down the thighs of the girl-women coming away from the man and his gloves. It only takes a second for me to weigh the consequences of action against the consequences of inaction—I turn quickly around, stepping into the other line. This is my first accomplishment in Auschwitz: no one gives me a gynecological exam.

The German women prisoners, who are obviously superior, toss woolen uniforms at us. There are Russian insignias on the breasts of the uniforms. We fumble, then try them on, quickly discovering that they are too huge for most women to wear. There is a tall woman next to me whose pants are too short. "Here, try mine on," I suggest. We trade. Around us, other women do the same, trying to find something that won't fall off. I balk at pulling the trousers over my body without any underwear on. Sniffing my dark green woolen shirt, I am nauseated by the dampness of the fabric. There are no buttons to close the shirt, but there are holes and reddish-brown streaks and stains. "They haven't even washed these clothes!" I remark. Touching a smear of dirt, I wonder if I can scrub it out later. But this is not mud. It is sticky. It smells sweet. My stomach lurches. I stare at the women around me who are already clothed. Still damp from the disinfectant, they are simply grateful for something to put over their bodies. Like myself, they do not notice at once, preferring to think that the cloth has been eaten away by moths rather than bullets. They do not see that the streaks are not dirt and mud but blood. We are like lambs being led to slaughter, following one another because we know of nothing else to do. Despite the sweet-sour smell of stale blood and scratchiness of the wool against my nipples, I modestly pull my shirt across my chest. What will be next?

In the last room there is a pile of wood slabs with leather straps across the top. These are supposed to be shoes. Again, we try to help each other find a matching pair, but they were not made in pairs. They're not even made for human beings to wear. Scuffling out of the block onto the camp road, I move into position. We stand in neat rows of five, bald, practically barefoot, and wearing dead men's uniforms. It begins to drizzle.

"Line up!" The drill is repetitive, mundane. We are capable of nothing but obeying orders. "March!" With one hand clutching the stench of my shirt close around me and the other hoisting up the pants which sag below my hips, still possessed by a false sense of modesty, I march.

We stamp our feet awkwardly, trying not to trip or lose our sandals. We pass the first four blocks before turning into Block Five. We are so busy trying not to lose our clothing that we do not notice the room we are led into. The door slams shut and a bolt falls on the other side. We are trapped, standing almost on top of one another in bloody straw. Bedbugs jump, making our bodies black. We hold our clothes up over our faces; they jump on our bare heads, our hands, all over any exposed patch of skin. In the straw, lice crawl hungrily between our toes.

We have gone quietly for too long. Suddenly there is a surge of dissension. Running to the door, we pound and pound. "Let us out! Let us out!" With both hands we beat the walls imprisoning us. "This can't be!" the voices around me scream. "Please, let us out. We did nothing wrong. There's got to be a mistake. Help us!"

I watch the anguish around me. We have revolted too late. It is no mistake. Joining the mass of betrayed girl-women, I pound against the oak of injustice. It beats thinking. Anything is better than facing the facts on the floor and under our feet.

I am tired of being vigilant. I am tired of watching the sun rise on despair. The girl-women around me mirror my thoughts; my face must look as doomed as theirs. The filth, the smell, the sounds of guard dogs barking in the distance—it is too much. The whole night I crouch on the floor, exhausted yet alert. There has been no water for over four days, no food, not a drop of anything. I don't fall asleep, but quite a few do. Dropping off into unconsciousness, they collapse on the floor, no longer able to feel the gnawing bites of these terrible bugs.

The door to Block Five opens at four A.M. I am still where they left me, wide-eyed and awake. We scramble into line and march out for roll call. We stand silently, being counted, unable to move from our neat and orderly rows of five. I do not turn my head. I do not shift my feet. I want to scratch at the bites and the irritating wool against my bare skin. My thumb twitches against my leg; it is the only movement I allow myself to indulge in.

They divide us evenly into two different groups. We are given a bowl for our tea, but there aren't enough; some people share theirs, but right away there are arguments and some of the bowls disappear. We march into Block Ten. It is late morning when we are finally given a little of something like tea, a piece of bread, and a pat of margarine, which they slap onto the open palm of our hands. I notice that everyone gobbles their food quickly, too quickly for their shrunken stomachs. Some get in line again, expecting more, but there are no seconds. They are beaten for being so presumptuous. I chew my bread, slowly spreading my margarine as if I were at a proper dinner. My tea tastes strange, but I do not care. I sip it slowly, forcing myself to make it last, telling my body that it is full and this is plenty to eat.

The first day we clean the inside of Block Ten. Moving in a daze, I hold my shirt closed and keep my pants up while dusting, sweeping, washing. We carry out our duties. I am simply grateful to be let out of the block, with all its lice and bugs. There is little else to do but watch and learn. The Germans are disorganized. I notice this immediately, but it means nothing—organized or not, I am at their mercy.

More girl-women march into camp and I spend all afternoon watching them come out of the barracks bald and dressed in uniforms like myself. With so many coming in, I cannot imagine

Danka avoiding the transports for long. Standing by the fence watching the line of newcomers, I am torn between praying that I won't see her here and praying that we find each other if this is where she ends up. I wonder if she will recognize me. I wonder if I will recognize her. Each new face is carefully scanned before I dismiss it for not being my sister. Lost in an ever-increasing sea of despair, my heart has one last hope that Danka will hide in Slovakia. My bones tell me she will be here all too soon.

I see my lovely white boots with their red trim on an SS woman across the compound. I want to say something, take them from her and put them on my own feet. Trying to control this impulse to take back what is mine, I start to return to the block. "Line up! Line up!" We move into neat rows of five. The sun sinks in the west as one thousand of us are counted.

A concrete wall divides camp. The men's blocks are on the other side of this wall, but from the second story of the blocks we can see each other through the barbed wire. In the approaching darkness I stand before the upstairs window looking at the same men I had seen the day before. At least they look the same. Each of the blocks in Auschwitz has windows in the front, and from the second floor we can open them and speak to the men on the other side of the wall. They are half-starved, eager to hear news of the outside world and to make friends with us.

I go to the window and spit on my hand. The reflection is dark and obscured, but I stand rubbing the dirt from my face, smearing the tearstains into my skin so they will not know they've made me cry. I rub my scalp as if I had hair to comb. It is a futile but comforting gesture, reminding me of Mama's hand brushing back my hair. I shut out these thoughts quickly; there is only one thing to remember—don't reminisce. My reflection in the window blinks back her tears. I want to rant and rave but I can only stare at the picture before my eyes. What have they done to us? The silent screams inside my head rip my soul apart. Who is this person staring back at me? The men in camp no longer look insane. They look like me.

"Is anyone over there Polish?" a man asks from the other side of the wall.

"I am," I answer.

"Can I help you?" he asks.

"I could use a rope to hold up my pants, and a nail." This is called organizing. Really it is scrounging, but organizing is more appropriate when you consider our circumstances and how dangerous having anything extra is.

"Run downstairs. I'll throw something over." This is my first care package, and with grateful admiration I retrieve a rope with a nail, wrapped tightly around a stone.

I spend the rest of the evening fraying the rope into four pieces. It does not take me long to figure out that resourcefulness is as precious as food in this place, and nothing passes under my feet unnoticed or unassessed for its potential. By taking a stone, I am able to hammer the nail through the metal rim of my bowl, then I thread one of the pieces of rope—my new belt—through the hole. To keep my shirt closed I tuck it in my pants and tie the belt tightly around my waist. This is how it is. My life depends on this precious bowl which I can drink from and wash in. I will work with it. I sleep with it. I always keep it by my side. It is red.

There are no showers, but there are three toilets in Block Ten and a place to wash our hands. For toilet paper there are scraps of newspaper, but these disappear quickly. There's always a line, so we don't have a chance very often to use the toilet or wash our hands, but at least it is possible. There are bunk beds which have straw mattresses on them and thin blankets. The first night we have two people per bunk, but there are empty bunks waiting for more girl-women just like us. They must be in Block Five tonight.

My bed is next to a wall with a window that is boarded up, but through the slats in the boards I can look into the yard of Block Eleven. The struggle for sleep is not hard after so many nights of sleeplessness, but somewhere in the middle of the dreamless night there are gunshots. Awake and alert, I lie on my pallet of straw pulling the blanket closer around me, but it cannot warm the chill in my spine; my cup attached firmly to my waist is no comfort either. I know somewhere someone is dying.

Roll call on the second morning comes just as early, just as rudely. It is four A.M. They shout for us to form a line in alphabetical order. Frantically we jostle one another, trying to get where we belong; anyone not in place is beaten into line. We seem to always be marching from one place to another and standing for a long time doing nothing. This time we are funneled into a barrack with benches and long tables. There are two sisters in the front of our line, I believe they are numbered 1001 and 1002. The tattooing is painful. The men prisoners do not delight in sticking the needle, like a shot, in our left forearms over and over. They know how much it hurts. Still, the Germans force them to hurry, so there is no time to be gentle or concerned. It is as if each stab will burst any shred of ego left. My number is 1716. Branded and numbered like cattle, we rub our arms as we had rubbed our naked heads, trying to make the pain go away.

The Nazis are starting to arrange things now. The kapos, who are German prisoners, are put in charge of us when we are outside of our blocks. We learn how to distinguish the kapos by the color triangle they wear: green signifies that she is in for murder; red means she is a political prisoner, and black represents a prostitute or asocial prisoner.

A young Slovakian Jew called Elza is chosen to be our blockowa, our block elder, and is in charge of us when we are inside the block. Her duties include getting us out to roll call and dividing the bread loaves which are assigned to each room. There are also sztubowas, room elders, who divide the loaves between everyone in the room and hand out our portions. Between them, the block elders and room elders steal bread for themselves. It is easy to see that they are doing this and I realize almost immediately that I have to be frugal with what I get. Sometimes there might be half the portion allotted for me and sometimes there might be the whole portion; it all depends on luck and whether the room elder and block elder are honest people.

From the window I hear a man outside and across the wall asking, "Where are you from?"

"Tylicz, near Krynica." I answer.

"Go downstairs," he instructs, leaning his head sideways to see which way the watchtower guard is facing before tossing a piece of bread over the barbed wire for me to eat. I run out the door and grab this morsel just as a stone wrapped with paper lands at my feet. I grab the note and run back in the door before the watchtower guard swings back toward the camp road. Panting inside the doorway, I put the bread in my pocket and crumple the note in my hand before walking nonchalantly pass Elza's room. In the corner upstairs, I unfold his note and read: *Destroy this note the moment you read it, in tiny pieces. 12,000 Russian soldiers were here when we came. 5,000 are left, 7,000 have been shot. Your clothes are their uniforms. I am from Warsaw.* Shredding the paper into tiny pieces, I return to the lower floor to stand in line for the toilet, where I dispose of the confetti.

Block Ten is now full. I sleep next to strangers who cry in their sleep. We seasoned prisoners of two days eat our bread slowly and sip our tea as the precious rarity it is. We have bowls tied to our waists and spoons in our pockets while the new women argue over these utensils. We seasoned prisoners have seen the new arrivals go up to Elza and ask for a bowl or more food and get slapped. We know to get up in time for roll call; we have already seen the sleepers beaten. We are fast learners.

Outside, I see the man who gave me his bread earlier. He nods. I have organized a scrap of paper and scratched on it, *Thank you for your note. Where are they killing the Russians?* I try to throw the stone over the wall, but miss. It takes three tries before I am finally able to arch it past the electric fence, where it lands at his feet. Turning my head, I try to pretend that I am doing nothing, breathing a heavy sigh of relief that no one has seen my poor attempt at communication.

Along Block One there is a new line of well-dressed women who have just gotten off the trains. On the other side of the barrack, a line of newly dehumanized girl-women wearing Russian uniforms exits. My heart begins to beat faster. Narrowing my eyes, I squint against the sun, scanning for a face in the crowd which my heart distinguishes long before my eyes.[4]

"Danka!" Her beautiful chestnut-red hair is gone, but they cannot remove her brown doe-like eyes or touch her pretty face. My arms itch to grab her. If I can just touch her I know I will never let her go, but there is nothing I can do because there is a man with a machine gun and a dog standing guard over the new prisoners. My feet hold their ground, forcing me to wait, but I see her and in that instant of recognition I find my reason and will to live.

There is a moment of general confusion while the new girl-women mill about. I take this chance to merge with their ranks.

"Danka!" I grab her frail shoulders. For a moment she looks into my eyes terrified and threatened by this stranger. The stone in my stomach hardens—she does not recognize my face. Then she throws her arms around my neck, sobbing. "Rena!" She falters.

"Fall in! Get moving!" the SS start yelling.

I loop my arm under her shoulders, preventing her from swooning.

"When did you eat last?"

"I can't remember. Oh, Rena, it was horrible. There were so many people on the train. We were sitting on top of one another and someone died who was sitting next to me. It was unbelievable." Her face scares me. There is no focus to her eyes.

---

4. "March 28 [1942]. . . . 798 Jewish women from Brunn [Slovakia] . . . receive Nos. 1999–2796" (Czech, 150). Danka is numbered 2779.

"How did it happen that you came here?"

"Because you are." Her voice is so naive, so young.

"What do you mean?"

"Our friends were going to hide me on a farm, but I had your letter and I told them I wanted to go work with my sister. You are all I have, Rena."

"Danka, you shouldn't have come. We should have stayed in Slovakia and hidden. This is bad . . . real bad."

"March! Get in line!" The block elders push us into line so they can march the new prisoners into Block Five.

"Follow me." I push her past the others, marching over to Elza. "My sister has just arrived and she is so hungry and tired." I beg. "She has had no food since Bratislava. Please, Elza, let her be in our block! I am afraid for her."

"Okay, your sister can share your bunk." We are lucky, Elza has a heart today. "You can help me with dealing out the bread and take an extra portion for your sister."

I do not ask what will happen to the girl who was sleeping next to me; I know already that one does not ask. This is a selfish act, perhaps, but I have a sister who I have to keep alive and she is all that matters.

I know this is going to be a tough assignment for Danka. I can see in her face a look of bewilderment and shock. I will have to try to be by her side every moment. As if I have the power to shield her from the SS. But I actually believe I can; I have to believe I can.

We are in Block Ten for the night. Staring at our surroundings with a frozen face, she asks me where we are. The man I have been corresponding with calls my name from the windows, tossing over a bit of bread and another note. I go downstairs and retrieve it with more expertise and less hesitation this time.

"Here, Danka, a little extra bread from a fellow Pole." I am grateful for the extra food. She does not notice the note, which I read and tear up quickly. *They are being shot in the Block Eleven, next to you. Tear this up immediately.*

I sit down on our bunk, taking Danka's hand in mine, looking into her face for an undisturbed moment. She is so tired she can barely keep her eyes open, but she tells me all that has happened to her.

"What about Zosia and the children?"

"I heard nothing."

"Maybe they will be okay."

"Maybe." It is a dim prospect, but we cling to whatever hope we can muster. There are tears streaming down our faces as the magnitude of what is happening around us begins to sink in. I am frightened. We are in prison. Our only crime is that we were born.

"We can't cry very much here," I say, dabbing her tears with my sleeve. "We can't let them know they've gotten to us. You see here—this is the enemy and we're going to have to be real clever to outsmart them. Are you listening to me, Danka?" She nods as I wipe the tears from her cheek.

"Then listen good to what I'm going to tell you. We're farmers' daughters. We're going to work, but that is what we do already. The work here will be nothing to us. And this is my dream, Danka—I am going to bring you home. We're going to walk through our farmhouse door and Mama and Papa will be there waiting for us. Mama will hug and kiss us, and I'm going to say, 'Mama, I got you the baby back.'"

"Yes, Rena." She lays her head on my chest, falling asleep in my arms.

I stare into the darkness cradling my sister until her breath lengthens and deepens and I am sure she will not wake. Gunshots crack open the night. Through the slats of the boarded-up window I watch Russian soldiers collapsing to the ground. There is so much I want to ask God for, but my lips are numb and my mouth is frozen open in disbelief.

I am wearing the uniform of these dead soldiers' comrades. To-morrow morning more girl-women will march through the gates;

they will be handed the uniforms of the men I have just witnessed die. My throat swells shut. I cannot tell anyone what I have seen. Only my whispers can be heard, but I do not believe that anyone is listening. "God help us."

❖   ❖   ❖

Four A.M.

"Raus! Raus!"

The room elders beat the bunks, poking the girls who are not early risers. It is Danka's first morning and she wakens with a start. I wish there had been time to prepare her for the ordeal of rising and roll call, but there has been no time to prepare her for anything. I have waited for my sister and that has kept me from thinking about much else.

"Rena?" In a daze she looks at me. How I hoped it was all a dream, a nightmare.

Today we will work. I have been eager to get busy and finish this prison life, and wonder if they will release us sooner if we work harder. Anxious to wash my face, I am in line for the toilet immediately. Danka moves slower, and as the line of women desperate to go to the bathroom lengthens she gets pushed back.

The kettle sits outside the door of the block. We hold out our bowls as the block elder scoops a ladle of tea into our bowls. We step into the dark. Our breath, the steam rising from our tea looks like specters and phantoms floating in our midst. We sip our tea quickly, hoping it will warm our insides, but the chill sweeps through our muscles.

The mist traces halos in the searchlight beams above our heads. It is eerie, like a scary movie. Shivering, I wonder where the monster is. I am not sure if it is the actual coldness of the morning, the lack of sleep and food, or abject fear that is making my knees and teeth knock together uncontrollably.

The SS walk up and down our rows counting our heads. They

seem to take a long time as they compare notes and lists. They are not sure of what they are doing.

"Rena, I have to go to the bathroom," Danka whispers.

"That's not allowed. You should have gone before roll call."

"I can't help it."

"You have to wait until roll call is over." Reality is cruel. She holds her legs together.

"Pick your kommandos!" an SS man orders. The kapos come toward us, sizing us up and down. I take Danka's hand, leading her back to our block where Elza is standing on the steps.

"Elza, will you please let my sister inside? She has to go to the bathroom, she has diarrhea."

"I can't do that. You know nobody goes into the block after roll call. There are rules! Besides, the room elders have already cleaned the bathrooms."

"Please, Elza. You know they will beat her if she messes herself."

"I don't care." Her eyes glare at me, defying me to argue with her.

"She has got to go!" I grab Elza's shoulders, shaking her. "How can you be that way?" I nod at Danka to run inside while I distract our block elder. "Don't you have a mother?" I yell. "A sister? Were you born from a stone? Who do you—*arghh!*" The words catch in my throat as the breath is slammed out of me and my collar is pulled back, choking me. Hurled through space, I fall roughly to the ground, seeing only the reddening face of an SS woman before her boot finds my ribs.

"You! *Scheiss-Jude!*" My arms fly across my face, my most precious possession. She pummels my thighs and my back, but I do not scream or cry. I have seen enough abuse in the past few days not to encourage it through pleas to stop. I bear her assault like a stoic as she steps on me again and again and again. When she finally stops, I crawl to my knees looking for someone to help me up. Danka has returned from the toilet and is crying without any noise. My legs are bruised, my ribs hurt, I can barely breathe, but I have my face, and after a few moments I can walk.

We join the ranks of still unchosen girls. A kapo points at us. "You there! Line up here!" I grab Danka's hand, pulling her with me. We fall in behind the kapo. She must have seen me get beaten and I wonder why she's chosen us. I have never been hit before and hide my eyes, ashamed to look into our kapo's face. I feel so small and insignificant. I feel completely worthless.

"March out!" The fog is rising. We follow the other groups out the gate, toward the fields, to work. Shuffling our feet so as to keep these so-called shoes on our feet, we try to march. Some girls are still holding their pants up; some, like myself, must hold our shirts shut. The wind pierces the bullet holes in our uniforms.

There is a draft at my knee and one by my heart. I wish I were not so sore. After three days of doing little else but cleaning and worrying, I had thought work would be a welcome relief. I want to show them what a hard worker I am and how proud a farmer's daughter can be of her strength. I ache all over.

"How are you feeling?" I manage to ask Danka. I know that worrying about her will take my mind off my throbbing bruises. She nods, afraid to answer. An SS man passes us. They are the monsters hidden in the mist, our nemesis dressed in gray. They are everywhere.

"Halt!" There is a pile of sand and dirt and stones before us. Our kapo orders, "You will sift this sand through these nets and load it onto those lorries. *Schnell!*"

We take shovels from the shed before beginning to dig the rocky soil and toss it through the net. It does not take long for our hands to ache and our shoulders to grow sore. Blisters appear almost immediately, and just as quickly they pop and make the shovel handles slippery. A young girl leans against her shovel to breathe for a moment. The whip cracks across the air, striking her on the cheek. Her cry is spontaneous. Shocked, she returns to her task with renewed vigor as a welt of blood forms on her cheek. I catch Danka's eye for a split second; we know not to stop.

Once the lorry is full we are ordered to push it up the hill, where we must unload the sand in a separate pile. We line up, four on each side of the lorry. The wheels are steel and made for railroad tracks. Forging forward, we hold onto the cold metal sides, heaving with all of our might. Movement is slow, but once the momentum is built we manage to complete our task. Unloading the carts, we push the lorries back down the hill with relative ease and start all over again. By noon we have completed many trips.

A huge cast-iron kettle is carried into the fields by male prisoners. Other kommandos arrive at the kettle and we line up for the noonday meal. Hungry and eager to have time to eat, Danka and I push our way into line. The kapos serve us. The servings are pitiful. We can see a few vegetables hiding deep in the murky depths of the water, but the ladle does not even graze them. It does not deserve to be called soup; it is barely turnip broth.

"Tomorrow we'll get in the back of the line," I tell Danka.

"Why?"

"Because the less water there is on top, the more likely we are to get a piece of meat or turnip."

We sip our noonday meal slowly, hoping to savor what little there is, hoping it will give us the energy we need to continue. My mind tastes these circumstances like strange food. For a moment I allow myself to brood. This is slave labor we are doing. I cannot accept this thought, though. Maybe it will get better. I am just hungry. Maybe they will give us more food tonight after a hard day at work. We are working toward a goal—freedom. We are helping the Germans build something. These justifications, no matter how small and insignificant, help me get up, get in line, help me continue working.

The weather is not encouraging as the afternoon labors on and a steady drizzle turns to sleet. The mud becomes like cement, grabbing at the wheels of our carts, and as the temperature drops the metal we cling to freezes to our skin. Whips snap above our heads, sometimes landing against our backs like stinging wasps. At least we have wool shirts on to protect us from the elements and the rawhide. Like a team of plowhorses we are prodded. A girl pushing the lorry losses her shoe. Our kapo pulls her out of line quickly, before the cart can lose its momentum. The girl looks in the mud for her shoe and then I do not notice what happens to her. We have our own shoes to worry about.

Somewhere in the late afternoon, as the gray sky above us darkens, we hear the blessed order to "Halt! Line up!" We stand in line, muddy and worn out. We are not the same girls who marched to work this morning; our heads hang lower, our eyes do not dart as quickly and alertly. Danka's cheeks are sunken, her eyes almost vacant. We march defeated to the blocks.

Evening roll call lasts forever. We stand in our neat rows watching the other details enter camp. Some of the girls are carrying bodies. I want to shield my sister's eyes from this sight, but I cannot move. An SS guard orders that the bodies be dropped in a pile next to us. They are counted. I am counted. Danka is counted. The living are tallied in a separate column from the dead. I think it is dark but cannot be sure; the lights from the watchtowers are a constant brutal sun which does not warm.

We hurry into Block Ten, our new home, in silent shock. The room elders dole out our crusts of bread. There is no extra food for the hard day of work; there is not a slice of meat or cheese, just a smear of margarine on our dirty hands. Sitting on our beds, we stare at this meal. How did it come to be called dinner? Slowly, gently, we begin to lick our palms.

"I can't take this." "Look at my hands." "I have blisters." "I'm starving. Why won't they feed us more?" The voices timidly emerge along the rows of bunks. Others are already curled up on their mattresses, weeping in their sleep. A few voices can be heard talking to the air and I wonder if I was right about the men I saw on my first day here. Maybe this is a place for the insane, maybe it will not be long before we are all talking to the air. It seems so long ago that I thought the men in camp looked like lunatics. It has not even been one week.

I go downstairs after eating, then wash myself. My nipples are raw and red from the scratchy wool shirt and the cold which corrodes my skin as viciously as the bugs I am infested with. Why didn't they let me keep my bra and underwear? I feel as if someone has taken sandpaper across my breasts until there is no skin left. I close the shirt and return to our bunk upstairs. Danka is already fast asleep. I try to lie down next to her but my side is too tender. Pulling my knees under me like a fetus, I crouch over my legs, allowing my shoulders to fall forward. My head rests on the mattress. I wonder how I will ever fall asleep but I am too tired not to. Like a small boulder I slumber.

Four A.M.
"Raus! Raus!"
We roll out of bed and race to the bathroom before the line is too long. We get our tea and drink it quickly while we wait for the SS to count our heads. The tea is not warm enough to warm our hands or our bellies. We line up behind Emma, our kapo. Somehow we have learned her name in the past two days. She has a black triangle. She is a prostitute. We march behind her in rows of five in the dark to the field where we will sift rocks and sand all day. The mud is so deep now that it is almost impossible to push the lorries. Still we haul our loads through the muck. Like Sisyphus, in the Greek myth, we are punished, forced to push that eternal rock up a hill.

Again at noon we are allowed a few moments of rest and some turnip stock. Even waiting at the end of the line does not assure any pieces of vegetable or meat, but the broth is a little thicker— or maybe we just think it is.

On Saturday, our Sabbath, we work. It is just another way that they undermine our faith and challenge our fortitude. We toil in the mud, forgetting that it is against Hebrew law to lift a hand in labor on this holy day. We shovel and push, sift and haul, from sunup to sundown.

On Sunday there is no roll call. It is the Christian Sabbath and they honor this day of rest, although not out of Christian charity. It is a free day, if anything can be called free in Auschwitz. We sit on our beds, speaking to one another for the first time. "Where are you from? How old are you?" Meaningless chatter that has no place in memory. We do not discuss our circumstances. Bashfully we try to rid ourselves of the lice imbedded in our uniforms and every crevice of our bodies, scratching our heads, brushing out our underarms. I take off my pants and run my fingers along the seams and pockets, pulling the bloodsuckers off and squeezing them between my fingernails until they pop or squish with my blood.

Within an hour my fingernails are black and blue from killing the parasites, so I toss them on the floor, squishing them with my shoes or just ignoring their squirming white bodies. If I think about what I'm doing, if I look at them for too long, I will vomit. It takes all day, this ritual cleansing. I wash my face and hands three or four times, hoping to feel clean again. It is futile. Finally I must lie down and rest. Sleep is not forthcoming, though, for there is the gnawing of the lice I have missed, the voices of Slovakian girls around me, my sister's heavy breath. She slumbers. I must keep watch. I lie on my bunk staring at the ceiling, waiting for sleep to take me away. Some nights it comes swiftly. Some nights it lingers just on the fringes, out of reach. Sometimes I hear the rifles firing at the wall in Block Eleven. Other nights I hear nothing, but this does not mean there are not Russians being shot. It only means I don't have the energy to hear or think about the dying next door.

I wake in the morning, before anyone else has even opened their eyes, knowing that something has changed in my body. I stare up at the bunk above me for a few minutes, wondering what I have sensed about myself; then it comes. The slow moistness on the wool against my legs. The cramp in my stomach. I sit up with a start and pull down my trousers to check. The stains on my thigh are unmistakable. I have my period.

Slipping downstairs to the toilet, I look for something to use, but there are no rags or sanitary napkins, only small squares of newspaper. The flow has increased since I stood up. As I check the searchlights before stepping outside, blood trickles down my leg. I remember *Mama handing me a soft piece of cloth and saying, "Go put this on and bring me the other one. Don't look at it!" "Yes, Mama." I obeyed her words. She didn't want me to be frightened by my own blood.*

I scour the ground looking for anything that might help me hinder the flow. There is nothing. The kettles are being brought to our door; I know Danka is up by now, wondering where I am.

I return to the block toilet and take a few squares of newsprint. Wiping them against my trousers to make sure they're clean, I shudder. Then, without thinking any further about it, I crumble them up and place the newspaper between my legs. I spend the day completely self-conscious, afraid of what getting my period means in this place. I cannot speak to Danka about it. Dealing with this curse means praying that it will go away quickly and never return.

There are more girls in our ranks today; a transport must have come in. Emma collects us for work and we march out to a large, open field. I am grateful that there are no lorries and sand for us to cart today. My back is still sore though the bruises on my leg are almost gone.

There is a large pile of bricks. "You will carry these to the other side of the field. You must carry ten bricks apiece!" Emma tells us. We pick them up one by one, balancing them in our arms until we have a full load.

Arms throbbing, pulled almost out of their sockets by the

weight, we walk carefully so as not to trip. The shoes impede us, slipping side-to-side underneath our feet. It's hard enough to keep the shoes on in the mud, now we cannot even see where we are going with so many bricks in our arms. The rocks and brambles grab at our feet as if we are making our way through a maze. We cannot drop one brick and pick it up without losing the whole load. Emma follows behind us, whipping us to work harder.

"Halt!" Emma stands by the kettle serving our noontime snack. We sip the broth hungrily. It is hard to slow the gulping tendency because the stomach craves more. We march back to the field, carrying bricks the rest of the day until we hear "Halt!"

We take our bread at the door. Am I imagining it or have the portions gotten smaller for Danka and me? The block elder's sister has arrived in camp and Elza has seen to it that she is in our block. I believe she's eating our bread.

"I'm going to go to the window to see what I can organize," I tell Danka, walking to the front of the block. It is a newly born bartering system, and what I trade with the men on the other side of the fence is simply being Polish. They long to speak with their countrywomen and Danka and I are two of just a few Poles in the women's camp; we have this one advantage over the Slovakian girls, who do not speak Polish.

"What's your name?" I hear a man's voice from the other window. He sounds sympathetic.

"Rena. My sister and I are here and we are both very hungry."

"Go downstairs. I'll throw you something."

I wait and wait by the door; nothing falls by the steps, though. Elza's door is a crack open. I worry that she will punish me for being downstairs after yelling at her the other morning. Something falls in the dirt. I check the guard tower. He is looking the other way. I dash out the door, grabbing my parcel. Inside I lean against the wall, breathless. It is hard to comprehend that such a mundane task means risking my life—I could die for something as insignificant as a piece of bread the size of my hand.

Four A.M.

"Raus! Raus!"

We roll off our bunk, slipping the sandals onto our feet. We divide the extra portion of bread and quickly eat.

"March!" Even though we are tired we try to march proudly, just as we are instructed to. "March!" Heads forward, we step in unison, playing the part of dutiful servants to the Third Reich, but there is nothing to be proud of. We organized an extra piece of bread; it means a lot to us, it is nothing to them.

"Line up across the field!" The pile of bricks has not gotten any smaller overnight. We line up wondering what this chore will mean.

"You go on the right side of me," I tell Danka.

"Face me!" We shuffle into position. We stand about ten feet apart and wait. Orders are barked in German. The girl in front of the line picks up a brick and throws it to the girl next to her, who throws it to the next girl. The whip cracks as the girl in the front shakes the cobwebs from her brain and grabs another brick. The girl to the left of me tosses the first brick into my hands. I toss it easily to Danka, turning back just in time to receive the next brick. At the front of the line we can hear the SS yelling, *"Schnell! Schnell!"* The tempo increases so that there is barely a moment between tossing the brick to our neighbor and receiving the next brick. Within twenty passes, blood begins to ooze from cuts on my hands. The rough edges of the baked clay slice into our palms, repeating the injuries over and over. Danka is slow at this chore and doesn't always turn in time for me to throw my bricks, but the girl by my side is not waiting for anything. She throws them anyway.

I want to scream at the pain in my foot when the bricks land on my arches or toes, but I do not. I do not do anything to call attention to myself. I throw the bricks as I have been instructed, but I do not throw them at my sister's feet, I do not inflict the torture on her that is being inflicted on me. I grab these bricks quickly from my feet and hold them until Danka can catch up; sometimes I am holding two or three bricks at once, sometimes I have four. Danka sees that I am in trouble and speeds up, but she is like me, unwilling to throw bricks at her neighbor's feet. We are lucky in one thing only, the SS do not see the bricks falling on our feet; others are beaten for the same offense. Last week our backs hurt from the strain of pushing and shoveling; today our sides hurt as we twist and sway with the weight of the bricks. Every muscle throbs.

Lunch comes hours after the sun has risen, hours after the first welt raised its angry head on our hands. Each a mass of rough cuts and torn skin, our hands hurt just carrying our red bowls full of gray-white soup. We sit for about twenty minutes before marching back to the line, to the bricks. Our stomachs and the pain in our hands gnaw like persistent rats at the last vestige of our humanity.

The afternoon drags on.

At sundown we march back to camp. We stand at roll call. We are counted. There are several bodies piled next to us. They look so alive, as if you could reach out and wake them. If they don't look dead, I speculate, could we all be dead? Maybe this is all there is, maybe there is no world beyond us. One can't think like this without going insane. I stop pondering any thoughts which might lead to insanity. I focus again on the present. The girl-women who carry bodies into camp at the end of the day are in work details under the kapos with the green triangles that signify they are convicted murderers. At least our kapo is not one of those.

Four A.M.

"Raus! Raus!"

We stand for inspection. We can barely keep our eyelids open except for the crisp German orders cracking around us in the night that is really morning. We line up behind Emma. There are a few missing and a few added to our kommando.

My heart sinks as we near the field where we worked the day before. The SS orders are derisive; if they could laugh at us they would. "Move this pile of bricks back to the other side of the field." We stand unable to move, unable to comprehend these orders. "*Schnell!*" The whip snaps, their slaves scatter.

Danka stands next to me, away from the pile we must move. I pray that the girl next to me doesn't throw bricks on my feet. The first brick slices into my hand as the sun breaks through the clouds. Pain and light. I toss it to Danka, willing it to land gently in her hand, pleading with the brick not to hurt my sister. This is useless! It hurts a lot more knowing that this work is futile, knowing that they see our labor as worthless. How long will this go on? Our hands will be stumps if it continues. This is not work. It is meant to destroy us. Like a thunderhead obscuring the sun, I blot out this thought.

After evening roll call, for some reason I linger outside, unwilling to run into the block for the night. Maybe it is the faint smell of spring in the air, maybe I am too tired to run behind the others and wait in line. Danka has gone ahead.

"Rena? Rena!" I look through the wire of the men's camp at a skeleton who seems to know who I am. I cannot move. Squinting my eyes, I stare and stare.

"It's me. Tolek." The bones of his skull seem to stand up out of his skin. His eyes bug out above his cheekbones. He checks the guard tower to make sure no one sees him.

"Tolek! What are you doing here? How long have you been here?"

"I was arrested a few days ago for smuggling people across the border."

"Did they hurt you?" His mouth does not speak but his eyes answer my question. "You look hungry," I say. "Wait here. I'll get you my bread. Lucky for you I haven't eaten yet!"

"I can't eat your bread, Rena!" He turns slightly so no one can tell we are having a conversation.

I turn away from him. "You and Andrzej saved our lives, Tolek. Danka and I would be dead or worse if you hadn't taken us to Slovakia. You have been arrested for saving people like us!"

"And look where it got you."

"We are alive and that is enough. You never took money for that trip, now you must at least accept my miserable bread." I start to walk away against his protests. "I won't take no."

My feet have hope in them again as I run to find Danka. I have seen someone from our past; we are not dead. I can help someone. I no longer feel helpless or at the whim of a fate governed by German SS. I run breathless and tired up the stairs to the bunk Danka and I share. "Danka! Tolek is in the men's camp!"

"Tolek?" Life flickers in her eyes. "Where?"

"Outside. Come on. He's very hungry. We will have to share your bread tonight." I stop, looking directly into her eyes. "He looks terrible, like he might drop of starvation. We must help him."

"Yes, of course." Her eyes are full of tears. We run downstairs and out to the camp road, throwing our meager meal high over the barbed wire. There are no second tries tonight; it lands at his feet.

"Bóg zapłać." Tears get caught in his throat.

"May God reward *you*, Tolek," we answer, moving away from the fence, unable to risk speaking further.

Danka squeezes my hand. "He'll be okay, won't he?"

"I hope so."

The next few days we hoard our bread jealously so that whenever we see Tolek we can throw him an extra portion. Then he stops coming to the fence.

On our fourth Sunday in camp they shave us again. We had secretly hoped they would let us grow our hair back, but after the weeks of itching stubble it is shaved off again. Between the lice, the bedbugs, and the hair, there is always a nagging prickle somewhere on our bodies. I long for order and neatness, any way to feel better and not so filthy.

More Poles have arrived. Some are Gentiles and put in separate blocks from us Jews. They are better than us. Some of the Jews are from the ghettos in Krakow. There is one young girl called Janka whom we all cherish. She is just fourteen but had the guts to lie about her age on the train platform. For one so young and pretty, it is hard to believe she is also so streetwise. Her young life has been war and the ghetto, and I think she can be ruthless, but then Auschwitz is a good place to learn to be ruthless. Janka is a rare bird. She loves to flirt with the men and they give up many portions of bread for her smile and because she has news of home, and perhaps because she reminds them of their own daughters.

Our kapo, Emma, is brunette. She pulls her hair back tight against her head and wears a babushka. She is taller than most of us. Her friend Erika has blond curly hair and a pretty round face. She is slim and of medium height. Our blocks go from Five to Ten. Emma, Erika, all of the kapos live in different blocks but they are in camp with us. Only the SS live outside of the electric fences.

I haven't seen Tolek in quite a while and am worried about him. It is dusk, time to be going into the blocks, time to be getting to sleep soon so we have energy for tomorrow, but I scan the men's camp for our friend's face.

Erika walks by and then turns back. "You want to come and see our block?" she asks me. I am startled but do not show surprise. This seems like a strange offer.

"I'm not allowed. I'm Jewish." I tell her.

"Yah, of course you're Jewish or you'd be living in my block, but come see it anyway. I'll take the responsibility."

Sure, I think, you'll take the responsibility, but I'll take the beating if we get caught. The sun glows red on our faces as I follow her lengthening shadow.

She opens the door for me and I step into a world of neatly made beds and rooms where there are sheets and pillows. There is a blanket that looks thick and warm. How I'd love to have a blanket like Erika's.

"Have you ever loved a woman?" she asks me.

I come out of my revery. "Of course. I love my mama and my sister, who is here with me."

Erika smiles benignly. "Would you like to sleep here tonight?"

"Oh, no. I'd be terrified! My sister would worry, too. It's not fair that I should get to sleep on cotton sheets while she has straw." Then, fearing that I have been rude, I quickly apologize. "Thanks for asking, anyway. I can't leave my sister even if staying here meant having a good night's sleep and being warm."

Erika laughs. "You go back to your block. You're not ready for this." She leads me toward the door. "Here." She slips me an extra portion of bread. I take it quickly, not understanding why she would offer me such a nicety, not comprehending anything that has just happened. The light from the kapos' block illuminates the ground and then is severed as Erika shuts the door. I disappear into the closing night.

In our block I split the extra piece of bread with Danka. The crisp, clean whiteness of the sheets in the kapos' block haunts me. I cannot bear to think about the filth I wear, the conditions in which we are kept. Where our hands were once blistered we have grown huge callouses. My chest and legs are always red from bites and the wool rubbing against my skin. I want to scratch and scratch at the dirt on my body until there is nothing left for the bugs to gnaw on. Suddenly I am struck by an idea and take off my pants.

"Rena, what are you doing?" Danka sounds concerned.

"I'm going to fold these horrible trousers and put them under our mattress at night so they have a crease down the leg."

"Don't, Rena. It's cold."

"I want to look neat, and there is no place to wash and iron these clothes." I spit on the fold and begin running my fingers down the material, squeezing it together. "If I can't be clean, at least I can be neat." My glance falls to the floor. My shoes are filthy.

Our poor feet are too miserable to look at for long. They are no longer pink with health but pale and dyed with reddish brown stripes left by the leather straps. Soon it will be summer and at least our feet will not be cold, but now it is spring and the weather is the worst it's been in years. I spit on the leather strap, using the inside of my pant hem to polish the leather. "I can clean my shoes first without dirtying my pants too badly!" I hold the first strap out for Danka to admire.

"You're crazy."

I return to pressing the crease into my uniform before motioning for her to move. Lifting the mattress up, I lay my trousers lengthwise, smoothing them until there is not a wrinkle. I place the mattress back in its place and let Danka get back in bed. She shakes her head but doesn't say another word.

In the morning we roll off our straw pallets. I lift up the mattress, retrieving my neatly pressed pants. Shivering a little, I pull them on, tuck in my shirt, and tie them with my rope. Smoothing my trousers down my leg, I smile; the leather strap has a sheen even in the dark. What I wouldn't do for socks, as well as a bra.

"You look nice, Rena." Danka observes. We head out the door. We rarely have to use the bathroom more than once a day because of dehydration, although I try to wash both morning and night. It is more to my liking to use the facilities in the evening than to wait in the morning line and chance a beating at roll call.

We turn over the dirt in a field. Shovel after shovel, we lift the damp dirt and rocks into the air, dropping them back to the ground. Sprigs of spring grass shoots stick up from the earth. When no one is looking we sneak these little blades into our mouths. The white portions of the grass are sweet and succulent. However small, they comfort our dry throats.

The SS woman over our detail today is gorgeous. Her raven-black hair gleams in the sun. She must have had a perm. I remember the last perm I had before I came to Auschwitz. She is dressed in gray. Her skirt is tailored to her waist and her boots are polished to an obsidian gloss. Her skin is alabaster, radiant against her rosy cheeks, and her lips shine with health despite the wind.

It is a cruel day. The wind is damp and nips at us between the holes in our clothes. Her black cape keeps snapping in the wind as if teasing us, saying, Look at me! Look at me! Aren't I gorgeous? Look how far superior I am to you. She stays far away from us. We have lice. We are poison to her sophisticated senses. I cannot help but steal a few precious glances. Her beauty holds my gaze. I am in awe. We are so wretched in comparison.

She is Reichdeutsche. Her German shepherd has fine bloodlines, too; his head is not too pointed and his ears are upright, attentive to her voice, her commands. He is gray and black. He matches her outfit. Together they strut outside of the postenkette, the work boundary that separates her from her slaves. Her whip cracks against her boot. The wind cracks her cape. We shovel.

Out of the corner of my eye, I see her take her army cap off her head. Her hair dances in the wind, against her cheeks. Her eyes are defiant as she looks at Emma, who is not, who will never be, her equal. She throws her cap outside of the boundary which we are restricted to work within. I quickly drop my gaze to my work. The wind is still.

"You there!" the SS woman barks. "Get my cap."

A girl looks up from her work, glancing at the rest of us, but we are busy. We are invisible. She is not. She puts her shovel down, running quickly across the field to obey the order. She does not think about it. She does not question it. She is a slave just as we all are. Hesitating before crossing the boundary to retrieve the Wardress's cap, she casts a glance back at the SS woman.

"*Schnell!*" The wardress cracks her whip. Stooping to retrieve the cap, the girl moves tentatively toward the Aryan. Her frail and skinny arm holds out the cap timidly.

"Attack!" The wind grabs the order with a hiss. The girl freezes, paralyzed between fear and confusion.

The dog rushes past us, snarling. The girl's hands fly to her face. I move in front of Danka. "Don't look."

He lands on the girl's chest, driving her into the ground. Her screams lacerate the sky, rending the breath from our mouths, splitting our hearts apart. We cannot cover our ears. We cannot breathe.

The screams, oh God, those screams. There is no sound on earth as horrible.

I glance, just once. Her bloodied arms flail the air. The dog reaches her throat. Cemented before my eyes, never to rest, is her spirit as it departs, separated from her body by a dog's jaws on her neck.

There is no silence like this silence . . .   empty . . .   silent.

The reverberation of death. I turn over the earth. Danka follows my lead. The girls next to us lift their shovels. Nobody breathes.

We work harder than before. As fast as possible we shovel, almost hysterical, faster and faster. Our muscles ache. Our ears weep with the echo of her screams. Only the sounds of the dying are immortal in Auschwitz.

The dog pants. The wind whips her cape. The wardress pats his head. He licks his paw. "Good boy." It begins to rain. We shovel faster and faster.

"Halt!" Jarred, Emma motions for two of us to carry the body into camp. The girl looks like a little spider somebody squashed underfoot—so thin, so fragile. I take her arms. They are not cold. They are sticky. We march. With every step I take her head flops against my back. With every tap of her head, every step I take, her screams tear my soul. I tighten my grip, afraid that I may drop her, afraid that I might damage her further, afraid . . .

There is no silence in my head. There is only screaming.

Four A.M.

"Raus! Raus!"

We roll off our bunk. My period has arrived again, even though everyone else's has stopped. I rush to the toilet. Today I am lucky; there are newspaper scraps. I stash extra in my pocket before hurrying outside to get my tea. We get counted.

Four A.M.

"Raus! Raus!"

It is Sunday. How many Sundays have we been through? We do not talk about it. Danka and I pick lice off ourselves. It is disgusting, but it is worse to have lice than to pick them off. We go outside for a look around. It is not hot yet, but summer is nearing. Some days are very warm, but I wonder if the chill will ever go away or if it is like the permafrost in Finland, always just below the surface of our skin.

"Danka! Rena!" We can barely believe our ears. Scanning the fence, we see Tolek. He is looking much better, more like the boy we used to know.

"Tolek! Where have you been? We have been so worried."

"Are you hungry?" Danka asks.

"No, no bread. I have gotten a good work detail emptying the latrines. We take the filth to the fields, where the local farmers take it to use on their crops for fertilizer. There is a kind farmer who sneaks me food from his kitchen whenever he can."

"That's wonderful."

"If you had not shared your bread with me I would never have been given such a good job. You gave me the strength to go on."

"You gave us hope, too, Tolek."

"I'm going to throw something over." That is the cue to keep our eyes peeled for danger and to be ready to hide the thing coming over the wires. The guard in the watchtower is looking in the other direction. The coast is clear. A large chunk of real bread falls at our feet.

It is manna from heaven.

"Thank you, Tolek." Danka flashes her beautiful smile.

"It smells like home." I slip the loaf under my shirt.

"Thank you both. I must go." We watch our friend disappear into the men's camp.

The smell of the yeast-risen dough drives our nostrils to distraction. "Come on, Danka, let's go back to the block and have a feast."

Huddled next to each other we divide the bread. This is not the sawdust-and-water biscuit-shit we get from the Germans, this is heavy Polish bread that comes from the earth and has been kneaded by a farm woman's hands. Our taste buds cannot cease watering. I imagine that the whole block can smell it. Our teeth tear at the dough and our jaws hurt after not chewing anything substantial for so long. There is a memory that surfaces just behind my eyes, something about bread and Mama. I push it back. I cannot think about anything dear or sweet right now. Tucking the thought back where it belongs, I continue the meal Tolek has shared with us. There is a constricting pain in my chest and something dampening my cheeks. I chew tenderly, wondering where my sniffles came from and if I've caught a cold, while wiping my nose with the back of my woolen sleeve.

Four A.M.

"Raus! Raus!"

Roll off the bunk. Stand in line to pee. Get a splash of tea. Step into the dark. Wait on the camp road. Stand for roll call. Get counted. The sun rises. Get counted. Step in line behind Emma. March out to the fields. Work until they say "Halt!" Get soup. Sit down for a moment. Get up. Get in line behind Emma. March back to the fields. Work until they say "Halt!" March in neat rows of five back through the gates, under the words ARBEIT MACHT FREI—the sign means nothing anymore. Stand in neat rows of five. Get counted. The sun sets. Stand in the dark. Get counted. Go to the block. Get a piece of bread. Stand in line to wash. Nibble at dinner. Make it last. Lick your hand. Lie down. Wake up.

Four A.M.

"Raus! Raus!"

At roll call a man called Himmler appears in camp. He must be important.[5] He watches the order in which we line up. The kapos are counted. They are prisoners too. He looks at his list. "One in the ranks has finished her prison sentence today!" he announces. Silence. He reads her name. There are a few shouts and hugs of congratulations among the kapos. We watch, stricken. No one will read our names at roll call, pronouncing freedom. We know this now. They are prisoners. We are slaves. They are human. We are not.

Summer. It is hot. We crave water. We work in the hot sun until we are burnt and blistered by its rays. The wool makes us sweat and scratches worse than before. There is no relief.

There is a rumor that Auschwitz is going to be used just for men again. We are going to be moved to Birkenau.[6] There are other rumors of a gas chamber and a crematorium.

"What is Birkenau?" We do not believe the other rumors, they were started by the Germans to dishearten us.

Four A.M.

"Raus! Raus!"

Roll off the bunk. Stand in line to pee. Get a splash of tea. Step into the dark. Wait on the camp road. Stand for roll call. Get

5. "July 17–18 [1942]. . . . Himmler inspects the Auschwitz camp complex, takes part in the killing of a transport of Jews, attends roll call in the women's camp, and approves the flogging of female prisoners. He also orders Rudolf Höss, the commandant of Auschwitz, to proceed faster with construction of the Birkenau camp" (Rittner and Roth, 29).

6. Auschwitz (Auschwitz I) is approximately two kilometers from Auschwitz II, often referred to as Birkenau; they are both a part of the same camp complex known as Auschwitz-Birkenau.

counted. The sun rises. Get counted. Get in line behind Emma. March out to the fields. Work until they say "Halt!" Get soup. Sit down for a moment. Get up. Get in line behind Emma. March back to the fields. Work until they say "Halt!" March in neat rows of five back toward . . .

Wait! We've turned. We are moving away from Auschwitz.[7]

Voices murmur through our ranks. We march. This is a change to our routine. The unknown is dangerous. Eyes vigilant, senses alert, we march away from Auschwitz, away from the walls and watchtowers. The sun sets. There are fences and more barbed wire towering before us. We march under a different gate with the same sign, ARBEIT MACHT FREI. We are not fooled. We stand in neat rows of five. Get counted. Emma and Erika and the other kapos go to their new blocks. They have moved with us to this new camp. We stand in the dark getting counted. We are assigned to Block Twenty, or is it Twenty-Two? It is dark when we step inside.

The floor is dirt. There are no bunk beds here; there are shelves, wood planks, three tiers high. We are suppose to sleep here? Where are the mattresses? Our beds look like horse stalls. There is a sour smell of human odor. There are rags for blankets. We stand, squeezing our bread in our hands, unable to cope, unable to move. A girl begins to cry. Like fire in a stable her fear grabs us, and like dried straw we burn inside. Tears cannot quench these flames of disaster. We are lost. This is Birkenau.

---

7. "August 5–10 [1942]. . . . The women's section at Auschwitz I is moved to Section B-Ia in Birkenau" (Rittner and Roth, 29). "Birkenau was a swamp fenced off by electrified wire. No roads whatsoever, no paths in between the blocks. . . . March to mid-August 1942 . . . about 17,000 women prisoners, most of them Jews, arrived at Auschwitz. A large number of them (probably about 5,000) perished before the transfer of women to the camp at Birkenau" (Strzelecka, 401, 394).

BIRKENAU

(Auschwitz II)

How will we survive this place? What do we have to do to in order to live? What does this life mean? These are not questions that abuse our thoughts every waking moment of every day, they are simply undercurrents, concerns that cannot be answered. What is there to know? We did not receive a ticket, when we entered Auschwitz-Birkenau, saying, You will leave on such and such a day, you will leave alive. There are no guarantees.

Birkenau is a cruel awakening. In Auschwitz there was a lot of death, but it was not such a daily fact of life. Now we see death every day. It is a constant like our meals. And there are not just one or two girls dying, like before, but tens and twenties and losing count.[1]

I know that I must be with my sister. I know that I must make sure she lives; without her I cannot survive. I do not admit that to myself, but I know she is a part of my truth, my being. We cannot be separated; there is danger in separation.

It is colder than it was yesterday, but lately it is always cold. Even in the heat of summer I did not feel warm. We are wet for

1. "Some 15,000 to 20,000, mostly Jews, died during these two months [July and September 1942]. The girls' camp suffered the most, as it was not fitted with sanitary installations, and the poor wretches were covered with lice. . . . Suicides were frequent and were mostly committed by throwing one's self against the high tension wires of the inner fence. This went on until they had dwindled to 5 percent of their original number" (Wyman, 32).

days after it rains; it penetrates everything. How does one measure temperature when there is but one temperature? It is a dull
chill, like the numbness in my mind—always there, taken for
granted, eventually ignored.

I used to love the warm, sparkling days of summer, but this year
it seems to have disappeared. Can it be fall already? How long have
we been here? What month is it? There must be trees somewhere
in the world that are changing color, preparing to welcome winter
with their fiery reds, oranges and golds, but I do not see any
changes here. It is always gray. I myself am gray.

We have a calendar in Birkenau. It is hunger.

The emptiness in our stomachs never ceases, just as the chill
never leaves. It is our only clock, our only way to discern what
time of day it is. Morning is hunger. Afternoon is hunger. Evening is hunger. Slowly we starve until we cannot make out anything beyond the gnawing of our intestines grinding against each
other.

A block elder asks me if I want to be a room elder. "No, thank
you," I tell her, but in my head I think, I can't take bread from others who are as hungry as me, I can't hit people suffering just like I
am. I repeat my private chant, Be invisible. That is one of the rules
I live by. Those who are too visible eventually get struck down, so
I stay in the background and try simply to get by.

There is only one thing that exists beyond the gates of
Auschwitz-Birkenau. It lies in wait for me like a beacon of light
shining through the fog. I hold it before me constantly, every second of every day. It is the only thing that keeps me going—Mama
and Papa. They beckon to Danka and me from the fringes of my
mind. Their hands wave against a backdrop of snow and winter
sky. *We're here!* they cry. *We're waiting for you to come home.*

We're coming, Mama, I remind them. *Don't leave us here
alone.* And they don't. I hear Mama's voice comforting my trou-

bled mind, soothing the worries of our existence. The only thing she cannot help is the hunger, but even that dulls in comparison to the knowledge that Mama and Papa are waiting for Danka and me to return to Tylicz. I frame this picture in my mind and hang it on a mental wall where I can gaze at it constantly. I know they are there. I work because they need me. I eat because they are waiting. I live because they are alive.

Mama, I brought you the baby back. I repeat it over and over in my head. It is the refrain to the song that keeps me strong and healthy and spirited: Mama, I brought you the baby back. My one great feat in life, my fate, is to survive this thing and return triumphant with my sister to our parents' house. My dream cannot be marred by German whips or chains or rules. I will succeed because I have no other choice. Failure does not even occur to me. We may die in the interim—death cannot be avoided here—but even that will not dissuade me from my sole purpose in life. Nothing else matters but these four things: be with Danka, be invisible, be alert, be numb.

I wonder if I will ever wake up to turn over in a real bed again. Will I ever open my eyes without German commands and decide to sleep in because it is raining out and I don't have to get up yet. Will I ever dream again? The days are long and hard but the nights are devoid of even the relief of dreams, the pain of nightmares. I crawl onto my shelf and pull a woolen rag around my collarbones. I pretend that it will warm me. Falling into unconsciousness, I am woken by barking, by gunshots, by nothing at all, . . . by four A.M. . . .

. . . *"Raus! Raus!"*

The room elders hit the girls who are still sleeping and those who aren't quick enough to scramble off the shelves we lie on. Is this place so different than Auschwitz? The room elders, the block elders, all have an edge in their voices that I haven't heard before.

For all their privileges, the extra food they pilfer from us less fortunate slaves, they also have a dirt floor beneath their feet. They
have cots rather than wood to sleep on, but they are in a converted
stable just as we all are.

"Come on, Danka." I shake her gently. "We have to get up and
find the bathroom." There is no toilet in the block, as we had in
Auschwitz; there is a bucket. The pot-bellied stove sits at the end
of the rows of stalls and toward one end of the block, close to the
block elder's room. There is a curtain dividing the block and room
elders from the rest of us.

"Where's the toilet?" I ask, ducking as the stick strikes for my
head. This is not a place for questions. We run outside. The kettle
of tea is sitting in its customary place by the door. We hold out our
bowls; the ladle splashes lukewarm tea across our hands.

Standing in neat rows of five in the dark, we eat our remaining
piece of bread and wait for the SS to arrive. We have noticed that
the day goes better if we can eat something before we work, so
Danka and I always eat only half our portion at night, saving the
rest until morning.

SS men Stibitz and Taube march up and down the rows counting
our heads. Wardress Drexler, the head of the women's camp,
watches; her buck teeth stick out even when her mouth is closed.
Roll call takes at least two hours this first day in Birkenau. We are
not used to standing for so long at attention; fighting the urge to
shift our feet, we must not even yawn. Every few minutes Taube
hits someone for not looking attentive enough, for moving her
feet, for no reason at all.

"Dismissed!" The orders crackle through the dawn light. I take
Danka's hand, stepping quickly toward Emma. I have had her in
my sight ever since she came out for roll call. With all the changes
in the past twenty-four hours, I'm determined to keep one thing
constant, and getting on Emma's work team is the only thing I
have the slightest control over. She spares us a brief smile as we

line up behind her. It is a small comfort to see a familiar face in such terrible surroundings. Emma's is that face.

We work all day and march back to the stables. "We should try to sleep here." I point to an area far enough away from the block elder's room to give us time to get up in the morning without getting struck by her stick. We crawl onto the shelving cradling our bread and clutching our blanket between us. Silently we chew half of our bread, hiding the remainder in our pockets. During the afternoon I have learned that Birkenau is where the Russian prisoners of war were kept. With a shudder I recall the bodies falling into the mud between Block Ten and Block Eleven. They must all be dead now.

These first few weeks we are barely surviving. The food is less than it was, which means it has gone from a crust to half a crust. The soup is so thin there is no use to wait at the end of the line for a piece of turnip or meat, and the tea is practically clear. Every morning that we wake up at least one girl has died in our block. There are no exceptions. We are dropping like flies.[2]

You have to have a brain to figure out all that is going on, the tricks to being camp smart: where it's the warmest, who's the most dangerous, who doles out a bit more soup. The new arrivals barely have time to figure out how to survive before they die.

After roll call you don't know about anything else that's happening. You can't keep brooding about what is befalling you and everyone else because then you won't have the energy to go on, and you have to keep going. The work you do may kill you, but if you don't do it you will be killed.

No matter what the detail, we work, we dig, we carry, we sift,

2. "As the history of Nazi Germany so emphatically shows, racism's 'logic' ultimately entails genocide. . . . Any consistent Nazi plan had to target Jewish women specifically as women, for they were the only ones who would finally be able to ensure the continuity of Jewish life. Indeed, although the statistical data about the Holocaust will never be exact, there is sound evidence that the odds for surviving the Holocaust were worse for Jewish women than for Jewish men" (Rittner and Roth, 2).

we push, we die. But Emma does not kill prisoners, this one thing I know. Every morning Danka and I run to Emma to get in her detail. Birkenau is bad, but Emma does not make it worse.

❖   ❖   ❖

It is Sunday. We stand at roll call, but then, rather than being dismissed, we are ordered into a block where tables are set up. As we step inside we are handed a postcard and a pencil.

"You will write your family and tell them that you are fine and like working here," we are ordered.

I stare at them incredulously, unable to believe that I must write lies to my loved ones.

"Dear Zosia," I scribble at the top of my card.

"You will write exactly as you are told: 'We are being treated very well,'" they dictate to us. "'We have plenty to eat and the work is not hard. I hope to see you soon. Love, . . .' Sign your name."

I remember Zosia's cries when she said Nathan's card meant he was in Siberia, and on the bottom of my card I jot quickly in Polish, *It's cold here, just the same as Nathan told you.* I pray she sees the truth behind my words. I pray she and her children will not follow us to Auschwitz. We turn our cards in and are excused. I feel weak, shaky from the ordeal. As hard as we toil every day, writing those few words to Zosia has taken more out of me. Danka and I do not discuss the cards we have written. We do not discuss family at all.

My monthly curse wakes me. In the confusion of moving from one camp to another I didn't even think of sneaking newspaper squares with me. I didn't think the latrine in Birkenau would be any different than the toilet in Auschwitz. How naive I am; newspaper is a luxury that we no longer deserve.

Once a month my period still arrives without any prior warning. It is something I dread and wait for, never knowing when it will make its appearance. Will I be working? Will I be in the shaving line on a Sunday, embarrassed in front of the men? Will today be the day I cannot find anything to stop the flow and the SS decide to beat me to death for being unclean? Will today be the day the scrap I find gives me an infection?

I hate the smell. I hate not being able take a bath. The sink in Auschwitz was a relief, but in Birkenau there are no sinks, just faucets. It is impossible to remove the dirt and grime from my body without soap. On Sunday, if there's time, I use my red bowl for a sponge bath, although there is no sponge and the water is nothing but cold. No matter how hard, nor how often I scrub, it always feels as if something is left on my flesh. I worry that the smell of blood will attract the dogs to me. Of all camp horrors, the dogs scare me the most. I pray that if I must die, I do not die screaming.

The routine has changed slightly in Birkenau. It is easier to use the latrine in the morning because at night, after the door is shut, no one can go outside. So I try to get up before the room elders and sneak outside before the line gets too long. If that doesn't work, I use the bucket under the cover of darkness and then slip back into the bunk next to Danka for a few more precious moments of rest.

As bad as Auschwitz was, I miss it. I miss being able to wash my face and hands, I miss the straw mattress and the little blanket Danka and I both had. Now we must fight for just one blanket, and that barely covers us. In Auschwitz, the bunk beds we slept on were spacious in comparison; now there are six women per shelf. We are crowded so close that we almost have to touch.

As if that isn't bad enough, almost every day there's another transport, and more and more girl-women are filling the camp. The girls coming in from Holland still have polish on their nails.[3]

3. "September 16 [1942]. . . . 902 Jewish men, women, and children arrive from Westerbork . . . Holland. A first selection took place in Cosel, where about 200 men were probably chosen by the Schmelt Organization. After the selection on the unloading platform in Auschwitz, 47 men and 29 women are admitted to the camp and receive Nos. 63825–63871 [men] and 19720–19748 [women]. The remaining 626 people are killed in the gas chambers" (Czech, 239).

There are so many more of us in this new camp than there ever were in Auschwitz; roll call takes twice as long as it used to. At the end of the day, when we're finally dismissed to our blocks, we run as fast as our weary legs can carry us to make sure we have a blanket and the best place to sleep. I have decided that we will always try to sleep on the middle tier of the shelves. The top is too high to climb up to after a hard day of work, and the bottom is too cold.

We take our bread, stepping into the dank block. Together we crawl onto the shelving, nibbling on half of our bread before collapsing into the despair of dreamlessness, crushing the other piece of bread in our hands for morning's breakfast. It is not safe in our pockets anymore. There are those who will try to pry open our hands while we sleep, to steal our food. There are those who will grab our blanket off our bodies while we sleep if we do not hold tight onto it. Some nights we come in from work and someone has taken our blanket already; some nights we wake up shivering because someone has ripped it from our hands. I cannot get up and do the same thing, though; taking someone's blanket while she sleeps is too heartless, so we huddle closer for warmth and wait until the next evening, when I will take a blanket off a bunk that has not been claimed yet. I have that right; someone has stolen ours.

In line for bread. The block elder calls out my name. "1716! You look sturdy. We're going to perform gymnastics on Saturday night. Can you do a cartwheel?" I nod my head gingerly. "Good! You want to earn an extra portion of bread?" I nod again, afraid to say no. "Then you and a few others will come with me and practice a gymnastic routine to perform for the SS this Saturday night." I hand my portion of bread to Danka and follow the block elder and about ten other girls outside.

"We'll start with some tumbling," the block elder instructs us. "Who here can do a flip?" Two girls raise their hands. "Somersaults? Handsprings?" I raise my hand with a few others. We line up according to our talents and proceed to work through our paces. "Smile when you finish that round-off!" she shouts. "Hold that pose after you finish the cartwheels! Thrust your chest out! Chin up!" It is beyond strange to be tumbling across the floor of a vacant block on a little stage. It is even stranger to try to pretend we're having fun doing these antics.

We work for about an hour before we are excused. "Okay, get some sleep. Tomorrow we'll practice a pyramid." We trudge back to the block sore and tired from the physical exertion. I can't believe they're going to force us to perform for the SS. We continue to practice our routines for two more nights.

Saturday night as we receive our evening's ration the block elder tells us, "I have gymnastic uniforms for you to wear for the show. After you eat, come to my room and I'll give you the clothes." In her room, we each get a sweatshirt and pair of shorts to change into. "You will get your extra portion of bread after the show." She reminds us of the reason we're doing this charade. "Now go change and meet me at the door in two minutes!"

A selected group of prisoners are allowed to watch. Danka is among them. The SS sit down in the back of the empty block to be as far away from the stage as possible. It was bad enough doing these tricks with no one watching, but now that the SS are watching the humiliation is ten times worse.

A bulb hangs over our performing area, lighting the plywood stage. The SS sit in chairs at the other end, eager to watch their monkeys perform. They chat merrily, enjoying their Saturday night out, as if this entertainment were the circus coming to town.

We march into the center of the lights and bow to the officers. They clap halfheartedly. The block elder beats on a drum she has organized from someplace, trying to give us a sense of rhythm. I do three cartwheels in a row. Applause. A girl does a flip. Applause. Somersault. Applause. I cartwheel in a circle. There is no smile on my face when I stand upright. Applause. The lips won't go upward no matter what I do. I can work ten hours a day, I can be starved to death and watch people die, but I cannot smile—it is impossible.

The wood under our bare feet is hard and unforgiving. I complete a round-off. Applause. A girl does a split. Applause. The bottom of the pyramid lines up. The second level gets on top of their backs, then the third. I vault on top of all of them, praying they don't collapse beneath me from fatigue. Then I stand up, raising my hands over my head, opening my mouth slightly. It is not a happy face I wear, it is a questioning face, a mouth hanging like a question mark. Why am I doing this? Is it really worth a piece of bread?

The applause is mediocre. I leap to the ground. We line up holding hands, bowing to our superiors, then turn around and march, chests out, chins up, back to our block.

In the block elder's room we return the gym clothes and take our extra piece of bread, like dogs getting a bone. "Good work." She praises us. "Next time," she continues, "I think we should try some more difficult flips." Eyes lowered, I scan the ground for some relief while splitting my portion of bread exactly in half to share with my sister.

There is not going to be a next time—can't she see how sick and tired we are? Just these few days of practice have taken their toll on our bodies. I'm afraid I have lost more weight; I know some of the other girls have. All for a piece of bread. We should have an entire meal for the work we did. I never want to do anything like it ever again. Crawling into our space on the shelf, Danka whispers, "You were good, Rena." Her voice is so sweet, so loving. My head droops. My eyelids fall. I disappear.

Somehow we figure out how many Sundays we have been in camp. This tells us it is Yom Kippur, and we fast from sundown to sundown. In my heart I pray: Oh, Lord, my Lord, please help my parents and protect them until we can return home. Tell them we are alive and that we love them. Tell Mama that I know she is watching over us through your eyes. Strengthen our faith and our bodies. Let us not falter from hunger. In your name, Lord, who is my Lord.

There is power in my prayer; it strengthens my arms and my back as we sift the sand all day. The knowledge that our God is near us lifts our spirits and we work with renewed hope in our hearts, ignoring the bread deep in our pockets and refusing the soup at lunch. In the evening, after sundown, we eat yesterday's bread for supper and save today's for morning. It is something to fast, but we are so hungry already fasting makes little difference to our stomachs. We simply do as we have done every year of our lives since we were old enough to fast on the holy day.

Danka is behind me, waiting for her soup, when the kapo accuses her of coming back for seconds, and hits her on the head with the steel ladle.

"I'm never going for soup ever again." She stands in front of me crying, her bowl empty.

"Danka, you have to get soup. They don't feed us enough for you to skip a meal."

"I'm never getting in that line again."

"Here, share mine."

"No, you don't have to do that."

"Why not? It could've been me who got hit. She just chose you because she's cruel and selfish and she wants your meal, too."

"I'm not taking yours."

"Well, you better, because I'm not taking any until you do, so you're going to let the whole thing go to waste. Come on, take some." We take our spoons, scooping together out of the same bowl. She sips it hesitantly.

"You didn't fill your spoon up as much as mine. Take some more." She takes a little more, smiling vaguely. There is a little tidbit of turnip floating around. I push it toward Danka. She pushes it back. And so we eat my portion of soup two spoonfuls at a time, splitting the turnip evenly between us.

The next day she refuses to get in line at lunch and I have to convince her all over again to take some of mine, and so it goes; we count our spoonfuls and share my soup. I wish she would return to the soup line but keep my mouth shut.

It is Sunday. It is fall. We get off our shelves. Get our tea. Eat our half piece of bread. There is a rumor that there is going to be a selection.

"What's a selection?" we ask among ourselves.

We groom ourselves all day, pulling lice from our armpits and clothes. There is no fighting these creatures; they are everywhere. I spit on my shoes and wet the crease on my pants. It is important to look good if there is going to be a selection—whatever that means. I want to look right. Sunday fades with the light of a pale sun.

Four A.M.

"Raus! Raus!"

We grab our tea as we step outside. I notice that something is different immediately. The guards do not count us at once. Instead they stand at one end of camp, ignoring our neat lines and perfect rows. We wait and wait. Well after the sun is up, we wait. The row at one end begins to move forward slowly. We strain our eyes to see what is happening but they are too far away. "They are selecting us." The whisper scurries down the rows, informing those of us who are not yet moving toward the SS.

"What's it mean?" Danka asks.

"I don't know," I lie. I have an idea, but it is not something I will share with anyone I care about. We stand in our lines, forced to contemplate what new Nazi trick this is.

"They're deciding who will live and who will die," the whispers confirm. Our ranks grow silent and still. How can this be true? How can they do that? We have seen how they step on us like cockroaches—why does this next thing comes as such a surprise? We move forward. I take Danka's hand, squeezing it reassuringly. "I will go in front of you," I whisper.

There are two sisters at the head of the line. I recognize them from the first transport. Like me, they've been here since the beginning. They step up to the table of SS officers. An SS points for one to go left and the other right.

"No! Please!" the one who has been chosen for life cries, falling on her knees. "Let me go with my sister," she begs the officer, careful not to touch him. She huddles at his glossy obsidian boots weeping for mercy.

He points. She follows her sister. Hand in hand they step toward the flatbed trucks.

I squeeze Danka's hand one last time before stepping in front of those who will judge me fit or unfit. Tomorrow may have no meaning for us if we do not pass this selection—and if we do pass? Tomorrow may have no meaning for us.

I hold my breath. The thumb points for me to live. Stepping forward hesitantly, cautiously, I wait for my sister . . .

The thumb points for Danka to follow me. I breathe.

Squinting for a last glimpse of the sisters, I suddenly wish I had gotten to know them, their names, anything about them. All I know is that they were in line before me when we got tattooed the second day in camp. I think their numbers may be 1001 and 1002. I look at my left elbow. The gray-blue ink blazes up at me. 1716. Their numbers were lower than mine. I haven't seen many numbers lower than mine since we came to Birkenau. I wonder how many of us are left from the first transport.

They push and heave the girls who have gone the opposite direction as we have onto the flatbed trucks. I haven't seen the dreaded trucks since my first day of arrival. Danka's face pales as the blood drains from her cheeks. Frozen with fright, she watches the girls scramble against one another as SS beat them with riding crops. Cattle and sheep are treated with more respect. I take her hand, trying to pull her away from the scene across the compound, but recoil at the touch of her clammy flesh.

"Come on, Danka. There's nothing we can do for them now."

"Where are they taking them?"

"I don't know, but it can't be good. They treat them just the same way as they did the people on the transport platform." Her eyes glaze over. The sun has sunk below the horizon. I cannot believe we've spent an entire day waiting for self-proclaimed gods to decide if we are fit enough to deserve life. That night there are fewer girl-women in our block. We do not ask where they've gone.

The following morning we line up for roll call, but we are not counted. In neat rows of five we wait. In the dark. In the morning light. In the noonday sun. We wait. The line moves forward. There is no pause for lunch, there is no break from standing and waiting.

We are "selected" again.

Four A.M.

"*Raus! Raus!*"

There is another selection.[4]

❖   ❖   ❖

One night after roll call the block elder gives Danka and me, and quite a few others, packages from the Red Cross. We stare at these packages, puzzled by their presence in this place. They even have our names on the brown paper: *Rena Kornreich* and *Danka Kornreich*. The stamp is from Switzerland. I stare at it for the longest

4. "October 1 [1942]. . . . A selection is carried out in the women's camp, Section B-Ia, in Birkenau. 2,000 prisoners are selected and killed in the gas chamber the same day. . . . October 2 [1942]. . . . A selection is carried out in the women's camp. . . . 2,012 prisoners are chosen and killed in the gas chambers. . . . October 3 [1942]. . . . At another selection in the women's camp in Birkenau, 1,800 female prisoners are selected. They are killed in the gas chambers" (Czech, 247–248).

time. It's colorful and ornate, and confirms that there is a world beyond the electric fences and barbed wire that surround us. It is proof that somewhere someone cares whether we live or die.

We tear open the brown paper, ripping open the boxes as if we are opening presents from family. There is a can of sardines, a package of crackers, and a sweet tea biscuit. Slowly we unscrew the top from the sardines. They are so salty. After not tasting anything with flavor in six months, they are a smorgasbord to our mouths. We stick our fingers into the oil and lick slowly, trying to make it last, but even if we could lick it all night it would never be enough. The crackers and biscuits we stick in our pockets to save until tomorrow.

I feel stronger that day, savoring the crackers with our soup at lunch and saving the biscuit for dinner. The sweet cake serves as an actual dessert after our meager supper. It plunges our senses into another realm, melting in our mouths, leaving them yearning for more. We've craved sugar since the day we arrived in camp; it rushes through our bodies, but then it is gone. We are grateful for these three semi-meals, but the next day our stomachs yawn and ache for more and there is nothing left to eat except bread, tea, and soup.

"Are you going to get the soup today?" I ask, hoping the care package will have encouraged Danka's appetite. She shakes her head. I treat her as gently as possible, but if she doesn't start eating more and getting her own soup again we will both turn into a muselmann, and from that there is no way back.[5] If we become emaciated we're goners. I try and try to get her to get her own bowl of soup, but her spirit is dwindling before my eyes. How do I get my sister to want to live? Without that desire there is no way we can survive, and I need her just as badly as she needs me.

5. *Muselmann* is camp slang for those who have lost not only body weight from starvation but the will to live, becoming living skeletons.

When we march out to work and return at night, now, there is a band playing and we're supposed to step in time to the music.[6] It is a paradox to everything else we do, a slap in the face to what dignity we have left. I think the Germans like the fact that it degrades us just one more rung down the ladder of life. The musicians have it better than we do, but we do not begrudge anyone who has the luck to find inside work. Besides, they're forced to play no matter what the weather, and they can be selected, just like anyone else, if they get ill or look poorly. They do not have it so much better. We're all slaves. One slave may have an easier job, but we're all still slaves. The only way to avoid sure death is to work inside, but even that doesn't mean you can escape death completely.

Four A.M.

"Raus! Raus! Schnell!"

We rise off our beds of icy, hard wood. It is difficult to move. We are stiff and worn out. Every joint and ligament cracks with fatigue. It is freezing. The tea has lost its steam in these sub-zero temperatures. Even the SS, who are so punctual in everything, take their time entering the gates, counting our shivering bodies. It is the first frost of the season and our bodies are not yet used to the chill in the air.

My mind moves as sluggishly as the blood in my veins. A temporary lapse of conscious alertness, being at the end of the rows, and a brief pause crossing the yard to our detail, and Danka and I are late for Emma's detail.

"I'm full," she tells us. An SS signals for her to march out. She shrugs her shoulders; there's nothing she can do. We stand there looking forlornly at the kapo we have adopted as our own guardian, but her kommando—our kommando—marches out, leaving

---

6. Wardress Maria Mandel, former supervisor of Ravensbrück, became head supervisor on October 8, 1942, and organized the female orchestra in Birkenau. (Source: Rittner and Roth, 29.) Mandel's sister, Wardress Elisabeth Hasse, is also in camp.

us behind. With a shiver I turn away, my sister in tow, hoping that Erika's detail is still open.

"Fall in!" A whip crosses my shoulder blades as our course for Erika is redirected and we're herded into the rows of another kommando. Snatched up by a kapo eager to fill her numbers, we line up behind this stranger and set off to work. Her eyes are bright and cruel. Her face is grim. She is all we have been trying to avoid. Her triangle is green. This kapo is a murderess. The tension in our ranks is palpable. We march in perfect unison.

"We have to be careful," I warn Danka, daring only the briefest of whispers. "Very careful."

It is a day without end. This kapo delights in finding fault and brutalizing us for it. She has a nose for the weak, and these she tortures unmercifully until they collapse and she can finish them off with one quick kick. By lunch she has killed three prisoners. She is as deft at killing as the SS man Taube. At lunch she merely splashes our bowls with broth; it lasts for barely a few sips. There are no regulations on food. No one cares whether she hoards it for herself, or does it out of cruelty. She is evil embodied, relishing every moment she can impose pain, a sadist at home in a world of victim-masochists. We are her personal peons.

Won't she tire of her abuses? No, she continues throughout the afternoon, beating, destroying, demolishing us like little dolls. One girl is crippled beyond belief, and then, as an added measure of spite, the kapo leaves her broken and suffering on the ground next to the dead, knowing her turn will not come until she is dragged to the gas. There are no mercy killings here.

When the order comes to stop working, the crippled girl is forced to walk with only the aid of one other girl. Her whimpers and moans accompany us as we carry the dead and the wounded back into camp: six bodies in twelve hours.

Like all kapos, Emma hits us, but she does not do it out of enjoyment, she does it for show. If the SS are around she has to act tough, but she never beats anyone to bleed and she never beats

anyone to death. She hits you if you're lazy or do something stupid, and she'll smack you so the SS won't think you're favored, but
the only dead we ever carry in from working under Emma's eye
are killed by the SS or have collapsed from starvation or illness.

No matter what work atrocities they give us, Emma rarely adds
to it. There are very few constants in camp, but Danka and I are a
constant to Emma, just as she is to us. The three of us are there day
after day. Maybe Emma isn't mean to us because she recognizes
us. There are so many prisoners now that there are always new
faces, new numbers, but we're the old-timers, standing in front of
her every morning, doing our best to survive.

Not until we suffer the kommando under the murderess's command do we realize how lucky we are to have this secret ally in
Emma. It is not that we are friends, or that she will do anything
out of the ordinary for us—we are Jews, after all—but I think
there is a place in her heart for my sister and me. I am counting on
it—what else is there to depend on? There is so much uncertainty.
Emma simply gives us one less thing to worry about.

Four A.M.
"Raus! Raus!"
At morning roll call I see the familiar faces of Erna and Fela
Drenger and their cousin Dina, from Tylicz. There's not time to do
anything but wave before we must hurry to Emma's detail, but we
have seen our best friends from childhood and work through the
day hopeful that we will find them that night. After evening roll
call I find them in a neighboring block.

"When did you arrive?" We hug each other.

"A few days ago," Erna tells me. "Where's Danka?"

"She's holding our space in the block and making sure no one
steals our blanket. Are you all okay?"

"As well as can be expected. This is some hell. How long have
you been here?"

"From the first. You've got to be real careful and always on the lookout," I warn them. "I'll try to help you any way I can, for now just remember to avoid the kapos with green triangles. They'll kill you for the fun of it. I'm going to try to get Danka into the White Hats. It's a sewing detail."

"Winter will be terrible if we have to work outside, and in these shoes," Erna observes.

"I'm going to organize some kerchiefs for Danka and me," I tell her. "You have to have white kerchiefs on to get into the sewing detail. I'll get you three, but you'll have to give up a portion of bread."

"Whatever we have to do, Rena. You know best."

"I don't know about that, but I've been here a long time and have learned a few things. I'll see you tomorrow or in a few days." I tell them which block we're in so they can find us, and then depart.

Friendly faces amid so many strangers is a comfort, but it is also a burden. I realize this immediately after I leave their block. Now I have three more people to worry about—how will we manage? Danka is the most important, of course, but we grew up with these girls. If we don't help each other, who will?

It takes me a few days to organize the kerchiefs, but finally a girl who is working in Canada agrees to bring me four white kerchiefs.[7] In exchange I trade her two portions of bread, one from Erna and one from me.

I hand the kerchiefs to Erna and explain the plan to her. "In the morning, stand as close as you can to the sewing kommando kapo. As soon as roll call's over, give them to your sister, Dina, and Danka, then get into the line as quickly as you can."

"What about you, Rena?"

"I'll keep working with Emma to keep the door open in her de-

7. The place where personal effects were stored after having been removed from prisoners and those who were condemned to die was referred to as Canada because that country symbolized abundance and a place far from the war. "Canada" grew from five barracks initially, to thirty. (Source: Rittner and Roth, 427.)

tail in case the inside work doesn't pan out. It's okay. Even though the work's outside, I'll be safe."

Four A.M.

"Raus! Raus!"

Danka stands next to Erna and Fela. We are counted. I stand farther away, separated for the first time from my sister during roll call. I do not like her being out of my reach. We are dismissed. I dash over to Emma's detail before it's full. Everything in Birkenau is first-come first-served. I stand behind Emma, keeping one eye on the sewing detail. Erna and Fela have their kerchiefs on, Dina is wearing hers. Danka looks lost, she doesn't have a kerchief on. My eyes sear into the back of Erna's head. Where's Danka's kerchief? my head screams. It's no use. Danka's thrown out of line. She looks across the camp for me, but it's too late; another kapo has signaled for her to get in line and they march out. I watch helpless as my sister goes to the fields to work without me. What have I done? Oh Lord, what have I done?

All morning I work, wondering if my sister is dead yet. I can barely finish my soup at lunch. And my stomach is so tied up in knots of worry that I don't appreciate the extra broth. I simply miss my sister and wish she were here to share it with me; I know she won't eat lunch today. Through the afternoon I try not to think about whether I will ever see Danka's smile or her beautiful eyes again. I cannot stand the time it takes for the sun to cross the sky. Finally Emma orders, "Halt!"

We put the tools in the shed and march into camp. We're the first back. Usually it is a relief to be in early, but today it is torture. Every kommando marching in seems full of dead or injured workers and they all look like Danka. My eyes play tricks on me and my mind follows. In one kommando she is being carried between two girls, her body is bruised and battered; in another she limps, leaning heavily on someone's shoulder. Weak from hunger, mad with worry, I believe that my sister has died a hundred times over. Then I really see her. She has been beaten, but she is alive. I cannot run

and hug her, I cannot move until we have all been counted, but I
see her and she is alive. Roll call ends and we reach each other
through the throng of milling girls heading for their blocks.

I hold her fiercely, unable to let go. "What happened?"

"Erna didn't have an extra kerchief for me."

"What? I gave her four!" I'm so angry when I locate Erna that
I can barely control my voice. "What did you do that to Danka
for?" I whisper hoarsely.

"I forgot I had an extra one in my pocket."

"Erna, this is no joke here." I grab her collar, wanting to shake
the sense into her. "Danka was almost beaten to death today."

"I'm sorry!" She weeps.

"What is sorry? I gave up my bread so my sister can have a safe
place to work that won't exhaust her and you almost murder her
by your negligence." I struggle to quiet my voice. "Erna, this is
serious. It isn't like going to school or Krynica. We can die!" I
point up at the watchtowers and whisper hoarsely, "See that! If
they say so, we are dead. There are no second chances. You have
got to use your head."

"I'm sorry. I'm so sorry. I was so scared that I forgot I had it. It
was stupid, a stupid thing to do. Will Danka ever forgive me?" She
takes the kerchief out of her pocket and hands it to me.

I hand it back to her. "Tomorrow she will be in the sewing room
with you. You will see to that—understand?"

"Yes, Rena. I promise. I won't make the same mistake again."

"That will be your forgiveness, Erna. Remember, mistakes here
are fatal."

The next day Danka gets into the sewing room. Now I march
out alone with Emma. I miss my sister terribly, but at night as I
wait for her at roll call I can relax a little, knowing she has not been
beaten. She is not dead. The sewing detail doesn't last long,
though; because the work is easier, everyone in camp starts organizing white kerchiefs and sneaking into that detail. We're getting
too smart for them. So they cut down on the workers they need

and Danka is one of the first to go. This time I'm watching closely, though, and take her hand, swooping her into Emma's detail. I'm not letting her out of my sight for another day of outside work; my nerves couldn't stand it.

Erna is a quick learner and manages to get Fela and herself into the detail in Canada. "This is good work, Rena," she tells me one night. "It's so easy. All we do is fold clothes, and when the SS aren't looking we can check the pockets and find all sorts of food left in them. We ate all day today. There were cookies and or-anges—I even found a chocolate bar! The best thing, though, is it's under a roof."

"There's a roof?" Chocolate is beyond my realm of imagina-tion, but a roof is something I can connect with. Finally a work de-tail that can protect us from the elements. It is our only way to survive, I know this; outside work is hard, but next to the SS, weather is our worst enemy, and winter is coming.

"I've organized two red kerchiefs for you and Danka." Erna checks the area before taking my hand in hers. "Tomorrow, march out with us. Only twenty-five can come, so be early."

I squeeze her hand warmly, retrieving the kerchiefs in a deft and invisible moment. I know she is returning the favor and that she stills feel guilty about Danka getting beaten. I enter our block feel-ing slightly relieved. Tomorrow we work inside.

Four A.M.

"Raus! Raus!"

We march out to Canada. There are mounds and mounds of clothes; I have not seen so many garments since Uncles Jacob's dress shop. There's a long table in the middle of the room, where we fold the clothes, pile them into bundles, and bind them with string.

"Where are these clothes going?" I whisper to Erna.

"Germany," she answers.

"What are you doing?" an SS man hollers.

"Nothing," a girl at the other end of the table whimpers.

His whip raises into the air, falling on her hands with a smack. "You were eating! You are here to work, not fill your filthy faces!" He strikes her again and again. A girl closer to me sneaks a morsel of food while his attention is diverted. Danka folds the clothes in front of her, staring into space. She is far away.

The whole day this SS man beats us to fold faster and work harder. There is not a minute when we can look for crumbs or candy in the pockets of the clothes.

I fold a Persian lamb coat. Touching its silky smooth fur, I lovingly reminisce about the last time I touched Persian lamb. Schani had promised me that someday I should have a coat as fine as my aunt's. I fold the sleeves behind the back, remembering how lovely Aunt Regina looked in her fur coat. I fold the front of it slowly over the arms, pulling out the shoulders so it won't wrinkle. The tailor's tag gleams up at me, white satin against the curly black fur. The words *Jacob Schützer, Bardejov* leap off the tag.

"No. Oh no," I gasp before I am able to quiet myself.

"What is it, Rena?" Danka comes out of her daze just in time to see that I am folding Aunt Regina's coat.

Where is the justice in it? Where are they? Where are Cili and Gizzy? Where is Aunt Regina? . . . Where is Uncle Jacob? . . . I cannot bear to stay in this place any longer. Looking outside, across the compound, searching for some relief from the horror in my heart, I see an SS man standing on a ladder. He opens a can, pouring something into a hole, then ducks down quickly as if he's avoiding something that doesn't smell good coming from the can.

"What's that man doing?" I ask, incredulous.

"Pouring the gas in," Erna hisses. "Don't watch."

I can't believe it, but I cannot avert my eyes. The rumors of gas chambers and crematoriums come back to me, plunging me into darkness. They are true? I stare and stare at the proof before my eyes. My aunt and uncle could be in there right now. I can see it but I cannot accept it. What does this mean? That my parents could be in there, too, right now, dying?

No, they are safe. They are waiting for me to come home. I can see Mama waving to me. Her babushka still draped across her shoulders. She is far away, but I know she is waiting for us. *I'm coming, Mama. Don't leave without me. I have Danka with me. We're all right.*

Blinking hard, I force myself back to the present. Bundling up my aunt's coat, I wish I could bury my head in it and sob; I fight back the tears in my eyes. The mounds of clothes glare at me. These coats and dresses and suits and hats have been taken from my people. Where are these people now? Are they even alive? Are they in camp wearing the same uniform that I wear? Are they dead or are they dying?

"You know what we have to pray for, Rena?" Erna's voice slices through my thoughts.

"What?" Smoke billows out of the chimneys on the horizon.

"Not that we don't get in there, but that when we do end up there they have enough gas so we die and don't go into the ovens alive."

"Oh, my God, Erna, we don't want to work here anymore." I imagine the screams of mothers and children and grandparents as they wither into nothingness just a few hundred meters away from where we fold their clothes to be shipped to Germany for Reich-deutsche to wear. "I don't know how you do it," I tell my friend.

We are from the same village. How is it she can take this barbarism in stride while I must turn and flee from it? I respect her nerve, but I'm not as strong as Erna. I cannot fold the clothes of my mother's brother's wife, watch the gas go down the chimney, and not die a little more inside. If my sister and I are to live, we will have to find another way; this detail will destroy our spirits if it doesn't destroy our minds first.

The next day Emma is waiting for us. She doesn't say a word about where we were the day before. We just get in her line and nod to her. She doesn't ask questions. And we pretend that nothing ever happened.

"Rena." Erna jerks her head toward the latrine. I lift my chin slightly upward, letting her know I'll meet her there. A few moments later we stand together next to the boards with holes in them that are supposed to act as toilets. She pulls a gift out from under her jacket, shoving it into my hand.

"Erna, you shouldn't have." But she is already slipping something else from out of her pocket. In my hands is something I have been dreaming of for months—a bra. I put it on hastily before anyone can notice, but cannot withhold my sighs. My poor nipples, scabbed and blistered from the constant rubbing of wool, are immediately relieved.

"Here, take these, too." Erna hands me a pair of underwear. "That's not all. We're getting shoes for you and Danka, too."

How? I want to ask, but knowing better I simply nod my thanks and whisper, "I am indebted to you." We exit the latrine separately.

I cannot believe the difference this one tiny luxury makes in my outlook, my mood. To have one less thing to be in pain about gives me less to think about, worry over; my focus is more clear and I am more alert. I think this bra helps save my sanity.

Erna has paid back the injury she did Danka with these gifts, although I think because we are friends she would have brought them anyway.

It is much harder to get shoes. But Erna thinks of a way, and in each shoe is a sock to prevent blisters and keep our toes even warmer. We have been working in sandals and bare feet for almost eight months and now it's November, I think. These shoes make all the difference in the world. They cover our feet completely, protecting them from the elements and the rats; they lend support, keep our toes warmer, and don't fall off in the mud. The only shortcoming is they do not dry easily. We can use the potbellied stove, but it would take the whole night guarding them to dry them completely. After a short time by the fire, we put them back on our feet and go to bed. The leather grows hard and inflexible, but that is a small price to pay for keeping one's toes. No one who is still wearing sandals will survive the winter. Except to dry them, the shoes never leave our feet; to leave them unattended for even a second would be to go barefoot. Shoes are a precious commodity. Danka and I are lucky to have friends as dear as Erna and Fela, who have brought them to us without even asking for a piece of bread.

I am concerned about Danka's depression. She doesn't seem to care about getting her own bowl of soup. This is something beyond her fear of the kapos serving the food. She seems so downtrodden, as if she's giving up on any hope of survival and this depression is eating away at her soul. She is absent; her eyes are glazed over most of our waking hours. I don't think that she's too far away, but I know I must try to do something before she goes beyond my grasp. Struggling with what to do about my sister's failing faith, I finally decide that there is no other course but to confront her.

It is late. The rest of the block is sleeping fitfully. "Danka," I whisper into the dark, "are you asleep yet?"

"No."

"What's bothering you? Something's wrong, I know it. Why're you so sad?"

"I don't know."

"Please talk to me. How can I help you if I don't know what's going on in your head? I feel you shrinking away from me. You have to tell me what's wrong."

"What sense is there to this?"

"To Auschwitz-Birkenau?" I'm puzzled.

"To everything." She pauses. "What if there's a selection and I'm selected to die?"

"What makes you say that?"

"You look better than me. You aren't losing so much weight and you're still strong. What if I can't make it?" Slowly it dawns on me.

"Remember those two sisters?" I take her hand. "And how the one begged to go with the other one? " She nods in the shadows. "I will do the same, if it comes to that."

"They don't allow it all the time, though. That was the first selection. They were soft. Now if someone begs to go with their mama, or sister, or daughter, they laugh and push them away."

"I will do whatever it takes, even if I must strike the SS."

"Then they will kill you immediately—that's no good."

There is something else lurking behind her eyes. It isn't dying alone she's afraid of, but I'm not sure which fear is possessing her. "What is it you're really afraid of?"

"Being thrown in the truck," she confesses. "They treat us like rotten meat . . . I don't want to be discarded like that, thrown onto the flatbeds . . . I'm afraid of what Erna said. Maybe there won't be enough gas, and I'll go into the crematorium still alive . . . What if they're trying to conserve the gas?"

I cannot answer that question. I cannot give her any promises or assurances that there will be enough gas to kill us when we arrive at the ultimate destination of all prisoners in Auschwitz-Birkenau. I cannot promise her that because I cannot lie to my sister, but I can promise one thing.

Everyone is sleeping around us, but with everyone talking out of their heads all the time anyway, no one pays us any attention— it's too commonplace to hear voices and screams in the night.

"Sit up, Danka. Come on, sit up." I hold out my hand. "You see my hand here." I put her hand on mine and look into her eyes. "Our parents are standing here in front of us and my hand is the Holy Book and on this book and before our parents I make this oath to you: that from this day on, if you are selected I will join you no matter what. I swear that you will not go onto the trucks alone."

It is pitch-black in the blocks, but I can almost see the light flicker back on in my sister's eyes as I make this promise. Exhausted, I release her hand and we fall back against the cold wood, pulling our blanket close around our bodies. Sleep comes swiftly, carrying us away to a land where there are no shadows.

At lunch the next day, Danka stands in line and receives her first full helping of soup in months.

I shiver under the thin blanket protecting us from the elements. There is something like ice touching my body. Recoiling, I struggle to return to the solace of sleep. I hate the rats that wander in between our bodies, chewing on whatever does not fight back. I jerk my feet; it is an automatic response to the varmints that cross our feet at night. Again I feel the pressure and push back against it. My jaw clenches shut as I fight to squeeze in a few more moments of unconsciousness. The ice brands me. Involuntarily my hand reaches out to shove away the weight lying against me, then recoils, recognizing the touch of human flesh. She is solid, devoid of all warmth, absent of life.

The room elders begin the morning ritual, banging on the sides of the shelves with their sticks, yelling and beating anyone within their reach.

"Go outside and get your tea." I move Danka toward the door. "I'll fold the blanket this morning."

"Why?" she asks innocently.

"Just go, Danka. Let me do this for you. We should start taking turns tidying our beds. This morning it's my turn. Go on, I'll catch up with you." I wait until she is outside.

"Somebody help me carry this body out?" No one wants to assist me. I understand their fear, but I don't want to be beaten for not removing the body. Tapping a neighboring bony shoulder, I ask, "Can you please grab her feet?" She nods reluctantly, helping me shift the corpse off the shelving. "I'm going to stop at the door. I don't want my sister to see."

Danka has her back toward me, so we take the body out, placing her at the end of the lines for roll call, where she will be tallied along with the rest of us. I am dying to wash my hands, but there is no time for that now; I must grab my tea and get into line next to Danka before roll call begins. Wiping my hands against my trousers repeatedly, I try to scrape the feeling of cold flesh from my body's memory. All day we work, and periodically I scrub my hands with dirt and then against my woolen pants, trying to get rid of the aura of death still lingering on them. The afternoon soup does not warm them; cupping them and blowing my hot breath into them does not thaw the morning's chill. Wringing my hands together until they ache, I cannot dislodge the obsession in my mind. I hesitate to take the evening bread before washing my hands but am too hungry to avoid the food. In the latrine I finally get a moment to rinse my hands and face, but there isn't enough water in the world to wash her frozen body from my mind. How I long for a hot bath, how I long for a cup of cocoa to sweep away the frigid fears devouring my mind.

"You should always sleep on the outside, next to the stall divider," I tell Danka as we crawl into our place on the shelf-beds. I never want her to be touched by death.

She blinks in wonderment at my statement. "Are you okay?" she asks.

"Of course." I pull the blanket up over our shoulders, snuggling as close to my sister as I possibly can, trying to avoid the touch of the girl already asleep next to me.

You cannot count on anything here. You cannot even count on the ground beneath your feet.

Danka has gotten scabies. Many have contracted this disease from living in such close quarters, and it's quite dangerous if it's on an area of the body that's visible. Fortunately, they're not on her face or hands and her legs are so covered by mud that no one notices anything beyond the dirt. But at the drop of a hat the SS can deem us unworthy to live, and the selections seem to be occurring on a more regular basis. I search my memory for a rem-

edy, allowing just enough of the past to return to my present so
that Danka can get well. I remember.

*We had gotten scabies at school and been sent home along with
the other children who had contracted it.*

*"Rena! Danka! Come into the kitchen and let me rub this sul-
phur onto your poor bodies." Mama opened up the door of the
stove, rubbing the lotion into our skin. "There you go. Now I'm
going to wrap you up and let you sleep by the stove tonight so the
salve can soak into the sores and make them disappear." We wore
our one-piece pajamas, the type with the trapdoor in the back.
Then Mama wrapped us up in old blankets and slid the bench out
of the szlufbank so it would make a small sleeping space for us.
Fluffing the down in our pillows, tucking us in, she hugged and
kissed us good-night. "Sweet sleep." The next morning she heated
water and used the big washtub to bathe us in, scrubbing us hard
with sulphur soap.*

*"Mama! You're treating us like laundry," we giggled. "That's
because I don't want a spot on you!" She snuggled us, wrapping
our little bodies up in towels and rubbing us dry. "Now you look
like two healthy young ladies again!" She unwrapped the towels,
revealing our creamy skin as fresh as a newborn's. "It's still
itchy," Danka complained, hugging Mama's leg. "It's okay. I'll
wash you one more time and then you'll be all ready to go back
to school."*

I hold out my bread to the block elder. "I need some sulphur."

"What for?"

"Scabies."

"Humph, better get rid of them soon." She disappears into her
room. She takes her time. As always, I must wait until she sees fit
to come out again, and crouch against the wall, dozing. Surpris-
ingly, she does not take hours to return with the lotion.

"Here. You know how to use it?"

"Yah." I take the salve. "Thank you."

We stand next to the potbellied stove in the middle of the block. "Do you remember when Mama wrapped us in warm blankets and had us sleep by the stove, when we were little?" I ask, rubbing the sulphur into her skin.

"We had scabies then, too," she answers quietly.

Our stomachs growl as we split Danka's portion of bread between us, speaking quietly or not at all. I wait with her, knowing she'll leave the fire too soon if she's tired, and I want to make sure the heat makes the ointment penetrate her skin. I feel like Mama as I go through the motions of mothering my sister, only this time there are no blankets to wrap her in, or flannel pajamas. The smell of the sulphur is strong but it is not so noticeable above the body odors we constantly live in. I determine that it will be safe for her to leave the salve on throughout the work day before we wash it off.

"How are you going to wash it off?" Danka asks.

"I'm going to have to use our bowls to rinse you, Danka."

"I can't eat from mine if you do that." She looks almost terrified by the thought.

Why not? I want to ask. What's the big deal? But I keep my mouth shut. I don't want to risk her refusing to eat again. "We'll use my bowl," I suggest. "And I'll share yours until Sunday, when I can clean mine out real good."

"Okay." The next evening I get some water and rinse my sister's body of the salve.

"They're gone, Danka."

"They are?" She checks her skin, relieved. Mama's angelic face floats on the periphery of my vision; I am grateful that there's no sign of infection from the sores.

Four A.M.

"Raus! Raus!"

We crawl off the planks. Our shoes are already on our feet because they are never taken off. We step into the neat rows of five, sipping our piss-warm tea. There is a new layer of snow that glimmers across the compound creating an illusion that it is clean. That fantasy will not last long, though; as soon as the SS begin counting us and we step out of our ranks and into our work details, the ground will once more become the frozen grayish-brown slush that it usually is. The ice breaks beneath SS boots as they walk up and down our rows counting, counting. Our breath mingles in the air without prejudice; the last few flakes dropping from the clouds fall upon our eyelashes without discrepancy. I stomp my feet to wake up my still-sleeping toes, making sure they don't freeze in the stupor of standing, waiting. The sky above us has not changed in the two hours of roll call; winter days are so short that we march out to work and return in the dark.

Trampling through the snow toward Emma, I look across the sea of girls getting into their lines for work and recognize my cousin Gizzy. She is looking at me as well. We wave but neither of us smiles.

"Gizzy's here," I whisper to Danka. "I'm going to find her after work tonight." Danka nods silently. It's too cold to speak.

Bread in hand, I find Gizzy's block without too much difficulty. She is already lying down when I arrive, and half asleep. Her breathing is hoarse and vague. She is ill. I dig what is left of my fingernails into my hands, mustering the courage I need to continue.

"Gizzy? It's Rena . . . your cousin." Her eyes flicker in recognition.

"Rena?"

"How are you?"

"Not so good."

"How long have you been here? Where is Cili?"

"We were in hiding. She escaped . . . I got caught . . . " She pulls her blanket up around her shoulders. "It's so cold." I cannot respond. From beneath the blanket her feet hang out like two huge blue balloons. There is a smell emanating from the flesh. I try not to breathe. "Rena, I have bad news for you . . ." She seems unaware of her legs.

"What?"

"Schani is dead." She falters. "I'm sorry to be the bearer of such sad news, but I thought you should know. He jumped off the transport train on the way here, and they shot him."

I feel the pit swallowing me whole. What a waste of human life. What a sweet man, Schani Gottlobb. My fiancé. Gizzy introduced me to Schani at one of the Zionist organization dances. So long ago.

She takes my hand in hers. I welcome her comfort but cannot bring myself to tell her about her own parents. Her eyes close, heavy with fatigue, and my gaze drops once more to her gangrenous legs.

"You need medicine," I tell her. "I brought you some of my bread. Here, share it with me." I divide my portion, handing half to her. "Would you like me to get you some water?" She shakes her head. "Everything will be okay, Gizzy, you'll see. I'm going to get you something for your ankles and we'll get you some shoes so the cuts on your feet won't get infected, or be so cold . . . We should get you working inside." I stroke her hand comfortingly. "I have to get back. It's getting late. I'll see you tomorrow after roll call."

"Thank you for the bread, Rena. Give my love to Danka."

"You'll feel better tomorrow, you'll see," I tell her before stepping outside into the winter night.

My eyes smart in the cruel wind, making my eyes water. Tears stream unwelcome down my cheeks. I stop fighting them. I do not know how long it has been since I cried and I am not even sure that this can be called crying. It is noiseless; my eyes feel like rivers and I cannot dam the flow.

There are so many things to mourn that I'm not sure which one I'm weeping for. Walking back to our block, I cry for Schani's death. I cry because there's not going to be a wedding, and I remember how when I first came here I thought there would be. I cry for myself and my sisters. I cry for Gizzy and Aunt Regina and Uncle Jacob. I cry because it is dark and no one can see me. I cry because there is no reason not to.

Four A.M.

"Raus! Raus!"

My face feels raw from the tears I shed secretly last night. I wish I had some lotion to smooth on my cheeks to protect them from the elements. Danka and I take our tea and step into the lines already forming for roll call. It has grown colder during the night and the clouds that covered the sky, preserving what snowy warmth there was, have dissipated. The stars glisten above our heads like bright icicles hanging indifferently in the heavens. I stomp my feet. The SS trudge up and down our tidy rows, counting, hitting, counting. The hours drag by. The sky does not change. I scan our ranks hoping for a glimpse of Gizzy, knowing that the chance of finding her face among so many thousands is slim. Roll call ends.

"I'm going to find Gizzy and bring her to Emma's detail," I whisper to Danka, wheeling away anxious to conduct my search. She is nowhere to be seen, though. I retrace last night's footsteps to her block and find her leaning against the wall outside. This is where they put people who are dying, so they can be removed from camp.

"Gizzy. It's Rena." I collapse in the snow, pulling her into my arms, trying to hold back the cold. Her breathing sounds like castanets. Squeezing her tightly, I try to warm her, try to protect her from the wind. "Come on, Gizzy, hang on . . . Fight it." Swaying her limp body back and forth as if I am rocking a newborn babe, I tell her over and over, "Live. You have to live . . ." Her bones dig into mine. "You will see, Gizzy, everything is going to be fine."

There is one more rattle. A final gasp. Her breathing stops.

I cannot let go of her body. As if I were falling upon the Wailing Wall in Jerusalem, I rock and weep. My heart howls.

It is time to go to work, my internal clock warns me.

Laying Gizzy's cold body gently on the ground, I kiss my hand and place it upon my cousin's brow. "Good-bye," I whisper before stumbling away through the snow. The tears stick to my cheeks, freezing instantly; they are bitter, tasting like the day we left Mama and Papa behind. Mama waves in the distance. I stare at the fences, the wires, the towers, but Mama is there, waving to me from beyond this prison. "Help us, Mama. Please. Gizzy's dead." The wind confiscates my words, abandoning them to the growing darkness in my heart. Pain and light. But her lantern's golden glow bobs across the roads and hills of Poland, and I know she's waiting for us to come safely home.

Danka stands before me. Her eyes reach deep into my soul, shaking it back from its silent sorrow. She knows. I say nothing. She leads me toward Emma. I cannot stop trembling, but her hand squeezing mine feeds me the courage to continue.

"March out!" We tramp through the snow, out of the gates of hell, to work.

It is Sunday but there is no rest today; it is shaving day. We strip. "Remove your numbers from your jackets so they can be attached to your new uniforms!" There is some excitement over the announcement. It's been approximately nine months since we put these clothes on, and longer since they've been washed. We gladly dispose of the stench and scratchiness of the woolen jackets and pants, hiding our underwear to retrieve later. We are shaved and disinfected for lice. We huddle closely together for warmth, while stamping our bare feet.

In line we wait, naked and freezing, for blue-and-gray striped dresses. We pull these rough, uncomfortable uniforms over our heads. They are hideous, cheaply made, and stiff as cardboard. They have no pockets. How can we work hard labor in dresses? But I forget—they don't care.

Danka and I are lucky because we have the underwear that Erna gave us; others have nothing to put on under these dresses. There are no tights or stockings that come with this new uniform, so the wind races right up our legs and beyond like ice demons nipping at our thighs. The burlap itself rubs our skin in a new and cruel way. I do not know how we'll keep warm in these clothes.

❖   ❖   ❖

We stand at roll call waiting to be counted. They walk up and down the rows counting, hitting, shouting. Danka shifts on her feet, so I quickly cast my glance sideways. She's fine, just sore and hungry as I am. My fingers reach out and touch her hand, reas-suringly. Her fingers touch mine. This is our check-in. Every morning, if it's possible, we send this silent message to each other—I'm okay.

We are in the front row today. This is unusual; normally we try to be in the back or the middle, hidden and anonymous. It's harder to watch or be prepared when we're among the first to receive whatever they have in mind.

In the distance I can see a column coming toward us. I have never seen anyone on this road before. My mind is churning as it wonders who is arriving in hell today. Their feet try to march but they're not doing a very good job of it. There is a whisper through our ranks: "They've emptied a Jewish orphanage."[8]

The SS have their rifles up on their shoulders. "March!" Their orders snap through the stale morning air. My heart stops. My eyes focus on the column. Hundreds of pairs of tiny children's feet file past me and my sister and every woman in camp. Some of their

8. "January 30 [1943]. . . . 518 children are killed in the gas chambers. . . . [On] Janu-ary 31 . . . 457 children are killed in the gas chambers" (Czech, 319). The children Rena saw may or may not have been from one of these transports, we do not know for sure.

little faces are buried in their toys, choking the stuffing out of these inanimate objects of comfort. The younger ones hold the older children's hands. Their eyes stare at us big as saucers, lost as lambs. There is a tearful gasp somewhere deep inside our row. Is it a mother reminded of her own dear baby?

Their innocent faces look around in wonderment at the fences, the buildings, the grownups. Do they think we are insane, as I did when I first arrived? Are they wondering why so many grownups looking like their mamas and papas do nothing to protect them? Are they afraid?

My mouth drops open. I cannot bear to look at this. I cannot turn away. They can't be serious. Why would anyone want to kill babies? How long will it take them to suffocate? Will they cry out in fear with no one to comfort them?

The SS march them toward the gas chamber. Clutching dolls and stuffed animals close to their hearts, they shuffle past in rows of five guarded by SS men with their dogs and rifles. What do they think these children are going to do—escape? Revolt? But it is a rule, always to the gas chamber the SS are posted every fifth row on each side of the column, and they always follow rules. They don't want anyone around; they don't want the truth getting out. We know the truth. It has taken a long time for it to sink in, but there is no mistaking it anymore—the evidence is in the smoke-filled air and the empty compound after a selection. Still, they want no one disturbing their plans. The Germans have a saying, "Order is order." They stick to their rules like glue.

I am standing there just like a ghost. Their little angelic faces, the white knuckles of their tiny hands haunt me. I fight back my tears, my rage. My heart screams, Stop! Stop this madness! They are babies! Clenching my jaw, I shut my eyes.

God? I rarely say *God* anymore, but seeing their faces reflected in my heart I must try to pray one last time: God, you are my God and I believe in you. Won't you strike just one of these monsters down? Smite just one SS for these children, your children. You, whom I obey and believe in so much with all my heart? I have never held so much as a penny in my hand on the Sabbath and since I was old enough to fast I have always fasted on Yom Kippur. Don't allow this to happen. Give us a sign that you have not forsaken these children, the children of Israel. Never mind my suffering. It does not matter the time I have been in this place. Never mind all the things I've heard about people being burned and gassed, all the things I've seen for myself, not wanting to believe any of it is true. Never mind about me. What about these sweet children? For them, show them you are our God and kill just one of these Nazis.

My hands are fists of fury tight against my thighs. My eyes squeeze shut, holding a vision of lightning striking the guards in their neat and orderly tracks. Not one adult can move to save these toddlers, only divine intervention can supersede now: Please, God. . .

They fade in the distance, nearing the gas chambers. My heart screams for them to stop. Someone passes by me, then halts. Her feet crunch against the gravel road as she steps back to look at our stricken faces. Her hot breath hits my cheek. I open my eyes warily into the cool cruelty of Hasse's stare. Her clean boots, her polished and shiny skin, stand before us in full Aryan superiority. She has seen our agony; she has read my mind.

I know from the moment I hear her voice that religion will never be the same. I will still pray, I will try to believe and have faith, but it will never be as pure and sincere as it once was. Her lips pull back into a grimace which I am sure is meant to be a smile. Her words are harsh and staccato, like machine-gun fire; they shoot us down.

"Where is your God now?" The life drains out of me.

There is no answer.

We are miserable. Roll call is endless. To work would be a relief, anything to take our minds off of the children, but there is no respite in this place. Smoke comes out of the chimneys. My nose quivers at the reek of burning flesh, the smell of little children being incinerated. The sun disappears behind a cloud of gray.

If children cannot be saved, what is the use of praying for anything anymore? Hasse's voice plagues my wavering faith, dogging every breath I take.

"Where is your God now?"

My spirit withers . . . I do not know.

"What's wrong, Rena?" I have been staring at nothing for days, going through the motions of survival, unable to shake the cherubic faces haunting me.

"Did you see them?" I ask Erna.

"Who?"

"The children"—my voice cracks—"hundreds of them." I cannot let myself feel this much pain and still survive, but it is a fresh wound, not yet disguised by the callouses I have learned to develop.

"I heard about it." She places her hand on my shoulder. "Fela and I will be moving to a different section soon. We won't be able to talk anymore."

I nod. I will miss my friend but I do not want a job in her new work detail. She does not talk about it and I do not ask, but I know it is not a job that I could do.

"We'll miss you."

"You must get out of Birkenau, or get in a kommando that is inside at least."

"We will."

She moves away. "I'll see you before we go." I try to manage to smile. Be brave—another rule of survival.

A few days later, Erna signals me to meet her in the latrine. "I have something for you." She reaches into her hem.

"Erna, you have to stop risking your life bringing me things."

"Yah, but we are moving tomorrow, so these will be the last gifts I can bring you." She takes my hand, slipping something long and smooth, and something else very small into my palm. "I know how clean and neat you are."

I glance quickly into my hand. There is a nail file and a small silver elephant. "They're beautiful." I am overwhelmed by her generosity.

"The charm looked as if it belonged to a child and I thought of you," she whispers. "Elephants are suppose to be good luck. I don't want it to go to the Germans."

"Thank you, Erna. I will treasure them always." Tears spring to my eyes before I can quench them. We embrace quickly, but we do not say good-bye, that is not something one says in Auschwitz-Birkenau.

I slip the trinkets into the hem of my skirt before departing from the latrine. The silver elephant is a reminder of the children I watched walk to their deaths. It is the only mark of their passing—a tiny gravestone in my hand. I place it under my tongue during selections so it can be spit into the dirt if I go to the gas or if I'm beaten to death. My commitment to this small child's charm is that it should never get into Nazi hands, that even if I do not survive, it shall.

On Sunday, sitting on our bunk, I take out the nail file. It is mother-of-pearl, and under an etching of a cathedral it says *Budapest*. Hiding it in my palm, keeping the file covered so that it looks as if I am wringing my hands, I begin to clean my nails. It is an elevated feeling, to have one's nails clean after being dirty for so long. This simple manicure becomes a part of my weekly ritual. My thin thread to sanity grows longer: be with Danka, be invisible, be alert, be numb, be clean.

I crawl off the bunk leaving a still-sleeping Danka behind and head for the latrine. My period does not last as long as it used to, and the flow is not nearly as heavy as it was in Auschwitz, or even a few months ago; for this I am grateful. Danka hasn't had her period since the beginning. She, as well as most of the girls and women in camp, lost hers almost immediately. Breasts and the cycle disappear as quickly as our fellow prisoners. It is something in the tea; I think they call it bromide. I don't know why the bromide doesn't work on me, but the starvation does. My period is slowly slacking off as the weight drops from my body.

Taking a cloth that Erna also organized for me out of my sleeve, I thank her in my heart again as I leave the latrine with a semi-clean kerchief securely in place.

Every three weeks, on Sunday, the only day we have even a moment's rest, we are lined up and marched outside to another part of Birkenau to be shaved.

"Strip! *Schnell! Schnell!*" The SS shout at us as if we were deaf. Undressing, we place our clothes in a pile. Sometimes we stand for hours without a stitch on, outside in the elements or inside in the drafts. Our own Jewish men, prisoners obeying orders, wait for us, clippers in hand. The line to the shaving is long, but I think compared to all the other horrors this is not so horrible.

This is not the worse thing that happens to us in Auschwitz-Birkenau. It is not nightmare-making, but it is consistent, like everything the Germans do. Every three weeks like clockwork.

Our own boys, our own men are forced to see our nakedness, forced to shave our heads, our arms, our legs, our pubis. Sometimes they are friends, sometimes they are relatives; mothers get shaved by their own sons, sisters and brothers suffer this embarrassment. Danka and I are lucky. We meet no one we know.

Why can't they let us shave each other? We are young women, virgins; it is not in our religion to bare ourselves even in front of our husbands. This is not life-threatening, but it is degrading. One more degrading thing they make us do.

The German officers parade back and forth looking at us as if we are interesting specimens in their insect collection. There is one beautiful girl whom they stare at unrelentingly. She keeps her chin up, her eyes down. She is gorgeous despite her baldness. How anger-defying it is to stand and be visually defiled by these murderers. What I wouldn't do for a tap with hot water and a scrub brush, to wash the Nazis' eyes from my flesh.

We are silent in our shame . . .

There is no discussion and little whispering. The clippers are heavy, like shears for sheep, and they nick our flesh easily. Our boys, our men try not to hurt us, try to be careful, but they must cut quickly so they don't see our eyes, see our bodies, get beaten for being too slow, too prudent, too kind.

"Schnell! Schnell!" Little streams of blood trickle down our legs and necks as the SS men hurry them on. We hurt on both sides.

It is so demeaning. I can't bear it. I become a piece of flesh staring through the body of the man shaving me, staring at the other side of the room. I turn off the emotions inside of me until I see nothing and feel nothing. It is quite conscious. I hear only the command to move when it is over and then it is only the flesh moving. I am gone.

It is the body that finds its clothes, shivering uncontrollably from cold and fear and anger, quaking from unshed tears of shame. It is the body that waits for its sister. The feet stand in line until they are told to march. The hand takes her hand and together they return to the women's camp. The body enters the block. The arm takes the bread from the room elder. The mouth opens and closes, chewing bread—or is it sawdust? Everything tastes the same. Everything feels the same. I know at some point I will return to the body, but it takes time, and time is measured by tea, soup, bread, tea, soup, bread. Whenever it gets too much for me and I am about to burst, I turn my emotions off like a faucet and let the body take over. Sometimes it is the body that wants to survive, more than the spirit. There are days when the spirit has been sucked out and only time will tell if it will come back to feel again, come back to life.

No, shaving isn't the worst thing. It isn't life-threatening. But it is bad.

It is Sunday. I walk around camp looking for any tidbits or anything that might be useful lying in the mud.

"Rena!" Someone calls my name. Looking around, I see no one and start to move away, thinking perhaps the wind is playing tricks on me.

"Rena." This time it is a hoarse whisper. I stare and stare at a skeleton leaning out of the iron bars. Barely recognizing the face, I search through my memory for the name which fits the chiseled features before me. It is Erna and Fela's older sister.

"Pepka? Is that you?" I try not to look as dismayed as I feel. "What are you doing in Block Twenty-Five?" I shudder. Block Twenty-Five is the place we avoid no matter what the cost. No one who goes inside those doors comes out alive. The people inside this block are starved to death or carted to the gas and then the crematorium.

She cannot speak easily but manages to whisper, "Water." I run to get her something to drink, trying to shake her image away from my eyes. Her face has fallen inward, collapsing into her soul. She is a shade, no longer human, no longer the Pepka I once knew. I wish Erna were still in camp, she should know about her sister, but there is nothing anyone can do.

I place my bowl, brimming full of water, into her skeletal hands. She drinks greedily, barely able to contain her gulp at life, before handing it back to me. Her hands tremble. Retreating into the darkness, her eyes plead for me to save her; her voice is silent.

I am helpless against the walls, the bars. I have no food to share with her, no medicine to heal her ills, no way to get enough water that she will never thirst again, no way to get her out of the Block of Death. She is doomed and I am helpless. Pepka's eyes become those of my own sister, Zosia. What if Zosia were in Block Twenty-Five, would someone take her water for me? Would someone tell me she were there? What about the children? If Zosia was in this hell would they already be dead? I wish for someone to share this burden with but must blot these thoughts out quickly before they find a home in my mind and drive me mad. Maybe the children are in an orphanage. Maybe Zosia sent us the packages from Switzerland and she is safe. Zosia and Mama and Papa will be in Tylicz, and when it's all over we'll be reunited again. My mind slows its whirling descent into despair. Fragile hope replaces the doom around me, this is all that matters.

❖   ❖   ❖

Selections are sporadic. There is no telling how often they occur or when we are going to march out to roll call and instead of working stand all day, in neat lines and rows of five, and wait to be selected. There is usually one SS man who stands in judgment while the rest of them watch, but sometimes there are two making the decisions. When there are two, they both must give you the thumb toward life, otherwise you go to your death. No questions are asked; there is no appeal process, just a thumb. Usually there's a physical test, so that if you do get the thumb toward life you must then jump across a ditch to prove you are worthy of their decision. With shaking knees and no room for the take-off, we try to vault across this last obstacle between us and supper tonight. Sometimes I think the only thing that saves me is the fact that I don't want to get dirty before I die and somehow that resolve levitates me beyond the filth and mud in the ditch. Very few do not make the jump.

Depending on the number of girl-women in camp, selections take anywhere from ten to fifteen hours. We stand without food or drink all day and sometimes into the night, waiting to discover if we will wake up tomorrow, if we will ever eat again. There are no last meals, like criminals get before they are executed; we are not as good as criminals. We are nothing in their eyes—we are merely pests to be exterminated.

When we first came to Birkenau there were six women per shelf; now, except after a selection, we sleep twelve or more to a tier. If we want to turn over in the middle of the night we have to pull ourselves up with our hands and twist our bodies around like a screw. Danka and I always wake each other when we want to turn; it's easier if we both change positions.

There's no way not to touch the girl next to you. My prayer has become that no one dies next to me—this is a selfish prayer based on a desire to stay warm. I don't want to be frozen by a cold body in the middle of the night, but it happens, over and over again.

When a selection is over there is plenty of room on the tiers to sleep, but the barrenness of the blocks is haunting and rest is kept away by sleep demons and the souls dying in the gas chambers. In the morning we wake exhausted, watching the new arrivals come in from the transports. We see their faces, stricken and in denial, their uncertain fates written across their brows. They're lost and scared. Uncertain about this hell they've come to, they still wish they had hair, they wonder where their loved ones have disappeared to. They think we look insane.

There is nothing we can do to prepare them—no orientation, no list of things to be wary of, no rules for survival. There is only tea, soup, bread—they have no bowls yet. The first night they can't find blankets and search for a place to sleep not realizing that they must cram themselves in among the bodies already sleeping on the tiers. Once again we're wedged in tighter than herrings, twelve to a tier.

Four A.M.

"Raus! Raus!"

We maneuver our bodies out of the group sleeping on our shelf. Slip outside with our tea and get into line for roll call. Last night there was no moon, and on nights when the sky is dark, those with suicide wishes use the blanket of blackness to dodge the search-lights and run for the fence. This is freedom.

Their figures look like dancers frozen against the shadows of abruptly awakened ghosts. Mouths gape open like question marks, as if committing us to bear witness that we heard their screams in the night. They hang, charred, on the electric wires of humanity.

Spellbound, I cannot tear my eyes from their grotesque forms. How I envy them. What is it that has driven them to grab the wire? What is it that drives me to stay among the ranks of the semi-living?

Taube marches along our rows, but he is not counting us today. He seems excited, as if he has something else on his mind. "What we need are calisthenics! Yah, exercise is the key. Healthy body, healthy mind." He turns to our row. "Do knee bends!" He orders. "Down! Up! Down! Up!" We bend our creaking joints and stand upright, again and again, exactly as he demands. "Ten, and down! Eleven, and down!" We count in our heads, trying to focus on something besides our weakening legs and trembling thigh muscles, twenty, twenty-one . . . "Twenty-nine, and down! Thirty, and down! Knees to the ground." We falter, not understanding his request. "Kneel!" He cracks his whip across a girl's shoulder blade. She sinks into the mud. "Lie down! Heads down!"

I grab Danka's hand, pulling her with me. "Put your face in it, Danka. Don't move. Don't look up," I manage to whisper before my mouth is in the mud.

Taube stomps towards our row. Noses touching dirt, eyes staring into the ground. His black boots pass us. His boots stop. Trying not to breathe. A girl nearby raises her head. I can see from the corner of my eye her upturned face gasping for breath. The boot falling onto her face, pushing it deep into the earth. The crunching of skull bones sickens the air. I want to vomit. He moves on. I cannot help but listen for the sound. A few rows away it rises from our ranks—the crunch, the silence. I blink. I am leaving my body, fleeing the horror around us. But I cannot get far enough away. I cannot allow myself to leave Danka behind.

Finally the word "Dismissed!" releases us from our hold to the ground. Roll call is over. Timidly, those of us doing Taube's version of calisthenics get on our hands and knees, turning our faces in horror at the smashed skulls of the girls who will never rise again.

"Don't look, Danka." I move my sister away from the girl next to me. Hand in hand, we find Emma, line up behind her, and march to work.

Weeks just . . . are years here.

If the war is going well for the Germans, once in a while we get a slice of meat in the soup or with our bread. And sometimes the very Orthodox girls will trade their meat for bread because they won't touch unkosher meat. I don't know how they can survive without meat for long. They have something that I don't, though; they have their faith. I do not know where my God is.

They slap the portions on our hands. We lick our open palms slowly, savoring the smear of margarine or mustard; occasionally there is a bit of smelly Limburger cheese. I despise the taste of mustard after the first few months; still, I lick it up as the precious morsel it is. When there is margarine we rub the residue into our hands for moisturizer. The skin on our hands and faces cracks in the cold.

Sausage is no more than bite-size, but we eat hungrily, unable to pause or slow down. Danka never wants to eat it. "We have to," I tell her. "Food is food and this is all we have to depend on." And there is never enough of it. Our stomachs ache constantly. Every moment of every day, awake or asleep, we are hungry. The constant gnawing caused by this starvation is exhausting. Between working ten and twelve hours a day and avoiding the SS, there is little energy for any other activity. Thinking is becoming impossible.

When the war is going badly for the Germans, it is worse for us. The bread is little more than water and flour and the portions are rarely larger than our hand. But lately it looks as if the Germans are going to be occupying the whole world, and, like giving a dog a bone, they toss us slightly larger portions. We take the food eagerly but receive it with the knowledge that this piece of cheese means the Nazis are in Holland, this piece of meat means they're in France. I don't know which to long for more—food or freedom.

It's Sunday. We lie on our shelves delousing ourselves or trying to rest, squeezing in a few extra hours of sleep. I clean my nails deftly, hiding the nail file in my hand while staring into space.

"Attention!" our block elder shouts. *"Raus! Raus!* Get out. Now!

We can hear Hasse's voice outside shouting, "Get out here, you lazy imbeciles! I have work for you to do!" Confused, we jump to the ground, running for the door. Some girls scramble for their shoes, others grab their bowls; Danka and I forget everything, thinking only of avoiding Hasse's whip. Our minds are buzzing. We arrive outside first, standing at attention as the rest of the block rushes into line.

"Rena, I left my bowl." Danka tugs on my arm. I look quickly around us. Hasse is not there.

"I'll get it." I dash back into the block. My heart racing, I grab Danka's bowl off our sleeping area and run out the back door directly into Hasse's path.

Her eyes glare at me. I freeze. She raises her gun. My heart stops.

A gunshot rips through the air.

I collapse to the ground. Mud splashes onto my clothes and up my nose. I feel no pain. I wish I could see my sister one more time before I die. There are sounds coming from above me, horrible guttural sounds.

Hasse is laughing. "The miserable *mist biene* thinks she's dead!" Hasse guffaws.[9] Her joviality plugs my ears. "I didn't shoot you!"

I raise my head, looking up at the SS woman's grinning face. "*Hau ab!* Get lost!" She waves me away.

What an idiot I am! Jumping up quickly, I brush myself off hoping Hasse doesn't change her mind and shoot me anyway.

"*Hau ab!*" she yells again.

We work all afternoon carrying stones, knowing this is worthless work only to keep us busy. We will miss this day sorely in the middle of the week. Next week we will be shaved again, another Sunday with no rest. How will we ever catch up? I wish we could have had the day off.

We work in the spring dirt, turning over the soil the same as we did the year before. The fresh young sprigs of new grass stick their white tips out of the soil, tempting us to gather them for a midday snack. The succulent, sweet juice of these grasses is a pleasant sensation to our tired taste buds and parched throats. We sneak them into our mouths when Emma and the SS aren't looking.

The girl next to me falters in her digging. I follow her gaze. Stooping to pick medicinal herbs, a group of broken souls moves slowly past our detail in blue-and-gray striped dresses with clean, white, pressed aprons. Their skeletal forms do not haunt me as badly as their bottomless eyes. We freeze for a moment of shock before returning to our work. Their knees quiver weakly, as if each step they take is their last. I shudder, surprised by the chill racing down my spine despite the warmth of the day.

I have seen many things between Auschwitz and Birkenau but

9. *Mist biene* is German for "manure bee" or "dung bee."

never have I seen anything comparable to this. I have seen despair and hopelessness, I have seen insanity at first onset, but I have never seen any face so devoid of life. Even the dead look more alive than these walking corpses.

"They are experiment victims," the girl next to me whispers. Danka's face pales. My hands begin to shake with fright. "They torture them until they are dead, or vegetables." She turns another shovelful of dirt over. "After they are done experimenting with them, they go to the gas."[10]

Of all the horror we see daily, of all the shattered selves we witness on a regular basis, they are beyond any realm of imagination. They look as if the spirit God breathed into their souls has been utterly sucked out. They're no longer human beings, having long ago ceased to be girls or women. They are a child's nightmare.

"Rena, I have scabies and terrible cuts from a beating I got." My cousin's wife begs, "Please, help me." I look at her without pity, without feeling. Still, I must help her. It is not in my heart to turn family away, despite how she treated me when Danka and I first arrived in Bardejov, when she invited me to her house and served me a cookie and cup of tea while still in her bathrobe and her hair in rollers. She kept fidgeting and acting like I was a nuisance, then abruptly told me she had errands to run, indicating it was time for me to leave. She didn't ask me about my parents, or how Danka and I were doing in her city. She was so well bred, so wealthy, I felt like the poor Polish cousin being swept under the carpet to avoid embarrassment.

I was not fond of her because of this incident in Slovakia. Then I heard she had made trouble in camp. She was caught on her

10. "April 30 [1943]. . . . 242 female prisoners are earmarked for experimental purposes . . . housed in the experimental station of Professor Dr. Clauberg in Block 10 of the main camp" (Czech, 386). "By the time [Dr. Josef] Mengele arrived in May 1943, Auschwitz was packed with almost 140,000 prisoners and stretched for miles in all directions" (Posner and Ware, 20).

hands and knees inside the soup kettle, licking it out, scraping what food was stuck to the bottom with her bare hands and feeding herself like an animal. An SS woman had found her and beat her for behaving so despicably.

I'm ashamed to say that I do not trust her now and am afraid to have anything to do with her. She has no self-control, and for all her airs and superiority she has become less than human, and people like that are dangerous in camp. I do not doubt she will do anything to save herself but cares nothing for me.

I look at the scabies on her face. She will die at the next selection if I don't help her. "If I'm going to get you any salve, you must promise not to tell anyone what I've done for you," I tell her. I do not want to have anything to do with her.

"I promise. Just this once. If you would help me I will never bother you again." I am cold-hearted, committed to little else but my sister and our survival. I do not turn away from her, but I am confused that she doesn't hand me her portion of bread to barter with when I go to the block elder, and since she doesn't offer it, I don't ask her for her food.

Taking my portion of bread to the block elder, I trade my only meal to get her the salve she needs. I know that if our roles were reversed she would not give up her bread for me, she will not even give me her bread for her own self, but I am expected to sacrifice mine for her.

She snatches the salve from my hand, hiding it quickly in her dress. "Thank you, Rena."

"You must be more careful in the future." I warn her. She disappears into the night. I do not feel virtuous or good about myself. I feel used and hungry, but I also know that I will never look back and regret trying to help my cousin's wife. There is little we can avoid in Birkenau, but trying to act with a little bit of dignity helps me, reminds me of home.

The Jewish beggars came to our door Friday, before Sabbath. Mama had Danka and me stuff burlap sacks with straw for them to sleep on in the kitchen. The day after Sabbath, Mama had to burn the straw, scrub the floors, and boil the sheets and pillow-cases to get rid of the lice and fleas they left behind. Danka and I didn't like cleaning up after these people, but Mama would remind us that they had children and were less fortunate than we were. The same was true for Gypsies and beggars; no one who came to our door ever left empty-handed.

This is my legacy, to treat everyone with compassion.

Four A.M.

"Raus! Raus!"

The horizon grows dark. The wind shifts. My nose twitches in the breeze. They don't smell like rain clouds.

I feel myself detaching from my body; it happens sometimes and I am helpless against it. The chimneys are smoking. I watch myself move away as if I were taking a step to one side, leaving my body behind. There are footsteps approaching. My eyes shift toward the sound; my mind remains stationary.

Hasse smiles like a hunter who has captured its prey and is about to skin it alive. That is how she feels to us, ruthless and capable of snapping our necks in two without the slightest hesitation.

She flips up her hand at the gray clouds covering the dismal sky. "Look how the French models are burning!"

It doesn't matter who you are, if you're rich or beautiful or elegant—if you're a Jew, you're nothing! She is always ridiculing us, gloating at us. I cannot fathom her cruelty. She continues down the line, counting and smiling, a sadist thrusting her verbal knife into each of our hearts for the fun of it.

We stand in line for selection. It is a long day; no food, no water. I haven't seen Adela Gross except for a few times in camp. We didn't know each other, but I recognize her as the rabbi's daughter from Hummene. I wonder if she was on the first transport as well. I do not remember.

The line moves, and I catch a glimpse of Adela stepping forward. For a moment I am struck by her beauty and remember how gorgeous her beautiful red curls were before her head was shaved. I am astounded that despite the hardships of camp she still looks pretty.

She steps up to the death squad. The SS stare at her. Her chin is tilted slightly, bravely upward.

The thumb points away. She moves toward the ranks of the doomed.

I'm confused. How can she be selected? She looks better than me. Adela should stay alive. It must be a mistake.

The next girl steps up to the death squad.

Furious at the self-proclaimed gods who rule our lives, I wish I could yell at them, make them see their error. But I must prepare myself for the thumb. Squeezing Danka's hand one final time before letting go, I march toward my fate. We are hot or cold, there is no in-between. We are hungry and miserable. In a few moments we may be dead. Not sick, not hungry, not hot, not cold—dead.

I step up to the death squad, chin up. The thumb points.

Danka follows my lead, stepping up to the death squad. The thumb allows us both to live for another day. The girl behind us steps up to the death squad.[11]

The trucks begin loading the girls, the women, my friend. Normally I don't watch, but this time I must. Running the selection over and over in my mind, I search for the reason in their decision. Why? Why? There is nothing wrong with her. She is a lovely young woman. She is beautiful. We are nothing but pieces of scrap wood.

11. "May 31 [1943]. . . . Nos. 123205–123234 are given to 30 men prisoners and Nos. 45681–45698 to 18 female prisoners. . . . The occupancy level of the women's camp in Birkenau is 20,542" (Czech, 409–410). By the author's calculations, if there were 20,000 women in camp and a selection lasted fifteen hours, then 1333.3 women were selected per hour, 22.2 women per minute, or one woman every 2.7 seconds.

The reality strikes me squarely between the eyes, as if Taube himself had hit me. Their purpose is not only to destroy and defile us, it is to make a mockery of every positive moral value we have. Adela is thrown onto the flatbeds with the rest of the women, but she turns to help those behind her. Her chin still tilts with courage and dignity. She is not afraid. Her arm encircles a weaker girl whose knees are failing her. The trucks spew their exhaust as they head for the gas chambers. I cannot wrench my eyes away from her departing form. There is a tearing inside of me, as if a cord has been severed in my heart. As the trucks drive away, part of me dies with Adela.

❖　❖　❖

We're working on the new blocks, digging sand out of a deep hole and sifting it through the mesh nets. It's old and familiar to us now, this digging and sifting. Our hands are hard. They no longer bleed from the long hours of work, except occasionally when we throw the bricks and the palms get cut once more. But that detail has become less frequent as they find real work for us to do. We load the lorries with the sand, pushing them toward a building that is closer to a men's kommando than our own. There are tracks for the lorries to glide along now, so pushing is not the horrific task it was a year ago. But it's still difficult, and as we heave the sand toward its destination I cannot believe we ever accomplished this task with no tracks, up a hill, and wearing slabs of wood on our feet.

We approach the men digging trenches to bury pipe in. Emma is watching the group sifting sand, and the farther away we move from her the closer we get to being within earshot of the men. There are no SS nearby or watching. It is a precious moment to exchange words.

"Is anybody Polish there?" a man asks from within the ranks of working men. We scoop the sand out into a pile next to the building.

"My sister and I are," I whisper back. Stealing words carefully. None of the other girls pay attention to our snippets of conversation.

"Where're you from?" The lorry is empty. Grabbing onto the side of the car, we push it back to the piles of sand and reload. It takes a long time to fill the lorry. I am warm and cannot tell if it's the warm weather or my nerves making me shake. I long to have a conversation with this stranger on the other side of the fence; I long to know his name, his place of birth, his family . . .

I push the thoughts of normal life back where they belong, gouging deep into the dirt and rocks that must be sifted. I notice that Danka has slowed and quickly double my effort by taking a scoop from her section every few minutes.

"Take this lorry," Emma instructs. I grab the side, making sure there is room for my sister to hold on. We push it back toward the men's detail and begin relieving the car of its cargo. My eyes check the area for SS.

"Tylicz, near Krynica," I answer. We dig. The sound of shovels grating against dirt and pebbles seems louder than before. They dig. Our silence magnifies the noises around us.

Finally I hear "Krakow." We dig. They dig. An SS man appears. Our conversation is doomed until tomorrow. We push the lorry back toward Emma and the rest of our kommando.

Four A.M.

"Raus! Raus!"

Anxious to get to work this morning, I have already been to the latrine by the time the room elders are hitting and yelling. Under a blushing sky we eat our snippet of bread and drink our tea. The days are growing longer, as do our hearts; not only do the seasons pass us by, but the longer the sun is in our sky the longer they work us. Sleep is just something slipped in between roll calls. Danka crosses her arms across her chest, holding her elbows. "I'm cold, Rena."

"The sun will be up soon."

"No, I mean I have a chill." There is a thick crust on her swollen lips.

"What is that on your lips?"

"I don't know." She touches her mouth. "I'm so thirsty." I hold her forehead in my hand.

"You're hot," I say, trying to quench the worry and alarm surfacing in my mind.

She nods. "You have a crust on your lips, too." I touch my lips, feeling the flakes brush off from beneath my fingertips. Placing my hand to my forehead, I tell myself I feel fine.

"Are you hot?" she asks.

"No, Danka. We work so hard and eat so little that the body must try extra hard to warm itself." I lie to my sister as I lie to myself. She is warm, too warm for the temperature outside this morning. She is ill.

I do not say anything about this knowledge; I just make a mental note to myself. I can be alert for SS and green triangles, selections and dogs, but disease, this is something I cannot foresee. It comes upon us despite everything else we do to survive. This is our second spring. I can remember almost nothing of last year, nor do I want to. Still, I run through what memories surface about the first camp to see if any illness was common then, at this time of year. All that comes to mind is the biting bugs and the itching bites; the clouds of mosquitoes which infested camp last summer. So much has changed since last year that I cannot pick one change that stands out from the rest and fear that there are no answers in the past.

We march out with Emma toward the sand. Suddenly I am overcome with the fear that it was all a trick. The kind Pole from Krakow speaking to me yesterday will not be there today. A million things could've happened over the night. He could be dead, they could've moved his kommando to another area. My friend is gone. My fingers twitch against the burlap dress I wear. Agitated, these thoughts race through my mind without reason or logic.

We're going to die. The pit yawns before me. Fear chases me to-wards it jaws. We will die not of selection or gas but in the hospi-tal. Which is worse? The hope that has given me strength and en-ergy to endure seems to run out of my fingers and toes and ears as all the fluids in my body drain away. We march toward the sand. My eyes glaze over.

Then I see them. The men are working in the same area they were yesterday. The pit disappears. We are safe once more—or are we? Danka is hot. The fever is gaining.

We push a lorry toward the building. I see the tall, skinny one and his shorter friend as we start unloading our cargo. The sun beats against our bare heads, keeping at bay the chill that sends shivers between Danka's scapula and spine. She is sweating too profusely. A stone falls to the ground a few feet away. I mark the place with my eyes without stopping my work. The lorry will be unloaded shortly. There are no SS. I focus on my work. I move a step towards the stone, digging, digging. In a few moments we'll be done. Digging, digging. I stoop quickly, my hand landing di-rectly on the note. Firmly grasping the paper around the rock, I let the stone slip from my hand. We stand along the sides of the lorry getting ready to push. There is a moment, a second, in which to move, and I quickly adjust my shoe in that split of time and stillness, slipping the note under my foot. We push.

The afternoon wears on. Danka sweats. There has to be some-thing I can do. The fears of the morning are gone. There is not time to fret over death. We are alive; all I can do is try to keep us that way.

"Halt!" We quickly put our shovels in the toolshed and line up. "March!" We march toward camp. "Heads up!" We raise our chins, lift our feet as if we are proud to be slaves of the Third Reich. The only thing we have to be proud of is that there is no one to carry in today. Today we have all survived the Nazis' whips and boots, but a secret enemy is among us.

Tomorrow, if nothing happens tonight, Danka and I will return

to Emma as we have done every day for weeks, months—over a
year, now. We will not recognize anyone in our detail tomorrow,
just as we did not recognize anyone today. We pay no attention to
faces. We survive by ignoring the temporal and have stopped looking for repeaters, those who work in our detail day after day; it is
useless, in vain, depressing. They don't exist.

After roll call Danka and I get our bread and excitedly read the
note from the man on the work team: *I'm Heniek. My friend is
Bolek. Your names?*

"Which one do you think likes me?" Danka asks.

"Look at you, all flushed by the thought of flirting with a boy in
camp," I tease her gently, afraid that she is flushed because of her
illness, not love. "I'm going to get a scrap of paper from the block
elder to send them a note. You wait here."

I had typhus when I was twelve and remember the symptoms
for that disease. Although it's the most common illness in camp
besides scabies, Danka doesn't have typhus. I do not know what
this enemy is. I have three missions as I leave Danka behind: one
is to get a scrap of paper, one is to find out if there is an epidemic in
camp, the last is to check outside for a morsel of anything edible.
Whenever I have any extra energy I scour the grounds, organizing
what tidbits I can.

Sneaking among the shadows, I pass the kitchen, all of my
senses on alert. Finally, just as my eyes and legs are about to give
out from weariness, I spy a piece of potato in the mud. Grabbing
it, I dart back to the wall. It is a small morsel of food, barely big
enough for one bite. I stare at it, looking for the proper place to
mark it in half. Finally I dig my fingernail into the pulp so I know
exactly how much I must save for Danka. My mouth waters but I
do not risk even a nibble before I can share it with my sister.

Back in the block, I go to the block elder's door. She seems in a
good mood tonight, handing me a scrap of paper and a bit of pencil.
"Don't get caught with it."

"Can I ask you something?" I figure it's worth a try. If anyone would know about what's going around camp it would be a block elder.

"What?" She doesn't seem to mind my intrusion into her time.

"Is there any illness in camp that causes fever and crusting on the lips?"

She peers at me closely, warily. "Swamp fever—malaria," she says, shutting the door in my face.[12]

I ponder her words while writing our note to Heniek and Bolek. I scratch our names out, then wrap the note firmly around a stone, sticking it into my hem for tomorrow. Back in our bunk, I hand Danka the pitiful piece of potato and we nibble on it, trying to make it larger and more savory than it can ever be. "Thank you, Rena." How I wish it could be more. I long to take care of her properly, feed her chicken soup, lots of water, bed rest, all the things we're not allowed to have. Her eyes glisten like glass in the dark. I am worried. The conclusion the block elder has stated is not an optimistic diagnosis. I say nothing to Danka, but I have heard of this happening in the whispers around camp. The mosquitoes are terrible this spring, and the swamp we live in makes our bodies their banquet tables as they suck us dry. There is no defense; between them and the lice infesting us, we are too weak from starvation to fight their gorging. I fall asleep feeling a wave of chills wash across my muscles in quiet spasm.

The stone lands close to Heniek. He retrieves it easily, bravely glancing at the note. He taps his friend. We dig. There are no SS nearby, so we slow the progress of unloading the lorry just a little bit in order to steal what bits of conversation that we can.

They dig. I am so concerned about Danka that for a moment I wonder if anyone can help us.

As if reading my mind, Heniek asks, "Can we help you in any way?"

12. "June 3 [1943]. . . . 302 female prisoners who are ill with malaria are transferred to Lublin (Majdanek) C. C." (Czech, 411).

"I think my sister has malaria." I'm not sure if I should continue. Quickly I glance across the work area; no one can overhear us. My shovel never falters from its movement. "Maybe if we had some tomato juice and a slice of lemon, we could wash the crust from her lips. It might break the fever." I have managed the impossible; I have communicated an entire sentence without interruption. Rock against metal scrape abrasively against one another. I can continue these movements for hours without aching muscles or fatigue—digging, digging. We work without faltering. We go back for another load. I work twice as fast, hoping to get one more load in before the men leave, before nightfall. I am shaking with nervousness. Emma signals for us to take the lorry.

"Be quick!" she orders. We push the lorry along the tracks. Our heads down, we unload the cart without looking at the men.

"You need quinine." He sounds so hopeful.

"Yah, sure . . ." It has been a long time since I felt any hope. He digs. We dig. The sun nears the horizon. The lorry is almost empty. We disembark from our task, preparing to push the cart toward the sifters and Emma, away from the men.

"Don't worry, Rena." I hear his voice fall across the fence and cling to it as if it is a life raft on an angry sea. For some reason I believe Heniek can help us; I do not know how, but for a moment I breathe easier.

The crust on Danka's lips is worse, but she does not feel as hot today. I wonder if the volatility of this fever is one of its dangers. We dig and sift all morning until lunch and never load the lorries. I want to scream at Emma to let us take the lorries, but all we do is sift and sift and sift. At least there will be plenty to move tomorrow, but that means they will patrol us closer if more groups are moving the lorry loads. Lunch comes and goes. There is a portion of meat in my bowl. I bite it in half, handing the remainder to Danka.

"Is it pork?"

"Eat it." I refuse to answer her question. It is meat, that is all that matters. The war must be going well.

All afternoon we dig and sift. The lorries do not move.

Four A.M.

"*Raus! Raus!*"

We line up at roll call finishing our tea, eating last night's bread.

"How are you feeling today, Danka?"

"Better." She sips her tea quietly. Her eyes gape open at the scene around us. A sea of girl-women holding cups of semi-tea chew last night's bread slowly, carefully, trying to make it last. The camp is overflowing. I have never seen so many women at one time; I cannot even comprehend the numbers. Roll call takes ages.

Finally we march out with Emma.

"Take the lorries," she orders us first thing. The sun is just breaching the horizon. There is a golden glow about us as shadows appear where night had been. Danka and I quickly take our place on the side of the carts, pushing the lorry toward the men's kommando. An SS walks by. No sooner is his back to us than a stone falls at my feet. I stoop nonchalantly down to the ground, checking my shoe, and then swing up my shovel quickly, helping remove the sand we sifted yesterday. The hand with the note holds tightly to the shovel. It is a larger piece of paper than the scrap I sent them, and it's so early that I must think of what to do with the note for the rest of the day. In my dress or in my hand? The shoes aren't safe enough for a whole day of work, so the debate continues. In my hem or in my hand? I wonder where to hide the note. My hands are too warm and the shovel slips in my grasp as I scoop the sand over the edge into the growing pile. The lorry is empty. Quickly I hide the note in the hem of my dress with no chance to read it.

It's a long day, a long roll call, but at last we enter the block, more eager to read the note than to eat our bread. It is long and written as if in great haste. *You saw pipes coming close to your detail. Stuff in ground—five steps from pipes—tomorrow.* I cannot believe the words before my eyes.

All day we eye the pipes. I can see that five steps from the pipe there is a little rise in the ground, but we must wait patiently. I watch the sky closely as the afternoon wanes. Our timing must be perfect. I nod to Danka. Slowly we dig, little by little, away from the group toward the pipes. We gouge the land, carrying large shovelfuls of dirt to the sifting net, each time returning one step closer to the pipes. There are no SS nearby. I wink, and Danka busily digs around me, loosening the dirt while blocking me with her body so no one can see what I'm doing. Working diligently, she puts on a good show, giving me the cover I need to retrieve our treasure. Quickly I tie a bottle of tomato juice underneath my dress, to the other end of the string, which also holds my bowl. In a bit of cloth there is a lemon and, to my great surprise, tablets. There is a note, too, and these I hide in my hem with the lemon.

"They've gotten us quinine." I whisper to Danka. She digs deeper into the dirt, throwing her back into the work. I was not expecting so much and only have the hem of my dress to hide things in.

"Hurry," Danka whispers, digging, digging. It is very complicated, smoothing the tablets out in my hem so the SS won't notice any lumps. I pray none will fall out.

"Done." We dig around the area, quickly obscuring the hiding place.

"Halt!" Emma yells. Our skin bristles in fear. We stop what we're doing, trying to erase any traces of anxiety on our faces. We look up at Emma.

"Line up!" she announces.

I cast a glance at Danka as we carry our last shovelful of dirt toward the sifting net before carrying the shovels into the toolshed.

My heart smiles proudly at my sister's glistening face. She does everything to the best of her ability, and despite her illness she's been more than stalwart today.

"Here, take one now." I slip a tablet into her hand.

"March!" Our hearts are pounding so loudly that I am sure the band must hear the timing within our chests. Our luck is holding out; for five days there has not been a selection. We go to the blocks, grab our bread, and take our place in the shelves. Holding onto our blanket, I give Danka the tomato juice and lemon.

"You have some," she offers. "You have a crust on your lips, too."

"No, Danka. You're the one who's sick."

"Rena, I can't take it all. You must share it with me."

"You're going to waste it if you leave it for me. I'm not going to take it." She sips from the bottle and sucks on the lemon quietly.

"Wash your lips with the lemon, Danka." I show her what I mean. The crust dissolves under the vitamin juices of real fruit. Her lips change dramatically as the brown crust that has encased them for days washes away.

"Use the rind." She hands me the lemon rind. I use it to scrub my lips as well. The flavor of the rind is bitter and sharp, but it makes my taste buds leap.

"I bet it took twenty people to organize this package," I whisper.

"Read the note," Danka reminds me.

Quinine three times a day, I read softly, out loud. *Watch the pipes—if mound by pipes, something there for you. In few days more juice. Be well. Love, Heniek and Bolek. (Bolek's in love with Danka. I'm in love with you.)*

Danka blushes and giggles slightly. It sounds so strange to hear mirth. "Thank you, Lord, for saving us once more." Danka squeezes my hand as she falls asleep.

Morning comes and Danka finishes the tomato juice and eats the lemon rind. I give her a tablet and plan to give her one at each meal until they're gone.

Pushing the lorries toward the men, I check the landscape and quickly toss the note I wrote last night: *Thank you. Danka's already feeling better. Bóg zapłać, may God reward you. Love, Rena and Danka.* We do not have anything else to give Heniek and Bolek but these words. Perhaps, like the tablets to us, love will give them what they need to survive. In this place we cannot be selfish with affection or gratitude. If we don't say it today there may never be another chance.

Over the next few weeks there is a rise in the dirt by the pipes three times. Each time there is tomato juice, a lemon, and a love note from Heniek and Bolek. One time there are more quinine tablets. Then one day we march toward the piles of sand and there are no men working on the other side of the fence. Our saviors are gone from our view but not from our hearts. We think of them often. We never see them again.

❖　　❖　　❖

"Rena?" I turn toward a familiar face from my past. A whirl-wind of memory tangles my thoughts. It is someone from home, a Gentile.

"Manka?" I question the face before me.

"Rena. How goes it with you?"

"I'm alive. How is it that you're here?" I look at her triangle. It is the color of a political prisoner, but I find that hard to believe. She probably talked out of her head without thinking; she was known for that in Tylicz. I feel myself growing wary—her eyes have that wild look one sees too often behind these fences. She is losing her mind. I remain cautious.

"I saw your parents killed," she says matter-of-factly. "That's right. They came back to Tylicz. They shouldn't have come back. One day the Germans decided to take all the Jews that were left, about eight, and they made them line up in the marketplace . . ." I cannot believe her callous intonation. "Then they tied their hands up with ropes to a wagon and ran the horses around the circle until every last one of them was dead." She sounds as if she's reciting the alphabet.

"Excuse me . . ." I start to walk away, but her voice follows me.

"They screamed for us to save them, but there was nothing anyone could do. They suffered terribly. They shouldn't have come back, but it wouldn't have mattered, would it? Everyone who isn't dead is here!"

Stumbling through the mud, I try to escape her voice, her hideous voice. I hate you! I want to scream at her face. I hate you.

The vision starts to fracture. The crack is long and deep, scarring my mother's patient and loving face. Mending it quickly, as if I am a bricklayer securing a fortress, I smear concrete across my memory. Mama is waiting for us. They are at the farmhouse waiting. They are safe. Only the rest of the world is in danger. Manka's out of her mind, I tell myself. She wasn't there. She's crazy. She's out of her mind, I repeat to myself over and over again.

The fences of Birkenau stretch before me. I do not get close enough to get shot, but I stand there staring out at the open spaces of my homeland. There are no tears on my face, I'm too dehydrated to cry, but my eyes ache as if tears were falling.

Sometimes I have serious doubts that they're alive, but sometimes I feel as if there's a physical presence next to me. I can smell her. I can feel her touch. I cannot see Mama but I know she's near. I have moments of common sense and clear thinking when I know this invisible presence means she's gone, but then my cloudy mind obscures that truth. There is less pain, living in a cloudy mind, so I don't allow myself to think about things too clearly unless clear thinking means saving our lives.

There is not much time for clear thinking in Auschwitz-Birkenau, but when I made the oath to Danka, that was a clear moment. If I'd been cloudy I couldn't have said, "My hand is the Holy Book and Mama and Papa are standing right here in front of us." I'd said it as if they were in a heaven, invisible entities watching over us. That means at that moment I knew they had to be gone, but I rarely allow myself to think that far ahead. These two minds have a symbiotic relationship, and as long as no one challenges the logic, each realm can exist.

I shut the door on Manka's account of their deaths. Mama and Papa are alive waiting for us in Tylicz, and Mama is the warm invisible presence guarding and guiding us. This is how it is. It doesn't have to make sense to anyone but me.

We arrive at Emma's kommando in the morning to find fifty middle-aged women going with us to work. We gape at them as if they are aliens from another world. It is strange to see women in their fifties; they usually select any women in their forties or older for the gas. But here they are, these fifty women staring at us, looking like our mothers.[13] Their sweet, wrinkling faces reveal the fear and trepidation this place forces on us all. They are probably thinking about their own daughters and sons and grandchildren. I cannot turn away from their faces. It is terrible to see elder women without kerchiefs on their heads and as bald as we are. For a moment I think how Mama would have felt if she'd been forced out in public without her wig or a babushka.

"Danka, look!" I point to a woman standing in line.

Danka gasps. "She looks like Mama." We squeeze each other's hands, smiling at the stranger. She smiles back at us.

Taking the kerchief from my head, I approach the woman who looks so much like Mama. "You will need this to protect your head from the sun today." I hand it to her.

"I can't take this from you," she stammers.

"You must. I won't wear it." I walk away, blinking hard.

13. "The flow of convoys abruptly ceased at the end of July 1943 and there was a breathing space. The crematoria were thoroughly cleaned, the installations repaired and prepared for further use. On August 3 the killing machine again went into operation" (Wyman, 18). It seems likely that the older women were brought to Birkenau during this time.

"March out!" We step forward, heading out of the gates. The band plays an out-of-tune polka. There are girls staring at our kommando. Mouths fall open as the mothers pass, marching out to work. The silent wake which follows us is the invisible weeping of each girl remembering and praying that her own mother has escaped this end.

This is the second year, so there are so many of us that one SS watches one kommando. The kommandos are divided into separate work details, each with a kapo to oversee it. Still, we don't always have an SS standing right over us because they're busy inspecting other work teams.

"1716!" Emma says. I lift my head without stopping shoveling to see why Emma has chosen my number out of the ranks. "Come up here." I put down my shovel, moving warily toward the edge of the postenkette.

"Stand right here, by the edge of the ditch and keep watch." She looks directly into my eyes. "I'm going to the latrine and I'm going to be longer than usual." I nod, knowing that she's going to meet a man there. "You stand here looking left and right all the time and if somebody is coming, jump in and start to work. If they ask where I am tell them I went to the latrine." I nod.

I stand above my sister and the rest of the kommando looking left and right. My eyes fall on the elder women, and again I look left and again I look right. The sun is hot on our heads. I wipe the sweat from my eyes. The woman wearing my kerchief blinks into the harsh sun as she gazes up at me. I cannot bear to have them working so hard, for hours without a respite. These women are so much like our parents and they have not had a moment to stop and breathe since lunch.

"Why don't you all sit down," I suggest. "Put your shovels down and rest while I keep watch." They all look up at me. "Go on, I can see if anyone is coming from up here." One by one they sit down, crouching or kneeling in the dirt. The woman who looks particularly like our mother smiles. I look left. The stillness of the girls and women below me allows me a moment of comfort. I look right. The dust settles around their feet and hands. Their heads glisten with beads of sweat and I can see where sunburn is turning their delicate skin red. I look left. I look right. But I do not look behind me.

"What is going on here?!" The horse gallops up from nowhere. Before I know what is happening, an SS jumps from his steed and throws me to the ground. He kicks me viciously in the back. I cover my face.

"Where's the kapo?" he yells, swinging his steel-tipped boot into my ribs.

"Ahhh!" My hands fly to my stomach. "She's in the latrine!" He kicks my face. Blood gushes out of my mouth.

"And you let them rest?" And again in the stomach and again in the ribs. "You who were suppose to watch? Liar!" And again in the back and again in my face. "Filthy *scheiss-Jude! Mist biene!* You should all be killed!"

I cannot see through the blood in my eyes. He pummels me as if I were a rotten vegetable for compost, but I refuse to cry or beg for mercy.

The girl-women and the elder women busily work, sifting sand, shoveling dirt, trying to ignore my grunts and groans.

"What's happening?!" Emma comes running.

"Where were you?" he yells.

"The latrine, sir!"

"And you let a Jew watch other Jews? You whore! Stupid bitch! I want this prisoner reported for letting your detail rest!"

"*Jawohl*, sir."

"Report her to Commandant Drexler!"

"*Jawohl!*"

"Perhaps next time you will think twice before you go whoring."

Emma takes over whipping me. "You dog! Get back to work!"

Her strikes are not as damaging as the vicious kicks of the SS, but that she would beat me injures what feelings I have left for her.

I scuffle away trying to be invisible, hoping he won't start beating me again, hoping he's grown weary of so much physical exertion in this heat. The hooves of his horse pound against the ground as he gallops away. Danka puts a shovel in my hand. Her hand is like ice. I dig blindly at the soil, unable to distinguish earth from sky through the blood and tears.

We work silently, quickly. Everyone is shaking with fear. We do not cease our work; there is not even a pause in the rhythm of our digging.

"1716." I turn toward Emma's voice, unable to see her face. "Take this." I duck the blow, but instead a rag falls in my hands. "Clean yourself up." Without another word Emma returns to her post.

I lean for a second on my shovel, wiping the dirt and blood from my eyes and face. The sobs inside my chest rack against my bruised ribs. I am so confused, a miserable "mist biene," just as they call me. I struggle for control of the turbulent emotions welling up inside me. My temples throb, my mouth aches. I cannot cry, not only because of work but because of the pain. It will hurt too much to let one sob out. I chose instead to think of Emma. Despite the fact she beat me, it was to save her own skin; the rag says more than any words she will ever speak to me. I focus on digging again, concentrating against the summer sun, trying to think the pain away.

We work. The woman who looks so much like Mama watches me the whole afternoon. Emma ignores the fact that I cannot work as hard as I usually do. She cracks the whip above our heads and acts tough, but the detail works slowly in the heat and the elder women are not capable of this hard labor. I bear the pain as well as I can, but it hurts to breathe and stand upright. Finally it is time to march back to camp. The two-kilometer march is agony in itself. I concentrate on making the pain dissipate, but inhaling still catches my ribs like a knife in my lungs.

The marching band is playing, but inside I am dying a hundred deaths, hearing only a dirge; for me it is over. Emma stands to one side of the band as her kommando marches through the gate.

"Wait here." She pulls me out. My eyes catch Danka's; it is a silent good-bye. The band plays horror to my ears. I am screaming with pain and still I must stand, knowing in a few hours I will be dead, knowing I have seen my sister for the last time marching through the gates of hell—knowing I have not kept my oath, knowing I have failed her. I dare not shift my tired feet. I dare not turn my head. Staring straight ahead as kommando after kommando marches in, my eyes do not register the faces of any individuals. Some who still have the energy to notice see me there; none has the energy to care. I am doomed in their eyes, another prisoner awaiting her death sentence. They do not need to be reminded about the tenuousness of all our lives.

For the first time in sixteen months of imprisonment I wish I were inside the gates of Birkenau, standing next to my sister waiting to be counted; at least that means I'm alive. I watch roll call begin from outside the gates, removed from all that is real. Floating away from my body, I gaze down at the sea of humanity doomed to servitude and wish I were among them.

The sky is dark. I am alone. Even the band has left me behind.

The door to the office opens and Emma steps out. The light from inside illuminates her head. Her hair is turning gray.

"Get into camp," she says matter-of-factly. I move away from her uncertainly, afraid she is joking. "*Hau ab!*" she orders, adding under her breath, "And make sure you're at roll call tomorrow."

"Yes, Emma. I will, Emma." I move through the gates, disappearing into camp to join the ranks of downtrodden girl-womanhood. I am counted that roll call. I am alive.

Danka is waiting outside our block with tear-stained cheeks. "Rena?" We grab each other in a fierce hug. "I thought you were dead for sure," she weeps.

"I was. Emma saved me."

"How is that possible?"

"We will never know." I thought there was no joy in Auschwitz-Birkenau, but there is—I am still alive, that is joy. There may not be presents, or parties, but the fact that one gets to be with one's loved ones again, that is a rare gift behind these walls. And this brush with death inspires rather than defeats me. "We have to see if we can get some kerchiefs for the elder women in our detail."

"Rena, you're hurt. You should lie down."

"I will feel better if I can help these women." We go from one block to another telling the block elders and room elders and other prisoners about the elder women, begging for kerchiefs so they can at least protect themselves from the sun.

"They can't stand the heat," I tell them. "Look how I got beaten for letting them rest. They are the age of our mothers and they're not going to survive if we don't do something." Everyone who has a kerchief donates one to our cause. With damp eyes, they give Danka and me a scarf in honor of their own mamas who are now mere memories in the ashen air. We get ten kerchiefs altogether.

"I have been looking for you." The woman who looks so much like Mama comes up to me as I am gathering the scarves.

"How are you?" I ask.

"I should be asking you that. I want to give you something. Will you please take this?" She holds out her portion of bread.

"No, I can't." I shake my head, retreating from her gesture.

"Please, you are young. I want you to live," she pleads.

"You're going to need it tomorrow. Please, save it and eat it in the morning. It's going to be another hot day. You have your kerchief. You can live. I know you can. Look, my sister and I have gotten more kerchiefs for your friends to wear in the sun. It's going to get better—really it is!"

"You can talk like this after the beating you had?"

"Oh, that. Next time I'm going to look all the way around and be more careful . . . You'll see, it's not so bad here," I lie to my Mama's face. "Try to eat the bread and drink the tea, for me. Please, try to live . . . Have you got your tea?"

"Yes, a friend is watching it in the block. I'm going to drink the tea but not the bread. You have it, I don't need it."

"I can't take it from you. That would be like taking bread from my own mama."

"Your mama wants you to have her bread, to live for her."

My eyes sting. "I'm sorry. Thank you, but I cannot take it. Please. Promise me you'll eat it." I hold her hand, folding it firmly around the crust that is so precious many would fight her for it.

"What's your name?"

"Rena."

"You're a good daughter, Rena." She smiles into my eyes. "I know it's unlikely, but I'm going to pray that you meet one of my sons when you are free. Either would be a good husband to you and if you're not going to meet one of my boys, I'm going to pray to the Lord that you have a husband just as good as my sons, and have a good life." Our hands slip apart slowly and she leaves me standing alone in the night clutching white and red kerchiefs to my breast.

"Rena, are you done?" Danka's voice pulls me back to the present. "We have to get inside."

"She has her bread," I tell my sister. "She'll be okay, won't she?"

"Who, Rena?"

"Mama. We'll see her tomorrow, right?" I fall into sleep.

Four A.M.
"Raus! Raus!"

We arrive at Emma's kommando after roll call, but the elder women are not anywhere.

"Where are they, Emma?" I have never asked her a direct question before.

"I don't know," she answers, humbly.

"Stay here," I tell Danka, hoping to save my place in the kommando. Running across the camp, I look for their stooped and tired bodies in the nearby kommandos lining up for work. Her face is not anywhere. Dashing into their block, I see the block elder. "Where are they?"

"Who?"

"Our mothers," I stammer. "The elder women!"

"Oh." Her voice is quiet. As hard as we have all become, these women have touched our hearts and made us feel again, but the wounds are deep and sore to the touch. "They took them late last night."

Words are stuck in my throat as if someone were strangling me. The block elder and I stare at one another in grief and shock.

"Get out of here before you get caught!" Her voice jerks me back to reality. I leave the block unable to run anymore. My legs are heavy as iron.

Emma's ranks are full. I stare at her, lost, unable to muster my usual gusto of self-assurance. I am slipping into the pit, about to be swallowed up, about to disappear.

Rolling her eyes at me, she jerks her head. "Get in!"

Stepping next to Danka, I shake my head and bite my lip. Heads bowed, we march out to another day of work and blistering heat. There are no motherly faces to comfort our losses, but Emma does not crack her whip today unless an SS is riding by. The pain in my back and ribs reawakens and I am unable to think anything away.

The numbness in my heart expands through my body. The body digs the dirt. The body sifts the sand. The body screams with pain as the lungs expand against bruised and maybe broken ribs. But it is the eyes which hurt most. They ache until it feels as if the head will split apart, bleeding across the barren land as we sift more sand to make more bricks and concrete, to make more blocks for more Jews. Despite the sun the sky is black.

We aren't living in Birkenau. We are always almost dead.

❖ ❖ ❖

Stibitz is in a foul mood, stamping back and forth cursing loudly at our hungry faces while we wait for our ration of tea and bread. We don't pay attention to the reason for his tirade; these outbursts of temper are nothing unusual. Even the SS have bad days. He picks the lid up off the teakettle, flinging it like a discus against a wall. It ricochets, flying toward those of us in line.

"Duck, Danka!" She swerves. *Smack!* It slices into her head, toppling her under the weight and sudden impact. Blood pours down her face and across the earth. The bone under the wound is visible, but this is a good thing, I tell myself, at least her skull isn't cracked. I pull the cloth I use for my periods out of my sleeve and press it hard against the gash, praying the blood will clot quickly, before any SS notice her lying here. She stirs. "Hold this to your head and press hard." She holds it as I rip a piece of my slip off, another gift from Erna long ago.

"Be still, Danka. Don't move until I tell you to." Her eyes wince with pain. Placing this new strip of fabric against the cut, I wring out the other one before replacing it. The girls in line hide us by moving forward for their bread. Obscured by them, I have a few precious moments to stop the bleeding, check Danka's breathing, examine her eyes. She's in shock; the wound is large and ugly, arching from the center of her forehead down to her eyebrow. My head begins to ache in sympathy with her.

"It's not too bad, Danka. We have to get something on it, though, some salve." I dab the blood gently from her brow. It's oozing more slowly now. "We're going to stand up now, and get

our tea." I direct her into line to get our tea and bread. We head inside our block.

"I'm nauseous."

"Eat anyway, Danka. You need your strength. It's the cut making you feel sick, not your stomach." She sips her tea slowly, stopping every few moments as if fighting the urge to vomit. I cover
her with our blanket before going to wait by the block elder's door.

"Salve for a cut." I hand her my bread.

"Let me see what I have." She takes my bread and disappears. I
wait, trying to keep watch on Danka from where I stand. My legs
grow tired of standing, so I crouch with my back against the wall
and wait. The block is still. My knees begin to ache in this position,
so I sit on the dirt floor, and wait. The door cracks open. The light
from inside falls across the darkness of the now sleeping block.
The block elder hands me a smear of salve on a piece of paper, then
shuts the door in my face.

I wash Danka's wound gently. "Am I going to die from this?"
she asks.

"No way. It's not so bad, Danka, really. But I know it hurts."
What I'm really worried about is infection, a scar, selection. The
wound may not kill her, but the effect of it can. I stamp out these
worries that divert my attention and resourcefulness. Smearing
the antiseptic salve on her forehead, I assure her, "We'll get more
tomorrow."

Four A.M.

"Raus! Raus!"

My stomach growls all day. The soup sloshes in my belly like an
ocean of waves with nothing to cling to. Danka is weak and I can
tell her head is hurting, but she manages to work. I trade my bread
for more salve to put on her cut and then step outside to go to the
latrine. It is in the latrine that information is passed and things can
be bartered for. I miss Erna, wishing for a moment that I had
someone to talk to, someone to share my burdens with. "Have

you heard?" a girl whispers next to me. "There's going to be a big selection. They're going to clean out camp." Another voice echoes the information. "There are too many of us."

I walk back to the block in a daze. All I hear, over and over like a child's nursery rhyme chanting in my head, is the rumor: There's going to be a big selection; there are too many of us. Like an itch I cannot scratch, it eats away at my silence. It's an ominous secret, an unshareable burden. I almost wish they hadn't told me. The worry about Danka's scar eats away at my morale. She'll be selected if they see the cut, and it's healing too slowly. My head churns until I am thinking of everything and nothing at all.

We march out with Emma, but the work worsens with the weather; this is our second fall. There are no days off for snow or rain, I know that now. They will always stand there watching us struggle to move bricks, digging, building. We march in from work, our hands and feet blistered from always being damp and cold; we wait to be counted, wait for our tea, our bread, always working—always waiting.

The SS are more agitated than usual. Swinging their whips and clubs more often, they beat us without any provocation. The work details are stricter and harder. It's as if they're trying to clear out those who won't make the cut when the big selection comes. I scan the rows and rows of women who share my fate. I've never seen the camp this crowded. "There are too many of us." I wonder how it makes the Nazis feel when they can't kill us quickly enough by working us to death. I wonder if they feel at all.

The SS walk up and down our rows counting the evening crew, making note of those who collapsed and died during the day. A hush descends through the columns of women. Dr. Mengele has come into camp. We know who he is; there are rumors about him. He stands before us, the glorious angel of doom. It's difficult to believe that anyone so handsome can do the things he's rumored to do.

An SS motions for a portion of our ranks to move away from the main group. Danka and I are in the group separated from the rest of roll call. Dr. Mengele walks slowly among us looking for the healthiest, most able-bodied specimens. It is a moment I have been hoping for; sometimes he chooses prisoners for inside work details, like the one Erna and Fela are now in. This may be our lucky day, the day we find a way to leave Birkenau. He walks by us like a butcher inspecting his meat.

He points at me but passes over Danka. I step out, walking to the front of the line, moving away from my sister. Danka is discarded with the rest of the unfit specimens. Roll call is dismissed. Thousands of women hurry to their respective blocks to grab their bread and a place on the shelves to sleep.

Fifty of us march away from the regular blocks toward the quarantine block. Turning my head, I catch a glimpse of my sister as the pit in my stomach grows wider and wider. The anxiety of not having her next to me is unbearable. I do not know if this detail is for life or if it is for death. I do know that the only way I can keep my promise to my sister, though, is to keep her with me at all times; too much can happen in a moment. There is no debate in my mind about my duty to my sister; the oath is the driving force behind all of my actions. Inside the quarantine block we are handed a standard ration of bread. There's no conversation or speculation about the detail we've been assigned. The girls I've been chosen with move to the bunks without conversing, while I dissolve into the background so that no one will notice my exit.

Erika's on watch outside, holding a paper with our numbers on it. This is good fortune, although there is always the chance she won't be nice to me. I don't care about chances. I go straight up to her. "Can you help me? I'll give you my portion of bread if you can get my sister into this detail with me." I thrust my only meal into her hand.

Erika looks at me as if I'm crazy. The decision in my eyes convinces her I'm serious, though. "What's her number?" She takes the bread, slipping it into her pocket in one deft movement.

"2779." I hold my breath. She might let Danka in. She seems sincere. She seems to care, but one can never be sure. "Can I bring her into quarantine?" I ask timidly.

"Yes." Erika looks around quickly, assessing the area. There is no one nearby. She crosses a name off the list. "Go get your sister."

"There will be too many, though. What will you do?"

"That's none of your business," her voice hisses. "*Hau ab!*"

Obediently I vanish, becoming one with the shadows, weaving my way toward our block. Danka is standing just inside the doorway, waiting for me. Only her eyes betray the absolute terror she's in. I take hold of her hand as I used to when she was little. "I got you into the detail."

"How?"

"Not now. Follow me." We step into the dark, sneak back across the camp toward quarantine. The spotlights trace the electric fences, looking for kamikaze prisoners with suicide on their minds. We move like ghosts, avoiding the lights, the guns, the eyes of those in the watchtower.

Erika is waiting outside. We do not step toward her; we wait in the shadows for her signal. She raises her chin slightly in a half nod before turning her back to us. We dart through the door to safety. Careful not to disturb anyone, we tiptoe to a bunk that isn't full and crawl onto the boards. Pulling up the blanket around our shoulders, I put my arms around my sister for the first time since we arrived in camp. I want to chase away the demon dreams which steal sleep from our troubled minds. I want to rest my weary bones and stop the incessant worrying that rattles against the insides of my head.

For the first time in a year and a half we don't stand roll call. In the morning they bring a kettle of tea into the block and the waiting begins.

We're served soup at noon and sit through the afternoon waiting for supper with nothing else to do but listen to our stomachs growl. I'm grateful we don't have to work and try to take advantage of this brief reprieve. We don't feel like speaking with the others and they do not feel like speaking with us. The first day of quarantine we sleep.

The second day we are not so tired and move about the room asking questions, conversing, asking out loud why we're here and how long they're going to keep us in this place. My hope is that this will be a detail working under a roof. It would be good to be inside on the cold and rainy days. I also hope it's not the kind of detail Erna and Fela have disappeared into, a job that cannot be spoken about.

Danka drifts off into a world of her own. I watch her become oblivious to her surroundings knowing that this is how she survives. Meanwhile, I listen to every bit of information I can gather; this is how I survive—always be aware.

"Maybe we're going to work in the kitchen!" one of the girls says.

"Oh, the food we could eat if we were in the kitchen!"

"I wonder what they'll have us do?"

"It could be anything. Better not to think about it."

Another girl chimes in, but her comment is more to the window than to those of us inside. "At least we're not outside. The weather is terrible today."

Our conversation is sparing. We don't speak to each other for long; we're too exhausted and we've simply learned it's better not to become close friends with people who may die in a few minutes. There's no sorority of sympathy or understanding. We don't discuss our plight or what we're waiting for. If we discuss anything, it is about where we are from, but even that is too painful. We sleep. We drink our tea. We sip our soup. We chew our bread. We wait.

By the third day we're starting to go stir-crazy and get on each other's nerves. The unknown eats away at what little morale we have. There's bickering among bunkmates. The rest has done us good; the little bit of food still leaves us hungry, but at least we do not burn it all off doing hard labor. We do not gain weight but we do not lose it either.

"*Raus!* Line up!" It's the fourth morning. An attendant from the hospital enters the block. "March out!" We follow her lead, stepping out of quarantine, marching across the length of camp toward another building. The sign over the door reads SAUNA. Inside, the kapo informs us, "Leave your old clothes in a pile here. You no longer need them. There are new uniforms on that table. *Schnell!*"

Stepping naked over to the table, we snatch up the new one-size-fits-all uniforms, pulling them over our bodies. They're exactly like our other blue-and-gray striped dresses, rough as unworn sandpaper.

"Put these aprons on, too!" We tie clean, white, pressed aprons around our waists as we line up again, filing out of the building in twos. We march back across the length of the compound in front of the rest of the women in camp already lined up for morning roll call. The next building we enter is in the middle of the camp; it's a small, one-room building across from our blocks. It's Mengele's office. Inside, the nurse orders us to hold out our arms so the secretary can write down each of our numbers on a list. "1716," she repeats under her breath, "2779." It's strange that we do not have numbers on our uniforms. Outside again, we line up facing the camp roll call, in neat rows of five, ten to each line, forming our new, exclusive work detail. I wonder where Emma is; I wonder if she will even notice that Danka and I are gone.

It is strange to watch regular camp roll call and not be a part of it. The sea of women before me is unbelievable; I've never seen so many people in one place. They look so miserable, so forlorn and dejected. The words *There are too many of us* echo through my mind until I shake my head to free myself of the warning. Out of the corner of my eye I see a woman with a list in her hand and make a note that her presence is odd. She comes from behind the building, nervously looking this way and that as if she's afraid. She stands for a moment, scratching something out on the list, then cautiously she takes one of the girls by the hand and leads her out the back of the line and behind Mengele's office. They disappear.

My heart races as the realization sinks in. "Danka, this is not a good detail to be in."

"What?" Her eyes bulge with fright. "Why do you say that?"

"One of the elite just took a friend or relative out of the line-up."

"Who?"

"I don't know who she is, but she's important enough to walk around while the rest of us are standing roll call. She would know if this was a bad kommando. We're not going to work under any roof. This is for death."

"You can't be sure."

"Yes, I can." I look around. My mind runs through every scenario possible. It takes less than a second for me to decide the course of action we must try to take if we are to survive. "Come with me."

Her eyes pop out of her head. "Where?"

"Back to the sauna." I look at the dreaded dresses we're wearing. How could I have missed the signs? No numbers on the breast, new dresses, clean white aprons exactly like the experiment victims were wearing. "Our only chance is to get our old uniforms back before they remove them and we're lost for good."

"We can't do that!"

"We have to." I am fierce.

"How?" My mind has catapulted beyond the situation we're in, to the particulars that could save our lives.

"We're going to pretend that we're just as important as any block elder or kapo. I'm going to take your hand and we're going to march across the compound and I'm not letting go until we're in the sauna."

"In front of everybody?"

"It's a gamble."

"We can't. They'll shoot us for sure."

"Danka! This is something for experiments. Remember the women with the faces?"

"Gathering herbs?" I nod.

"You want to be a zombie?" I glare into her face.

"No."

"Well you're going to be if you don't come with me now. We have one chance to live and one chance to die. If we cross the compound we might live or die. If we stay here we're dead for sure."

She wants to follow me, I can tell, but fear has her feet rooted into the ground. "I can't," she whispers.

I lean very close to her ear. "I'm going to break my oath to you. I swore I'd die with you, but that was only if you were selected, not if you chose to die. I don't owe that to you anymore!" Our voices are sparse and speculative. The SS are busy counting the prisoners on the other side of the Laggerstrasse. "If you don't want to listen to what I'm saying, then you're deciding to give up your life—but I'm not. I'm going back to the sauna whether you come with me or not." I pray I've scared her enough to come with me.

"What do I do?" Her voice wavers.

"You just walk with me. That's all you have to do. Keep your chin high and believe you're important." Her eyes glaze over. She will do as she's told. "Now give me your hand." Like cold, clammy fish her fingers wind around mine.

Briefly, I check the direction the SS are gazing. Taube is beating someone. Their attention is elsewhere. Gathering my self-esteem around me, I imagine the cloud of God descending down upon my sister and me, just as it did on the mount to speak with Moses. We take our first step out of line. Past roll call, past the watchful SS, past thousands of other female prisoners, Danka and I walk hidden in the mists of Zion.

Passing Stibitz and Taube, we walk with the air that we are doing exactly what we've been told to do. My fingernails dig into her flesh; I'm not letting go of my sister's hand. We walk, convinced that no one will stop us. We are important; we have been ordered to return to the sauna. I repeat this to myself over and over. Chins up, eyes forward, never look back.

The distance seems to remain the same. The sauna gets no closer. The lines and rows of prisoners seem to continue on forever. Through the desert of Birkenau we walk invisible.

Seconds slow to hours as our feet trudge through the mud. Our heads held high, our gaze never veers from our path. Danka's hand turns blue from the tightness of my squeeze. Chins up, eyes forward, never look back.

I open the sauna door without looking behind me. There are no voices behind us ordering us to halt, no gunshots firing at our backs. There's only roll call, the lifeline that we must grab as quickly as we can change our clothes.

We step inside, shutting the door behind us. The silence of the sauna is dense as steam.

"Quick, Danka. We have to hurry!" I whisper urgently. "Undress and give me your clothes and I will do the rest." Tearing the uniform of an experiment victim off my body, I search the pile of discarded uniforms in my underwear. Danka cannot move. She stares at me like a small animal frozen by fear, incapable of helping me, as I fumble through the clothes looking for her number, repeating "2779, 2779" over and over, out loud. My hands tremble uncontrollably as my nerves unravel.

There's no time. Our lives depend on getting back to roll call and being counted before anyone notices we're missing from the special detail. I see her uniform and place it on the floor.

The pile seems to have multiplied since I turned my back. Shaking uncontrollably, I dig through the clothes looking for the one uniform out of fifty which is mine. They are all identical except for the numbers—what if I passed it when I was looking for Danka's? What if it's not here? Finally I locate the sleeve 1716. Stuffing the new dresses and aprons under the pile of old uniforms, I run to Danka.

"Can you put your arms up?" I ask gently. Her arms float upwards. I pull the old lice-infested burlap onto her arms and over her head. My fingers quiver as I button her into her old uniform, the number 2779 in its proper place. Then with a shudder I pull the comfort of anonymity over my own head. The number I've hated so much is now my refuge, my only link to life.

I open the door, carefully peeking outside. The SS are just a row away, coming our way. We have a few minutes to spare. I shut the door—catching my breath, waiting for them to pass.

"Ready?" I don't wait for an answer, pushing Danka out ahead of me and into the neat ranks of five. "Please move up," I whisper to the girl-women around us. "Please move over. Make some room, please." No one pushes back, no one argues. The rows of fated women we depend on move as silently as water, swallowing us into their bosom until we are one with the ranks. The SS move up our row. We hold our breath.

They pass us. We have been counted.

Roll call ends and Emma is waiting. I nod to her as Danka and I take our places in her kommando. She raises an eyebrow at our presence. I think her mouth turns upward slightly, too, but can't be sure; all I know is it feels good to be safe with Emma. Even the nip of fall in the air makes me grateful that I am outside digging, building, rather than in Mengele's hands. It feels good to be chilled, to be alive.

❖ ❖ ❖

Danka remains in a daze for a few days. Everything she does is automatic, without thought or contemplation, but sometimes I believe she looks at me with amazement and maybe gratitude; sometimes I am not sure where she is.

Rumors still haunt the latrines. There are more voices murmuring, "There's going to be a big selection."[14] We're not safe. We're never safe. We just narrowly escaped death for one day—what about tomorrow?

A girl in the latrine asks, "Remember that special work detail they selected last week?"

I watch her warily, wondering what she knows, wondering how much bread she is going to blackmail me for in order to buy her silent allegiance.

"I think so," I lie to her face.

"I heard from someone working in the infirmary that it was for sterilization and shock treatments. He took half of the girls and put hot plates on their stomachs to send electric shock into their bellies over and over again until they fainted. When they came to, they did it again and again until they died." I feel weak, nauseous. "The rest he cut open in order to take their female organs out. Some of them are dying from infection now. The lucky ones are already dead." I move away from this stranger's voice, the blood draining from my face.

"Rena, what's wrong?" Danka comes up behind me.

"Nothing, Danka, nothing. I must be hungry." I head back to our block.

"You're not getting sick, are you?" I shake my head. She watches me with concern.

14. "October 1 [1943]. . . . The occupancy level of the women's camp is 32,066" (Czech, 497).

There is a pressure screaming for release against my eyes. I don't cry. It takes time to cry and there is no time. I fight to find a reason, but there is no reason in this place. What did they do when they discovered there were three numbers missing in the experiment detail? Did the woman who snuck her cousin or sister out of line just put somebody else in her place? Why didn't they search us out?—they had our numbers written on a list. Why are we alive and the other girls we were selected with not? Will there ever come a time when we can thank God for being alive today before we have to ask the same privilege tomorrow, and the next day? Is life a privilege or a curse?

Rumors of the big selection increase. One thing after another tumbles across my brain. As if we were never in Mengele's clutches, I go back to worrying about Danka's injury again. The scar's not as angry as it was a few weeks ago, but it is still red enough to attract the bitter eyes of SS selection officers.

"Tomorrow," a voice whispers in front of me. I pass the information down the line. This is how we send news, the same way we toss bricks, from one to another. Usually we're in the soup line or waiting for the evening bread. "Tomorrow."

Taking my bread, I turn to Danka. "I'm going outside."

"For what?"

"For anything I can find." I'm irritated. It's not her fault. We're both nervous, weary with the exhaustion living on the edge brings. I need to scour the grounds, I need to do something besides think that tonight may be my last night on earth. Walking past the kitchen, I scan the ground for potato pieces or anything that might be edible. I wish we had some extra food for the selection. Beyond food I don't know what else to look for, and tonight the rats and other prisoners have beaten me to whatever scraps may have been here. Much to my surprise, a light-blue-and-red wrapper with the word *Chickory* on it peeks up out of the mud at me. For a moment I stare at it simply enjoying the familiarity of the logo and the memory it brings with it. Picking it up, I bury my nose in the wrapper, allowing the aroma to carry me back.

"Rena, don't play with that, it will turn your fingers red," Mama scolded sweetly. *"Look at your hands! Don't touch anything. Go wash it off quickly. The ink stains."*

"What's it for, Mama?"

"It makes the coffee smooth and not so acid on the stomach, just like Papa likes it."

I can smell freshly brewed coffee in the night air.

A familiar redness has left its stain on my fingers. I stare and stare at it, then carefully fold the precious paper into what is left of the hem in my dress. "Thank you, Mama." I head back to the blocks.

I force myself to sleep by telling myself that I need to be fresh for whatever test they give us. Sleep comes fitfully at first and then deeply, until I am no longer conscious of the sounds outside, the screams, the gunshots. Many who hold no hope in tomorrow will risk the moon in the sky trying to reach the fence, and tomorrow morning the SS will have a few less to select for death.

Four A.M.

"Raus! Raus!"

Morning comes too soon. There is no tea. Fear as thick as fog has descended upon our camp. The dead we carry out each morning have always been pitied by me, but today I feel differently; they have passed away in the bliss of unconsciousness. The bodies on the fence usually make me feel sad, but today I respect them for choosing to rob the Nazis of their secret delight. This is mercy in Auschwitz-Birkenau, to die by your own hand.

It rains, pouring sometimes, sprinkling others, as if heaven cannot make up its mind. But the selection team has no trouble making up their minds. We stand for hours on the Laggerstrasse in rows of five. The line stretches the length of the camp. The morning downpour changes to drizzle. The noonday meal passes without any soup—there's no sense in feeding people who are about to die. In their shiny boots and pressed gray jodhpurs, standing there like gods of the universe, their thumbs jerking this way to death and that way to life, the SS officers stand before their peers judging our inferiorities.

Taube and Stibitz walk down the rows.

"Miserable *mist bienes*," Stibitz yells. "You *scheiss-Judes* get down on your knees!"

My skin bristles. Catching Danka's eye, I warn her in advance.

Taube turns to our row. "Kneel down!" I pull her into the mud. His club swings into the knees of a girl who does not know she's supposed to kneel before him. Her scream pierces the air. He and his cohort walk away smugly. Our knees ache. We do not shift or sway. We kneel without faltering.

Taube's face glowers. He relishes his power. "Lie face down. All the way. Heads down!"

We fall on our stomachs into the mud. Danka needs no warnings for this portion of the exercise; we have seen the results of Taube's version of push-ups many times before.

"Up! Down!" Faces in the mud, we push our frail bodies into the air and drop back to earth for as long as he orders.

"Up! Down!" I have no idea how many push-ups we do; my mind stops as long as my body is in motion.

"Halt!" Taube yells. We collapse in the mud. "Don't move!"

Please don't let the girl next to me raise her head, I pray. Taube moves away from us, heading further down our row. I avoid listening for the sounds I know will follow. They no longer wait for someone to raise her head as an excuse to demolish someone's brains. They simply choose the skull they fancy and crush it before moving on to their next victim.

The waiting is impossible, the terror indescribable.

My eyes stare into the ground, boring holes into mud and muck, locking my gaze into the earth. We barely breathe. It is forever. Finally they release us from our "exercises." Helping each other up from the ground, we avoid looking at the bodies that will not rise again.

We move up, edging away from those who didn't know about Taube's exercises, those who've been selected by a foot rather than a thumb. We get closer and closer to the SS gods, trying not to think about what each step means—that someone else has been chosen to live or die.

I look into Danka's face. The mud on it inspires me. First, though, I spit on my sleeve and wipe the dirt and grime off her skin.

"My turn." She washes my face, taking care to wipe away all smudges from the Taube episode. Our faces clean, I stoop to the ground and take a fingerful of mud.

"What are you doing?" she asks, alarmed.

"Covering up your scar." I smudge it across her forehead. "That works, Danka. I can't even see it, and I know it's there." We edge closer and closer.

"Do you want to go first?" It's time to decide in what order we should go before our judges.

"I don't know." Her voice trembles.

"If you go first and they select you, then I can join you more easily."

"How?" We can now see that there is a ditch that we must jump across.

"I can fail the test or look miserable."

"What if you go first and they pass you and then select me? What will you do?"

"I'll run after you pleading with them to let me die with my sister."

"But that doesn't work all the time anymore."

"Then I'll attack a guard and be shot, then at least you'll know I died too."

"You can't do that, that won't work at all. I can't bear the thought of seeing you shot. I want us to be together or not at all."

"Then you go first." I put her in front of me.

She looks at the ground, ashamed. "I'm afraid to, I don't look so good as you do."

"I'll go first, then, Danka. I'll go with my head straight up and you go very close behind me. That way they'll be blinded by me and think you don't look so bad at all." She doesn't look bad, she has lost flesh but her face is prettier than mine; still, she does not have that sparkle in her eyes which says, I'm going to live.

"Okay, you go first. I'll be braver if I can keep my eyes on you."

I open my hem, pulling out the treasure I found last night and have been protecting from the elements for over ten hours. "Give me your face." Opening the chickory wrapper up, I lightly paint her cheeks. The dye from the paper adds a blush to her pallor. Spitting on my fingers, I blend it in so it looks natural and step back amazed at the instant transformation. "Beautiful. You look a picture of health now, Danka."

"My scar."

I take a little more mud and trace my finger along the cut. "It's healing very well," I assure her.

"It is?"

"Yes. You look very good indeed." We edge closer. "Don't watch the others, just tell yourself that you will fly over that ditch into my arms. That's all you need to think." I turn my back to her, leaving my hand behind me to hold hers until the last possible moment.

We don't have far to go; twenty, maybe thirty girls stand in front of us. The girl in front of me turns around. "You're going to make it," she says in Slovakian.

I stumble for words of encouragement but am at a loss. "You will too."

"Please take this." She takes my hand, passing something cold and round into my palm. "It was my mother's wedding band. I don't want them to have it," she whispers.

"I can't take this."

"You have to. Don't let them have it. Promise!" Her eyes are like steel beams, forcing me to swear I will protect her past.

"I promise." I cannot believe I have said the words. She steps towards the guards. I do not know what to do with this gold in my hand. I can be killed for having it. I wipe my mouth, slipping the ring under my tongue, next to the elephant.

The thumb turns away. The girl whose family heirloom is hiding in my mouth moves toward the side of the condemned. She looks back wistfully. Our eyes seal our fates across the compound. I will never know her name.

I step up to the tables.

"Halt!" My heart is pounding in my ears.

Their eyes are on my forearm—number 1716, from the first transport. They cannot believe I'm still here. Will this work toward my advantage? Or will it be my downfall?

The thumb jerks for me to jump the ditch.

I walk past them, my chin out, my shoulders straight, toward the ditch. There's no running start, there are only a few feet on either side for our take-off and landing. The ditch is a few feet wide and a few feet deep. Whoever falls in is covered by mud from the rain and has lost the last chance for life.

I fly over it with inches to spare, hugging the wall at the other side to give my sister plenty of room for her landing, but I cannot bear to look back and watch. Seconds stretch into the abyss of not knowing.

I wait, holding my breath, my eyes shut tight, listening, with my entire being hugging the wall, wishing it were my sister. I imagine that there is a thread between us that pulls her toward me. I do not think of her falling in the ditch. I think only of her being beside me.

There is silence . . .

Two hands slip around my waist, sending a little squeeze. I breathe again. Holding her hands to my belly, I pray I will never have to let go of them again. We do not speak, we do not rejoice; our victory is small in the face of so many failures. The sun is finally breaking through the clouds. It is pale and slight, but Danka and I lie in the damp grass letting it warm us, worn out from the hours of tortuous waiting. Our hands lightly touch, just enough to remind ourselves that we are still together. I take the ring and the elephant out of my mouth—two gravestones hidden under my tongue.

This is all that is left of her family. This ring is her immortality wrapped in gold and memory. Silently I vow to keep it safe from the Germans as long as I am alive. We stand up as the sun begins its descent toward the horizon. Shadows lengthen across field. There are still hundreds, maybe thousands, waiting in line to be selected.

We move away, unable to watch or think about what has happened today, wandering through the empty camp in a daze. No one dares to speak to anyone. A teenage girl eats a lemon while her mother begs for a bite. Her eyes glare at her mother angrily as she devours the already squeezed pulp like a wild animal. Her teeth sink into the pale rind, ripping it apart. I turn away, dismayed. She eats the whole thing without sharing it with her mama.

What have they done to us? The piece of potato I find I eagerly share with my sister—how else can we survive if we do not care for one another? I do not understand the selfishness before me, but then it does not matter what I understand.

It is late at night. We stand on the other side until the last woman falls in the ditch to her ultimate demise. We are not excused. The last truck heads for the gas chamber. The death squad departs from camp, ignoring us. We stand waiting for a command, but for the first time in a year and a half we're not ordered to do anything. We go to our empty blocks. The block elder's not here; we can only assume she was among the thousands who were selected.

Bread is doled out. Our stomachs are grateful for the food but our hearts are not.

Should I pray? Should I thank God for saving our lives again? How can I thank or praise a Creator who allows this to happen? There are five hundred of us, maybe a thousand, left in camp. This is not a miracle, to be alive—it is a tragedy. How can I praise the miracle that Danka and I live while thousands of our fellow girl-women prisoners are gassed and cremated just a few hundred meters from where we have life?

Four A.M.
"Raus! Raus!"
We take our tea and stand at attention for roll call. It will not even take an hour this morning. The smoke from the chimneys never ceases. A dull haze encompasses Birkenau. Ash fills the air, covering the roofs of the blocks and the ground we stand on. We march out with Emma, work all day, and return. Evening roll call takes a little bit longer; there are new shocked faces to be beaten into submission. A new flock of Jewish girl-women who do not know about straight lines, silent attention, and gas chambers. The transports are coming . . . The Germans have been very busy.

Four A.M.
"Raus! Raus!"
Camp is full.

❖   ❖   ❖

Winter is closing in on us and as fall slips away from our grasp so does our hope for survival. Yom Kippur has passed us by without notice. A few of the new ones fasted; we know better. We stand in the growing darkness for evening roll call. I am having trouble keeping alert to all the potential dangers; the hyper-awareness that has served me so well is starting to fade from fatigue. I fear that with the onslaught of winter Danka and I are going to be in for real trouble soon. How long can we keep on going like this? Someday we're going to drop from sheer exhaustion or worse illness. I am so helpless. Our fates lie in their whims.

Mengele is here again. He has made other appearances, but for some reason this night we notice it.

"Danka," I whisper, "the cold is coming and last winter so many got frostbite. We have the shoes and socks from Erna and Fela, but how long will they last in the mud and snow? How long will we last working so hard?"

Danka knows what I'm going to ask before I ask it. "Please, Rena. I can't take a special detail ever again."

"What can I do? I'm just hoping we get chosen. I'm not doing anything." I direct my eyes forward, but I cannot keep my tongue still. "Think about it," I whisper. "If we get chosen, and it's for inside work, we might make it. If we don't get inside we're going to die for sure this winter. No one can survive as long as we have here. We have got to get a good job, with a roof over our heads." I smooth my stubble of hair and straighten the stripes of my dress out so they fall in uninterrupted lines.

"Rena," Danka hisses at me. She knows what I'm doing. I check us both, nodding to myself. We are hardy. We still look pretty good. There is still some meat on our bodies, and for some reason I still have a bosom. I stand with my chin out, eyes forward. Danka, unwilling to be left alone a second time, copies me.

His alabaster skin and glistening black hair gleam with care. His gray uniform has been neatly pressed and the pleat falls straight down his leg. I notice things like this. He steps closer toward our row. He doesn't know who we are. We have that one advantage, we are anonymous faces in the throng. We have used our anonymity to be invisible and escape his clutches, now we must stick out. Somehow he must see that we are good girls, clean and orderly, organized, all qualities the Germans admire, even in Jews. He has chosen us for life many times during camp selections. Only once has he chosen us for death and experiments. What will it be this time?

Mengele points at me again. Chin up, eyes forward, chest out, I hold my breath, stepping forward hesitantly.

He points to Danka.

I exhale. We move in behind the other girls already chosen. Dina is in our ranks; I catch her eye. Is this for life or is it for death?

Mengele finishes his selection and orders an SS man to take us to quarantine. We march toward the isolation block—again. A feeling of dread washes over me the moment we enter the block. Danka's face is white. We move to the beds we slept on the last time we were in this place. Is this for life or is it for death?

There is nothing I can do to save us. I sleep through the day, unable to bear the depression that seeps into my mind. Erika is not outside the door this time . . . what if this is for experiments, like the other one? Danka and I speak sparingly, quietly, unwilling to discuss what might be.

"Rena?" Dina wakes me up. "What do you think this will be for?"

"I don't know, Dina."

"We've made it this far. It must be good." She has a naive hope that warms my heart.

"I hope so, Dina. For all of our sakes."

"You've been here the longest. You really deserve a break."

"They don't give breaks, do they."

"No . . . maybe we'll just be lucky." She leaves my bunk to go talk to someone else.

On the third day we receive new clothes again. These clothes are not long dresses with aprons, like the ones the experiment victims wore, these are simply another version of the striped dresses we have been wearing. The only difference is that they're cleaner.

"Rip off your old numbers. You will sew them on your new uniforms later!" Hope trickles into my heart.

I slip the elephant and the wedding ring under my tongue; the nail file hides in my hand. Nobody knows where we're going, so I must take care that they won't be found. We dress as quickly as possible and line up. We march into the scribes' block to have our numbers written down. When we are let back outside it is under strict SS guard; there is no escaping like the first time. We march immediately outside the gates of Birkenau, down a road, past the train tracks.

We march for what seems forever—but everything seems far away when you're weak. I do not know where in the complex of camps we are heading. I reach out for Danka's hand. We go into a building, marching down a wide stairway into a basement. The room is large and remarkably warm and there are windows that let the sun in. There are real bunk beds set up in neat rows with fairly clean straw mattresses like we had in Auschwitz I.

"This is the new laundry detail," the guards announce to the block elder. She looks us over, shaking her head. Despite our new uniforms we must look terrible.

"I'm Maria," she tells us. "These are your new living quarters. The laundry is across the hall. You will be assigned positions tomorrow." She leaves us alone, shutting the door to her room behind her.

Slowly we move toward the bunks to claim our new beds. Danka and I take the bottom so that we don't have to climb up anything in case we're tired at the end of the day. On the straw mattress, a sigh of relief escapes from my chest. There is a blanket for each of us; they're old but they're not rags. Dina takes the bunk next to ours. We hug our blankets solemnly, not sure what to make of these luxuries. The beds hold two people rather than three or twelve, like human beings instead of herrings. It is warm. There is central heat in this building and only a few drafts. I have forgotten what warmth felt like.

"There's a toilet!" a girl announces excitedly. "And a sink!" I squeeze Danka's hand with a little pulse of hope. We are no longer in stables for horses, we are in a building for people. "There's even a shower!" We are in heaven.[15]

15. "December 16 [1943]. . . . Men are given Nos. 168154–169134 and the women Nos. 70513–72019" (Czech, 548). "Of 28,000 prisoners brought to the camp in 1942, barely 5,400 remained alive at the end of the year. In 1943, some 28,000 women prisoners died in Birkenau; the highest monthly death rate was recorded in December— about 9,000 women" (Strezelecka, 401). Rena was most likely moved in October 1943.

Sara Kornreich (Mama)

Danka, Mama, Zosia, Papa, and Rena

Zosia, Mama, Rena, and Gertrude

Tylicz, Rena's hometown in Poland

Rena (age 15) and Danka (age 13)   Zosia Kornreich

Danka, Dina, and Rena (with bear) in Krynica

Rena, Herschel, Mama, Zosia, Ester, and Danka
(last group photo taken of the Kornreich family)

Andrzej Garbera

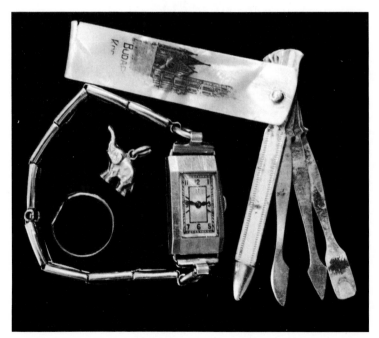

The silver elephant and nail file from Erna; the chrome watch Marek gave to Rena before the death march; and the ring given to Rena during her last "selection" in Birkenau (photograph by Karen Abato)

Rena, 1945

Danka, 1945

Eli and Danka Brandel, Rena and John Gelissen, with Rena and John's
first two children, Sylvia and Joseph, 1951

Rena and Danka in 1992, with Rena's granddaughter, Julia

Rena at Auschwitz, 1991

STABSGEBAÜDE

(Staff Quarters)

From the distance through the iron bars
freedom is laughing at us. . . .
But the sun's still not shining.

From a song sung by prisoners in the camps

We wonder what is going on here, but anything is better than Birkenau, so we keep our questions to ourselves. We are put in a basement with seventy-five Jewish girls who work as secretaries in the SS offices, the Politische.

Our new detail is in the SS laundry, to replace fifty Polish Gentile girls. They were sent back to the Polish camp in Birkenau because the SS learned that the Polish men working in the SS kitchen were sneaking food to the girls. I feel sorry for those girls but at the same time am grateful for this chance at life.

Our first morning in staff quarters we are assigned to our new positions. Our block elder is German and her triangle is red; she's a political prisoner. Political prisoners are more likely to be kind, as they've been imprisoned for being against the Third Reich. Our friend Mania is chosen as the block scribe, and works for Maria personally. Mania's sister, Lentzi, is placed in the sewing room. Janka, whom we knew in Auschwitz, is in the handwashing laundry. She's responsible for washing and ironing the delicate clothes of the women officers. She also takes the clothes to the quarters of the SS women, and she's Maria's favorite because she's so young.

The only people who have not been sent back to Birkenau are the Politische secretaries; they are the lucky ones. They were chosen on the transport platform when they first came to camp and most have never lived in Birkenau. Edita is the only Jewish kapo that I know of in camp and is the head of all the secretaries. Aranka, whom I know by sight from Bratislava, is one of the scribes. Rumor has it that when she was brought in from the transports to be shaved and disinfected the SS guards stopped to stare at her—that's how beautiful she is.

We still have roll call, but there is a roof over our heads now, and there are only a hundred and twenty-five girls to count, so it does not take hours. Our first morning in this heaven roll call is conducted in the hallway outside our sleeping area, across from the laundry. It is not four A.M. when they wake us, it is five A.M. We get a whole extra hour of sleep and roll call does not last for over two hours in rain and sleet, it takes less than half an hour. There is no marching a kilometer or two to and from work, either; we are only a few steps from the laundry.

"This is where you will work." Maria instructs us on how to run the laundry. "You will wear these shoes while working here and leave your other shoes on this shelf." The shoes we are shown are wooden and have straps across the arch just like the ones we wore when we first came to Auschwitz. "This is the hot water you will use to wash with." She shows us a large kettle on a coal-burning stove, which is already steaming. There are tubs with scrubbing boards in them and baskets of dirty clothes to wash.

Wardress Bruno enters the laundry to inspect us. We all immediately stiffen at the presence of the SS woman. She has a stern look and a formal, military manner. She points to a girl. "You will be responsible for the water in the kettle and keeping the coals hot."

So we begin our first day in the SS laundry. The stone floor is cold and the water sloshes against our calves and knees. We scrub long johns and undershirts against the washboards, rubbing them hard to remove the stains. It's hard work—nothing in Auschwitz-Birkenau is easy—but we are inside. There is so much water being dumped into the drains that they back up. We wade through the water as if we were fishermen instead of charwomen. Then we put the damp clothes in the baskets and someone carries them away.

"Halt! Roll call!" We leave the laundry, lining up in the hall, where we are counted and handed a portion of bread as we enter our sleeping quarters. The bread looks bigger than it was in Birkenau. We get a slice of sausage; it is small but welcome. Our legs hurt terribly after that first day but no one is complaining; there are no dogs, no SS men beating us unmercifully, no immediate deaths.

I rub my calves before lying down to sleep. I wonder if so much water is good for them and worry that they will become swollen or infected. I check my skin for abrasions and cuts; everything looks fine. Danka is already asleep. I roll over, pulling my blanket up under my chin, staring up at the bunk bed above me. My eyes droop under the weight of the past few days. Suddenly I want to pray but cannot remember any words.

I feel as if Mama were there, tucking me in . . .

"Did you say your prayers?"

"Yes, Mama." *The feather comforter, already warm from the hot brick Mama used to slip in at my feet, makes me forget the harsh winter wind rattling our shutters.*

"Sweet sleep." *She kisses my cheek. I snuggle down into down.*

When Wardress Bruno enters the laundry followed by a kapo, everyone stiffens and works more diligently than before. Her face is hard, her demeanor severe; she walks directly up to me as if she knows what she wants. "You speak German?"

"*Jawohl*, Frau Wardress." I straighten my shoulders, looking forward but not directly at her.

"You will be responsible for taking the laundry out to dry. Pick two girls to help you carry the baskets."

"*Jawohl*." I point at my sister and Erna's cousin. "Danka and Dina." I call their names.

"Ilsa, they are in your charge," Wardress Bruno orders. There is an audible sigh of relief from amid the washers and sounds of sloshing water when she departs.

Ilsa is about fifty years old but wears a black triangle. I have trouble imagining her as a prostitute and have to stifle a smirk that creeps across my lips as I look at her red-orange hair and bowlegs.

"Take these baskets. I will show you the way to the drying place," she says in German.

"Danka, you and Dina hold the outsides," I instruct. I am afraid that the baskets will be too heavy for my little sister, so I decide from the very first that I will always be in the middle and step in between the two baskets heavily laden with wet clothes. We look at each other, reaching the handles simultaneously and hoisting them up, following Ilsa out of the cellar.

We step outside onto a road and follow it toward two buildings. My shoulders begin to ache. We pass the SS kitchen. My arms feel as if they're being dragged out of their sockets. We turn left into an open field beside another building. I stare and stare at the expanse before us. As I inhale deeply the air bites my lungs. It is pure; there is no smell of burning flesh hiding in its odor. There are lines set up, with a little bag of clothespins.

"This is the *trockenplatz*, the drying place." Ilsa announces. We set the baskets down, put on our aprons, and obediently begin hanging the clothes up to dry. Then we wait.

There is a very handsome man who stands outside in front of a water pump which he operates. We each sneak a look at him while we work. There are SS going back and forth along the road regularly. I fidget among the clothes, smoothing them, making sure they are perfect and straight on the line. I am afraid there is something we aren't doing that we might get in trouble for. Danka and Dina follow me, copying my obsessive antics. Ilsa informs us when it's time to return to the block for lunch. We take the clothes that are dry back to the laundry and after our turnip soup return to the trockenplatz with fresh wet laundry. Finally Ilsa signals us that the day is over. We sort out which clothes are dry and which are not, carrying them back in separate baskets, but we bring in all of the clothes for the night. When we arrive in the laundry we leave the partially dry clothes in the baskets and place the rest on a table for folding.

We can see the Polish men working in the kitchen when we pass by each day, but because of Ilsa and what happened to the Polish Gentile girls, nobody dares to communicate with us. The man at the water pump, however, is so close to us that we manage to whisper to each other.

"What's your name?" He asks.

"Rena, my sister Danka, and our friend Dina. All three of us are from Tylicz."

"I used to ski there. It's beautiful. I'm Tadziu."

I can't help but wish that Ilsa would move farther away so we could have some conversation, but we are watched very closely these first few weeks. I guess we're on probation. The days lag as Ilsa watches us watch the clothes and we smile secretly at Tadziu. I think he is a shy man.

My fingers feel as if they are about to be peeled loose from the handles of the baskets, spilling the clean clothes across the dirt road; I struggle to keep them clenched closed. My shoulders ache. Ilsa is far behind us.

"Look at your kapo," Tadziu says to us as we put down our baskets. We look down the road and see her coming toward us on her extremely bowed legs. Her red hair gleams in the sun above her curving limbs as if she had a huge ball between her knees. She waddles towards us.

Tadziu teases, "Here comes innocence between parentheses!"

Like a bubbling gurgle of water, a sound wells up from inside of us, erupting quietly from our chests. We are completely surprised. I barely recognize what is happening or what we are hearing and doing . . . we laugh.

The quaking feeling in my chest has not been caused from fright or sorrow, but from mirth: prisoners are laughing—in Auschwitz—though not too loudly.

Ilsa is getting closer. We try to stifle these strange sounds, which causes our eyes to squirt tears down the sides of our faces. And the closer she comes, the funnier she looks. We hide our faces, but every time we catch each other's eyes we start giggling all over again. It is terribly difficult to act austere and serious when all we can think about are Ilsa's bowed, parentheses legs and how innocent she isn't; the rest of the day we silently shake whenever we look at our kapo. Danka's face lighting up gives me a momentary sense of relief. We have not laughed in I don't know how long. This laughter, which is so strange to us, is as valuable as bread; it eases our hearts of just a little pain and gives us something to smile about secretly.

Two weeks later Ilsa is no longer coming with us to the drying place; I guess that either she has completed her sentence and been pardoned or she's been moved to another place in camp. I become the one responsible for taking the clothes and there is no one watching us for the first time since the beginning. Now when we carry the baskets out to the trockenplatz I stop and have Danka and Dina change places so they can switch hands. I do not allow myself to exchange positions.

We take the clothes out to hang no matter what the weather. Wardress Bruno believes that fresh air is essential for clothes, so even on inclement days we stand in the rain or sleet and watch the clothes get as soaked as we do. Only if it looks as if it will rain all day do we stay inside and wash clothes to dry the following day; on days when it rains sporadically we hang the clothes up in hope that the sun will come out later. Hanging wet clothes in the cold nearly bites our hands off. We stick our fingers in our mouths to warm them, and then continue. Some days the clothespins with springs are too difficult for our fingers to press open and we have to use the ones with just slits in them. It is strange that after everything we went through to get inside work, here we should be, outside, with winter coming closer with each day.

I worry that the burlap dresses we wear are not nearly warm enough for the temperatures we will have to bear. And we have no gloves to warm our hands, either. I think briefly back to last winter in Birkenau, while staring into space. I cannot believe we survived it.

On the way back from the trockenplatz one night, the window to the SS kitchen opens and a friendly face asks, "Where are you from?"

We slow our steps down. "Tylicz, Poland," I answer in a low voice.

"All three of you?" He sounds glad that we're Polish.

"Yes, Polish Jews." I want to turn and face the person I'm speaking with, but that is an impossibility. I shift my eyes sideways without moving my chin.

"I'm an actor, from Warsaw. My name is Stasiu. Stop tomorrow in this same spot and I'll throw you a piece of sausage." I catch a glimpse of his face just before he moves from the kitchen window. He's old, at least for Auschwitz—he must be in his forties. We pick up our pace as if nothing has happened.

The next day we stop outside the SS kitchen just as the window cracks open. Danka and Dina switch places as I busily rearrange the clothes, making a hole in the center. A package lands neatly in the basket and I cover it up. Our hearts pound as we pick up the laundry and continue our trek. Inside staff quarters, while Dina and Danka unload the laundry I disappear with the package, hiding it under our mattress, hoping and praying that nobody will catch me. We wait until dark; then, when everyone else is asleep, we divide the piece of sausage Stasiu sent us three ways and devour it.

❖   ❖   ❖

There's a men's kommando working in a field close to the macaroni factory and I notice that one of them seems very interested in me. He's quite handsome. We steal glances. Danka and Dina have gone back to the laundry to take back some clothes that are already dry and fetch another basket while I guard the SS underwear.

"Where're you from?" the man asks when his kapo is out of sight.

"Tylicz." I hang up a pair of SS long johns.

"Warsaw." He works. I work. "How old?"

I have to think for a moment. Have I really had two birthdays in camp? They have passed unnoticed. "Twenty-three," I answer. We do not dare to exchange more words.

The next day I nod to Danka and Dina so they can see him. Danka stares at him, smiling faintly. We hang the clothes, trying not to look too anxious for him to start the conversation—if you can call snippets of words passed across a field a conversation.

"My name is Marek." I hear his voice from between the legs of long underwear.

"Rena," I answer, busily smoothing the wrinkles from the undershirts already hanging.

Danka steps to one side of the clothesline. "Danka. Rena's sister."

"Dina." Dina and Danka hang something up together. There is a slight breeze catching the clothes and teasing them about in the air. Contact has been made, names have been shared. It is moments like these that help us feel alive. There is another living being who knows we are here; it is a relief to speak to anyone outside our own narrow prison. I am slapped gently by the flapping clothes.

We're hanging the clothes up to dry when I notice a window at the top of the macaroni factory open for the first time ever and out comes a bag of macaroni. There is no one to see, no one to thank; it is a silent gesture. Quickly we cover it with the clothes already in the basket and smuggle it back into our quarters. Our hearts are pounding as we enter the block.

"Janka," I whisper to our young friend, "we have some extra food. Can you organize a potful of water and slip it into the coals after roll call?"

Janka's eyes narrow craftily. She nods. There are coals left each night in the stove in the laundry room on which we can cook, if we can find anything to cook and if we are careful not to get caught. We stand at attention for roll call patiently, trying not to fidget, trying to stop our watering mouths and the rumbling in our stomachs. We march into our sleeping area, taking our portion of bread and breaking it in half. We lie down after our meal, feigning sleep. The sounds of deepening breaths and snoring filter through the dark.

I tap Danka. We roll quietly off our bunk and tiptoe to the door. We are the first to arrive at the stove in the laundry room. I empty the contents of the bag into the simmering water. We sit and wait. The door to the laundry room opens slightly. Silently, Dina enters. Janka slips through the portal as stealthily as a cat, then Deborah, Mania and Lentzi, Aranka and a few others. Our excitement is impenetrable. "I got a bit of salt," one girl offers, pouring it into the steaming pot. We are smiling despite the danger we're in. We sit around the potbellied stove watching the kettle boil. It takes forever. The floor is cold beneath our buttocks, but we sit anyway, waiting.

I use my spoon to taste one of the noodles. "Done," I whisper to my coconspirators in the dark. Dividing the noodles evenly into their waiting bowls, I figure, accurately, that there are five tablespoons for each girl, then pour the hot water on top, making sure everyone gets some. Danka and I are served last. The rest wait until we are all served; then in silent unison we begin to eat the warm, nourishing macaroni. We take our time. No one is urging us to hurry, so we linger over each spoonful slowly, as if we were at a dinner party in some wealthy family's house. The water the noodles were cooked in is delicious. It tastes like home.

Aranka nods to Danka and me before slipping back across the hall to her bed. Slowly, soundlessly, the laundry room is emptied of its secret habitants. Janka stows the kettle so no one will find it in the morning, and together we tiptoe back to our beds, our bellies no longer rumbling but still hungry.

Dina and Danka have returned to the laundry to get more clothes. I stand watch, eyeing the garments and Marek's work team with the same glance. He tosses a rock with a note wrapped around it in my direction. The note is full of niceties: *You're a pretty girl. Too bad we're not in the free world, but maybe someday we're going to be free . . .*

"How many boyfriends did you have?" His voice slips across the field.

"Many," I tell him, trying to remember how to flirt, and then feel bad that I have lied to him. It is not a bad lie. I had three boyfriends; that is almost many. "I was supposed to get married two weeks before I came here." I clip up two pairs of underwear and a pair of socks. When I glance back towards Marek, his back is to me; his kapo is nearby.

Marek is not in the field every day, and I miss him when he isn't sneaking words with me or risking his life to send me a note.

It is starting to get bitterly cold outside as winter arrives. "Do you think I should go ask Wardress Bruno for better clothes to work in?" I ask Dina and Danka as we hang the clothes up in a snow flurry.

"I'm afraid of her," Danka answers. She stomps her feet for warmth.

"I'm afraid of her, too, but we've been here for a while and it's starting to snow. We have to take a chance. It's too cold for us to work without gloves and jackets." I rub my hands together to get them supple again so I can open the clothespins.

"You'll have to go on your own, she makes my knees turn to pudding." So it is decided. I am going to approach the wardress with our request as soon as I get up the nerve. It takes a few days.

"Wardress Bruno?" My words chatter with nervousness. Her black hair and chiseled features frighten me, her blue eyes are serious and look as if they could be mean, but I have to go on. "I would like to report that it is getting quite cold on the trockenplatz. And could I request warm clothes for me and the two girls helping me?"

"Yes, I'll arrange that," she answers. "I'll take you after roll call." She dismisses me. My jaw gapes open like a monkey's. I cannot believe our good fortune. She is not mean at all.

The next morning after roll call, true to her word, Wardress Bruno takes us to another building. She leads us upstairs to an attic, where we pick out skirts, thick stockings with elastic on the top to hold them up, jackets, boots, and gloves. I pick a black-and-white checked jacket, a man's shirt, and a woolen skirt, trying very hard not to think about where these clothes have come from. I try to remind myself that it is better for us to have them than for them to be sent to warm German bodies. In this way we are set to go outside, looking very much like human beings except for the white crosses painted across the backs of our coats and our numbers sewn on the left sleeves.

Marek's detail works diligently all day long. We haven't had a chance to speak, but finally he edges his way towards me, tossing a stone. We are stealing words between us, looking as if we're working in case the SS are watching from the macaroni factory window or come riding their bicycles along the road.

Do you have any boyfriends now? the note says. I shake my head to answer no.

The next morning our conversation continues. "Have you had any intimate relationships with your boyfriends?"

"No." He is going to embarrass me for sure if he keeps asking these questions.

"You're a virgin?" He almost stops working. He is looking at me as if I'm not real.

"Yes!" I whisper proudly. He chokes on his laughter; he tries hard to keep working but is in a fit of chuckles.

"I come from Warsaw, where I've never met a virgin yet." He has to walk away to cover himself.

"I think you're exaggerating!" I hide in the laundry, my face hot as an iron. Men! I decide to ignore him the rest of the afternoon.

I avoid his eyes by hanging the clothes quickly so I am blocked from his view and ducking behind the hoards of long johns bleaching in the winter sun.

He moves closer, digging busily. "You're blushing!" I hear his voice peek-a-booing over the clotheslines. Shaking my head and moving farther away, I hang an undershirt between his face and mine.

"We're in Auschwitz and you are embarrassed?" There is laughter in his voice.

I smile to myself, not allowing him to see that I'm also amused by this thought. With everything we have been through, with everything we have seen, I am still self-conscious.

"I'm glad I've given you something to laugh about."

"No one will believe it," he says. "Wait until I get back to the block—a virgin at twenty-three!"

The next afternoon he throws a third note. I stick it in the hem of my skirt and wait anxiously to read it until after roll call. Sitting on our bunk, I read, *When I was fifteen I lost my virginity. There was a married woman at a public swimming pool who asked me up to her apartment and she introduced me to it.*

"He's making it up!" Danka giggles.

"What am I going to do tomorrow if he's there?" We smother our chuckles under the blankets, trying to fall asleep. I cannot wait to see him again but I'm too shy to face him.

It is easier to bear the weather with our new clothes. The gloves make a huge difference in our ability to hang the clothes up, but sometimes the rain still soaks us through to the skin. It seems so ridiculous to do nothing but stand in a downpour and guard clothes, but there is nothing else we can do. I eye the awning on the back porch off the SS kitchen with envy; if we could just stand there we would be a little dryer after a day of rain or snow.

"Should I ask Wardress Bruno if we can stand there when the weather is bad?" I ask.

"Wait a week, Rena," Dina suggests.

"That's a good idea. We just got the clothes, we don't want her to think we're taking advantage." The decision is made, but I am terrified to ask for anything else.

"Wardress Bruno? I would like to make a report." I stand before the SS woman whose looks are so harsh.

"Yah?" She looks at me with semi-interest, as if I were more than just a number. After being a number for so long it is unnerving, and I must remind myself that one cannot trust the SS. She could change her mind about me in an instant. She has the power of life or death.

I begin my report. "We hang the clothes out for fresh air everyday rain or shine or snow."

"Yah?"

"There is an awning behind the SS kitchen. I can see the whole trockenplatz from there. If it would be acceptable to you, could we please have permission to stand on the porch when the weather is bad?"

"Yah, you can do that." She dismisses me. I breathe a sigh of relief. I tell Danka and Dina the good news—we have cover. It is just in time. Winter has arrived.

How strange it is that after all my hoping to get a job inside I should be standing outside, but I am simply grateful to be away from Birkenau with my sister, still alive.

The first rainy day after my request we stand under the awning all day. Sometimes I lean my elbows on the railing and scan the fields before me, where there are no fences. A train passes in the distance. I am careful not to make contact with anyone in the kitchen. This is my first day using the porch for shelter and I do not want to lose the privilege, so I keep to myself and my private thoughts.

The next day as we bring the laundry back from the drying place a stone lands at our feet. "Change positions," I whisper. Danka and Dina stop. We put the baskets on the ground and I retrieve the note adroitly.

We wait impatiently through roll call before I can read the note. Danka peers over my shoulder as I unfold the paper, but there are no words; it is a pencil drawing. We are slightly giddy about it and I am flattered that someone should take the time to sketch me: I am leaning forward and my skirt is hitched up a little too high around the curve of my legs.

"Does my skirt ride up that high?" I ask Danka.

"No, Rena, it doesn't." We giggle.

"He makes my legs prettier than they are, too!" I wish I could hang the drawing up or hide it somewhere safe, but there is no place that is safe enough. Besides, it is signed: *Stasiu Artista*. He has also scribbled in the corner, *When you walk by the window to-morrow, lean back a little bit and slow down. I'm going to throw something to you.*

The next day we stop in front of the kitchen and Dina and Danka exchange places while I look busy arranging the clothes. Smooth as clockwork the package lands in the underwear. I cover it up without a second lost and we pick the baskets up without looking back.

After roll call we discover that the package Stasiu has sent is a bag of sugar. "Let's share it," Danka suggests. Dina and I nod in agreement; this is too precious to hoard selfishly. We whisper to twenty of our closest girlfriends to come to our bunk after everyone is asleep.

"We have a surprise for you," we tell them. "Bring your spoon."

Sitting with the bag of sugar in my lap, I take the spoon from the first girl in line, carefully leveling it off, making sure that everyone gets an equal amount. When it's all gone we rest on our bunks in the dark, licking the metal of our spoons over and over, trying to squeeze out every last bit of savory sweetness.

It is sleeting. I have come to enjoy inclement days now because they give me a chance to whisper with my new friend, Stasiu Artista. Sometimes I long for a conversation that is face to face. One that is real and long and not dangerous. It's silly to long for something that is impossible, but I miss the days when I could flirt and walk down the road with a beau and just talk about whatever comes into our minds. That shouldn't be a crime, but it is.

"How did you like the picture?" Stasiu asks through the window.

"It was very nice, but you made the skirt too short. You were dreaming."

I hear a sound like soft laughter. "You are beautiful."

"My friend, I am alive, and here that is beautiful. Thank you for the compliment, though."

"How long have you been here?" he asks.

"March 1942."

"That's too long . . ." His voice suddenly sounds very sad.

"How about you?" I hear him moving away from the window and fall silent.

It seems silly sometimes, especially when it's sleeting, to act as a sentry for clothes, but I have my orders. The afternoon wears on slowly. The gentle tapping against the tin roof above my head sounds like a lullaby. The crispness of the air seems to capture the smells from the SS kitchen, dangling them before my nose. Whether it is the smell of meat roasting or the sound of sleet I do not know, but suddenly I am transported back through time. How wonderful our house used to smell the night before Sabbath—the goose, the kugel, the potato cakes. I long for real homecooked food and actual meals that take place at a table with white linens and silverware, meals that last for hours because there is so much food. I long to sit across the table from friends and family enjoying genuine conversation and togetherness. I long to see Mama with her white silk scarf draped over her head, lighting the candelabra on the dining room table for Sabbath.

She says the Sabbath blessing out loud, her arms stretching out from her body over the flames and back toward her heart—twice. Then, covering her eyes with both of her hands, she prays silently. Danka and I watch her with awe and anticipation. It is a solemn moment, with nothing but the golden flickering light upon mama's hidden face to indicate that time is passing. Her hands lower slowly, tears shine on her cheeks. There are always tears sparkling in her eyes after the Sabbath prayer. "Git Shabbes," she wishes us, radiantly. "Good Sabbath, Mama." Danka and I run into her arms. Papa returns from temple and we sit down for a feast; we feel so blessed, so loved.

My mouth waters for the tender meat of roast goose. I sigh.

The note falls close to my feet. I reach down and pretend to adjust my stocking while reaching for the message. I wish I could just read it immediately without having to wade through the rest of the afternoon until we get back to Stabsgebaüde. My palm itches, but I tuck the note well into my jacket, ignoring the nagging desire I have to read it. Glancing quickly at the window, I see Stasiu scuffling away. Once again I am alone with the skittering sound of sleet.

That night we read Stasiu's note as if it were the day's newspaper; that is how important these communications are to us.

I have been here since 1939. The chef is number 45. He has been here the longest of anyone I know who is still alive. We stare at his words seeing the naked truth. It is impossible to believe that years could go by and we might still be here, but Stasiu is proof. We are proof. I crumble his note while walking slowly to the toilet. It swirls downward, dragging with it all prospects for a life of freedom.

❖   ❖   ❖

After roll call, ten packages are given to us from the Red Cross. There are no names on them as there were in Birkenau, but Maria tells us, "Divide these up between you the best you can." We stare and stare at the packages, eager to tear open the brown wrapping paper to see the goodies inside.

"I think we should take a vote to decide who is going to divvy up the food." Mania suggests.

"I think Rena should do it," Janka volunteers. "She's very particular and honest."

"All for Rena, raise your hands." I cannot believe my eyes; every hand in the room is up. All one hundred and twenty-five girls vote for me. We open the packages as if this were a holiday, even though it's not a feast for so many. I put everything into separate piles: twenty cans of sardines, ten sweet cakes, ten loaves of wheat bread, and bags of sugar cubes.

"Somebody get a knife from Maria and someone else got a measuring tape from the sewing room so I can be exact." My hands shake. This is the biggest honor I have ever been given, more important than being chosen, the first Jew and the first girl, to recite a poem before our entire village on Poland's biggest national holiday when I was eleven years old.

We lay the measuring tape across the cakes; each one is about six and a quarter inches long. I divide the length of the cakes by one hundred and twenty-five and figure that each piece should be half an inch thick. With two girls holding the measuring tape taut, I mark off thirteen sections of cake and then carefully slice each piece at the premeasured mark. Our mouths water. We measure the wheat bread in the same way.

My hands tremble as I slice each section of cake. These are hungry people; everyone must receive exactly the same portions. I cannot show favor to anyone, not even my sister—not that I would even think of cheating another hungry person out of such precious food.

There are twenty tins of sardines and between six and eight per tin, and I figure that there are enough sardines for each girl to have one tablespoon. "It will be easier to divide the sardines up using our spoons so we do not lose the oil," I tell the girls. They stand in line, holding out their spoons as I meticulously scoop out the fish so that each spoonful is level. The sugar cubes are counted out as well. When it is all done, everyone takes her piece of bread, spoonful of sardine, and her nibble of cake and goes to her bed to eat in grateful silence.

If you knew there was a million dollars somewhere and you could take it, would you? These pieces of bread and cake are worth a lot more than that amount of money. I have never stolen from anyone in camp. Every scrap of food is a matter of life or death and I can never bring myself to cheat another human being. I remember how it was in Birkenau—when I found even the tiniest morsel of food, even if it was a potato peel on the ground, I divided it with my baby sister. Even though it was burning my hand because I was so hungry, I always brought it to her to share.

I consider myself an intelligent person, but I am so obsessive and prudent about food, it is ridiculous. This is what starvation can do to one.

The girls in the SS offices are constantly complaining about the Jewish kapo, Edita. She's always reporting them for the littlest thing and then punishing them too severely. She is a tyrant and treats them more severely than some of the German kapos. None of us understands why she is so mean, but the secretaries come up with a way to get back at her.

"We have a secret mission," Aranka tells me. "Do you want to join it?"

I look into the faces of seven of the scribes. "For what?" I ask.

"We can't tell you. Have you got guts and are you strong?"

"Yes, I've got both. Is this something that will endanger my sister's life?"

"No," they assure me. "We're going to pin Edita down in her sleep and beat her." I nod. It sounds like a worthy cause. "You want to beat her or hold her mouth?"

"I'd better hold her mouth. I don't have the chutzpah to beat a person," I tell them.

"Tonight, then." We shake hands.

While the rest of the block sleeps, we sneak into Edita's room, gathering around her bed silently. Then, on the leader's signal, two girls grab her arms and two grab her legs as I pull my hands over her mouth and another girl covers her eyes. The two who are going to beat her begin to strike her over and over on the stomach, where no one will see the bruises. It's hard to keep the pressure on her mouth as she struggles to get free, but I press my hands into her face to prevent any groans or noises. When they are done pummeling her they nod to us and we release our hold, dashing back to our bunks. Our covers are already folded back so we can jump into them, pull them up to our chins, shut our eyes, and look just like everyone else who is sleeping.

I force my breathing to be as slow and even as Danka's, but I am sure it is audible. What if she checks the room? What if she turns on the light and demands that the guilty parties step forward? I try to shut my brain off. What if we get caught? But Edita does not check our bunks. The next morning she walks stiffly out of her room without looking at anyone. Nothing is reported to the SS, and no one investigates because she doesn't tell anyone. She has learned her lesson. She stops berating the scribes and starts to act with a little shred of humanity toward her coprisoners.

Danka is on the outside basket and leans back as Stasiu throws us a piece of sausage and some bread. Out of the corner of my eye I see an SS man riding by on his bicycle. I swear that he's seen us, but we do not pause, look guilty, or do anything that will arouse more suspicion. We bury the food deep in the clothes and walk back to the laundry as quickly as possible. The whole way back we think that the SS man's going to come and catch us and then we'll be done for. We are jumpy and irritable, our nerves frayed with fear. First there is the joy of having extra food, then there is the possibility of that food sending us back to Birkenau or worse. We would gladly give up the meal to avoid that end.

We hide the food as soon as we enter the block stairwell and, sure enough, the baskets are checked thoroughly, but no one accuses us of anything. After roll call I sneak back to the hiding place and share the sausage and bread with a few other girls. It doesn't taste as good as it did before; our fear has flavored it differently.

The next morning one of the Poles who delivers our tea whispers to me, "Stasiu Artista just got twenty-five lashes for stealing a sausage for one of you girls." I try not to show alarm. I'm glad he gave me the information because I can prevent the story from spreading and getting us in trouble. I also know that Stasiu has not given up our names to the SS officer who caught him. We are safe.

Three days later, as we march in from work, Stasiu signals me from the window.

"Change places," I whisper. We stop. Danka moves as the sausage lands in our basket, and Dina takes her place.

"You're going to get into worse trouble than before," I scold him. "You better not do that again!" But he doesn't care. Every few weeks out comes a little bit of sausage, out comes an extra piece of bread—manna from heaven.

❖   ❖   ❖

It is spring. We do not allow ourselves to feel spring, but we cannot ignore the fact that it is here again. This is our third spring in captivity; except for the smell of the air, it has all but lost its meaning. All spring really means is that we have survived another winter. Marek and his detail are back working along the fence, and trains race by across the field. I enjoy the noise as they pass; it reminds me of freedom and far-off cities.

Danka and Dina and I hang the clothes up silently as a train passes us in the distance. I turn from my work to watch its journey, and for one moment my mind is transported beyond the walls and work fields of Auschwitz-Birkenau. There a woman bedecked in a white hat and white gloves, her chin leaning on her pristine wrist, is looking out the window, looking at me, looking through me as if I were not there. She is clean and refined. She looks as if she might be going to visit somebody and that the greatest burden on her mind is what to serve for dinner tonight.

I am so controlled always, never do I let the emotions catch up with me, but there is no stopping the tears pouring from the corners of my eyes. Where is she going? I ask myself. Why does she have a life and I have nothing?

"There is a world out there," I gasp, giving way to the deluge in-side of me.

There is a song we sing in camp. It never leaves my mind for one moment, always I am singing it inside my head:

There used to be tangos, fox-trots, and fanfares
sung by dancing pairs.
There were tangos of dreams and lovers,
but now we're at war. Nobody writes songs.
It's a waste of our young years.
So sing this new song, our heads held high.
Sing, sister, behind the German iron bars
this tango of tears, suffering, and desperation—
what the war means to us today.
Our hearts are crying hot tears.
Are we ever going to see the sun?
Are we going to see the beautiful world again?
From the distance through the iron bars freedom is laughing at us
and about freedom we are constantly dreaming.
But the sun's still not shining.

It is so impossible, but there it is, just a few kilometers away. Even in Stabsgebaüde, even if I can't see it, the smoke is still belching from the crematoriums. We aren't out of it, and the Ger-mans are so efficient, and they're winning the war. We are surviv-ing because we have a hope for living, but admitting to this hope is insane! In my heart I want to believe I will be free again someday because I don't have the strength to stand up and live without that hope. But death is too imminent; the crematoriums are too op-pressive. Hope is only there because we cannot survive without it.

"What's wrong?" Marek's voice invades my sorrow.

"That train, . . ." I answer, my voice wavering and unsure, "there were people on it, all dressed up, sitting there as if there is no war . . . as if we're not even here." I disappear behind the clothesline to wipe my tears on SS underwear so no one will know that they have gotten to me, again.[1]

The rock lands a few feet away. It is a simple note, just a few words: *Why don't we try to escape?*

And go where, Marek? I wonder. We are Jews, and nobody is for us anymore. Despite the spring my youth is gone. We work, we are temporarily safe, but I feel no passion for life anymore. I sit in the dark fighting the overwhelming urge to cry. One good long boo-hoo—even that is not allowed. I clench my hands and jaw until the desire to weep recedes, like the ocean tide. Someday, if we survive, I will cry for a week, maybe more. But not today, not here.

Marek's work detail is no longer by the macaroni factory. I notice his absence the way I do anyone's disappearance in camp: I fear that he is dead.

It is a warm day. Summer is nearing and the clothes dry quickly. We have checked the shirts to see which ones should be folded and put in the basket. I bend down to pull a few tender shoots of grass to nibble on, when a shadow falls over me. Squinting my eyes, I look up at the horse and its rider. Her blonde hair has lovely, graceful curls which tumble across her shoulders. Her boots are like mirrors reflecting the sun. I have seen her before, riding across the fields of camp. She is quite beautiful, and I feel small and insignificant in comparison.

1. Written in April 1944: "[Of] the Jewish girls deported from Slovakia in March and April 1942, [there were originally] over 7,000. . . . Now there are only 400 of these girls left and most of them have been able to secure some sort of clerical post in the women's camp. About 100 girls hold jobs at the staff building [Stafsgabaüde] in Auschwitz where they do all the clerical work connected with the two camps. Thanks to their knowledge of languages they are also used as interpreters. Others are employed in the main kitchen or laundry" (Wyman, 5, 32).

She allows her horse the reins. He shakes his head eagerly, lowering it toward the shoots of grass I was just gathering. Surveying the area for a moment, she allows him to graze. Then she pulls the reins up and clucks to her steed. They gallop off across the fields, her hair bouncing against her back. Pangs of memory shoot through me: I used to have long hair . . . I used to have curls . . . I used to sit on our plowhorse . . .

Danka and Dina return to the trockenplatz. "Wardress Grese was here," I tell them. We have seen her many times riding across the fields, and ever since she came to camp she has been whispered about because she is so beautiful.

"What did she want?" Danka asks nervously.

"I don't know. She certainly isn't going to speak to me."

"Was she on her horse?"

"Yah." We hang up the new load of laundry.

Marek returns to the work detail by the macaroni factory, and tosses me a note which is very long. I retrieve it, slipping it into my jacket. It must have been hard for him to organize a piece of paper so large. *I am an officer in the Polish army. I was trained to be a doctor in Belgium and then returned to Warsaw where I received the post of an officer. I have some contacts in the underground who are willing to build a double floor in the train that takes clothes out of Auschwitz and into Germany We can hide in this space which will be small but we can escape. You would have to leave your sister behind, we cannot risk more than one other person as one scream or cry could mean death for all of us. I would like to escape with you and make a life with you. I believe we can do this.*

I crumble the note, tearing it into little pieces, and go to the toilet to wash it away. Marek. So sweet, so eager, so naive. I swallow back the lump in my throat. I swallow the words of my friend.

I can't do this, I write back to him. *I cannot leave my sister in this place alone. Besides, I am not brave enough. Thank you for thinking of me, though.* I throw the stone across the field when no one is looking and turn away to hang the mounds of SS underwear that it is my duty to watch and clean and fold neatly.

I do not see Marek as often, but occasionally he sends word through the kitchen workers who bring our morning tea. I miss our correspondence and his voice drifting on the wind among the clothes. I miss his kind face across the field and his concern for my welfare. The trains still pass in the distance, but I refuse to look at them.

Mala is the messenger girl for the Birkenau camp. We have seen her many times walking from one office to another, exiting from the gates to take a message to one of the other camps. We all admire her, not only because she is beautiful but because her position is extremely important. Despite the fact that she's a Jew, they have given her almost free rein of the complexes and allowed her to keep her hair. She speaks seven or eight languages and takes messages from Wardress Drexler to the hospital, the SS offices— wherever they need her to go. We have always taken pride in her job; she is a symbol to us that we are of value, we are human. Still, even for her, with all her privileges, camp life was too much.

We hear about it from the men who bring us tea in the morning. In hushed whispers all day we gossip and fantasize about Mala, who has escaped from Auschwitz with her lover.[2]

Speculating, we imagine how they did it. "She must have had contacts in the outside world."

"Yah, sure. How else could they get out?" Late into the night after we have eaten our portion of bread we discuss the fates of Mala and her lover.

2. "June 24 [1944]. . . . Mala Zimetbaum (No. 19880) . . . escapes from Auschwitz II, together with Polish political prisoner Edward Galiński (No. 531) . . . who was brought to the camp with the first transport of Polish prisoners . . . on June 14, 1940. [Also on this date] six prisoners (male) . . . receive Nos. 189229–189234. [And] two female prisoners . . . receive Nos. 82064 and 82065" (Czech, 650).

"He was Polish. He had the contacts."

"I heard his name is Edward."

"I heard they stole German uniforms from the laundry, and someone built a false floor under one of the trains shipping clothing out, for them to hide in." I remember Marek's plan.

"You know a lot." For weeks we whisper and pray that these two brave souls are never caught. In our hearts they live happily ever after, they escape from Nazi Germany and make it to England, or Switzerland, or America, anyplace in the free world where there is safety for a Jew and a Gentile. We stoke the flames of our own courage as Mala becomes our beacon of light. If she can reach freedom, someday maybe we can, too. If she is brave, we can be brave. Oh, to flee this place and be with one's love. We dream of it. We cling to it. It makes the free world seem real again. It makes us remember what freedom was like. And then it makes us sad.

"The SS punished the camps for Mala's escape," the men carrying the teakettle in the morning whisper. "The prisoners in Birkenau were forced to stand roll call for twenty-four hours. Many dropped from the fatigue of standing."

I thank God we are not in Birkenau anymore.

We are just finishing hanging the laundry when Irma Grese appears again. This time she is on foot and wearing a beach jacket. She waltzes past us without the faintest sign of recognition, throws a blanket on the ground, and proceeds to remove the cover over her bathing suit. Nervously I check the garments swaying in the breeze. She lies down and begins to rub cream over her legs and arms. Danka's eyes widen in alarm. Dina steps back. I move away cautiously.

"You there!" I freeze at the sound of her voice. "Would you put some lotion on my back?"

I am shocked. I have never been *asked* to do anything by an SS; they always order their slaves. Not only that, but she has asked me, a Jew, to touch her! I move toward her, afraid that I might do something wrong, afraid to touch her gorgeous skin. Trembling, trying hard to still my hands, I gingerly smooth the cream over her shoulders and down her spine. Then I stand up, moving back toward the clotheslines, the safety zone, the place I know I belong. Busily we check the fabric for dampness, keeping our hands busy and our minds silent, pretending this SS women's presence does not unnerve us.

I remember:

Danka and I wake up early on Sunday morning. Mama has cheese Danish for us in a little sack. We put on skirts to hide our shorts underneath, because Papa forbids us to wear shorts. She kisses us at the door, hands us our picnic, and tells us to have fun. We hike into the mountains until we reach the stream. Then we take off our skirts. Folding them neatly and putting them some-place to stay dry while we play in the water and sunbathe. Around noon we open Mama's Danishes, still warm from the oven, or maybe the sun kept them warm, and eat them while languishing in the sun.

A wave of homesickness revolts in my stomach, making it flip-flop. How I miss lying in our forbidden shorts eating Mama's homemade sweets.

Throughout the afternoon Wardress Grese suns, then abruptly she dresses, folds up her blanket, and disappears down the road. We watch her depart, folding laundry quietly into our baskets, each of us lost in her private thoughts.

The morning tea comes, and with it the news. "Mala and her lover have been captured." Rumors escalate through the day; everyone is whispering about what has happened. That night, after the lights are out, we discuss her fate in the dark.

"They were caught eating in a restaurant."

"They had changed into civilian clothes, but an SS was eating there and recognized Mala."

"She's too beautiful for someone not to recognize."

"They shouldn't have stayed in Poland."

"They should have fled the country."

"And gone where?"

"She's going to be hanged."

"They will torture them first."

"Poor Mala." I shudder under my wool blanket. Our dreams are shattered.[3]

Grese comes often to the trockenplatz and always asks me to put lotion on her back while ignoring Danka and Dina. Sometimes she speaks to me, telling me about the war and asking me about myself. She is so congenial to me. Pleasantry from the SS is so strange. It is not rare—it's impossible. I do not know what to make of Grese's kindness, but I think perhaps she is lonely.

"How old are you?" she asks as I spread lotion across her shoulders slowly and carefully, making sure it is perfectly even.

"Twenty-three, Frau Wardress," I answer meekly.

"So am I." I do not miss a beat. I do not fumble, stunned as I am by her words. We come from such different worlds, we are in such different circumstances—but we are the same age.

"Where are you from?"

"Tylicz."

"Never heard of it."

"It's very small . . . in the Carpathian Mountains." She is quiet. I do not instigate conversation. I know my place. I am still a slave, no matter how friendly she seems.

"You know what's going to happen when the war is over and we've conquered the world?"

"No, I don't." My skin grows cold despite the blazing sun.

"All of you Jews will be sent to Madagascar." She doesn't use a mean tone of voice, she just says it matter-of-factly, as if she knows that without a doubt this is the way it will be. "You'll be slaves for the rest of your life. You will work in factories all day long and be sterilized so you can never have children."

3. Mala and Edward were captured on July 6, 1944. (Source: Czech, 710.)

My heart droops. Standing up slowly, I try to break away from hearing more without allowing her to see the bewilderment in my face. I have a feeling she does not approve of emotional weakness—no SS do—so I move toward the folds of underwear swaying in the summer breeze and hide.

There is a roaring in my ears, a train rushing through my head. Why don't I just die right now if I'm going to be a slave for the rest of my life? I stumble blindly away from her voice, fighting the dryness stinging my eyes. What's the point of going on if this is all there is? I hide my face between clean white undershirts and shorts. I want to tear them off their lines and scream at the encroaching clouds darkening the sky above us. I want to end it all, make the endless monotony cease . . . make everything stop. I want to sleep forever and never wake up. Then I hear myself saying, Come on, Rena, you don't even know if you're going to survive tomorrow—why worry beyond that?

The train barreling through my head stops. My thoughts quiet and slow. The sky has not changed, the sun still burns brightly and Wardress Grese still lies on her stomach as if she has said nothing to destroy my world. I could die tomorrow—I will worry about the rest when and if I make it that far. I hang up an undershirt, smoothing the wrinkles from the cotton, trying very hard not to think about Madagascar, watching her beautiful body tan.

It is harvest time. My birthday must be near, or maybe it has passed. I do not know. I only know that a farmer is crossing the field with his wagon full of cabbages, so it must be late August. He slows down his horse just a little as he passes us, then clucks and jerks the reins. The horse starts with a jolt and off roll five heads of cabbage. Danka grabs my arm with a squeeze.

"Dina," I say. "You and Danka keep watch while I nab a cabbage. Next you go, and then Danka." They nod in agreement, turning their backs to me, hanging up the clothes and keeping their eyes peeled for SS. I walk toward the bounty the kind farmer has left for us and quickly retrieve it, carrying it back obscured by my clothes and hiding it in one of the baskets. Within minutes we have obtained three huge cabbages, their leaves luscious and warm from the sun.

"What about the other two?" Dina asks.

"We have enough. We could get caught if we're too greedy. Besides, I'm sure some other hungry person will find them."

That night we dole out several leaves to our dearest friends while everyone else is asleep. They are sweet and crisp. The juice runs down our throats as we consume them. They are so fresh you can almost taste the earth they come from, and so full of vitamins that our bodies feel immediately revitalized, however momentarily, and that permanent hole that lives in our stomachs is partially filled.

The next day I notice that the other two cabbages are gone. A few days later we see the farmer and his wagon coming across the field again. His head down, he slows the horse and then clucks, just as he did before. Off roll a few more cabbages. I cannot prevent the smile that emerges as I say a prayer of blessing to this man before nodding to Danka and Dina. This simple farmer does the same thing for us one more time during the harvest season, and always we share the bounty with our friends.

As the fall moves in on us again the news becomes more and more positive, hope begins to seep into our pores and our dreams. Morning tea is our favorite time of day because the men from the kitchen who bring the kettle whisper news of the war to one or two of us. We sip our tea sharing the latest information: the Allies are pushing back the Germans; the Russians are closer; the Allies are going to bomb the train tracks.

We wait each day for more good news, more hope, which comes in on the radios smuggled into camp. This is food for the soul, and even those weak from hunger feast on this free meal of information, holding it close to their hearts as one would an extra ration of bread. This is good because the portions are shrinking once again and Stasiu is throwing less food, less often. The SS seem more tense and irritable, so we must be extremely careful not to annoy them. There are rumors that the laundry is going to be moved. We've heard planes overhead.

It must be September and the air is changing. The farmer with his cabbages no longer crosses the trockenplatz. Harvest is over. We hang the clothes out to dry in the cooling wind and whisper about the events outside our world, wondering where the laundry will be moved, wondering when and if the war will ever end.

At morning roll call we are told to line up and march out. There is anxiety at first; we eye each other nervously. Danka grabs my hand for a reassuring squeeze. We leave the basement guarded by SS. Please don't let it be Birkenau, is the prayer each girl repeats in her heart. Anything but Birkenau. We head down the road praying they will turn down another path. There is a fence and watchtowers in the distance, but it is not Birkenau. Our fears are quickly relieved. We assess our new compound; the fence is not electric, there are eleven blocks.

We march into Block Four. "This is where you will sleep." We enter our new living quarters hesitantly. The hair on my arms is raised, my skin is prickly: these are the new blocks, the blocks that Danka and I helped build when we were in Auschwitz and Birkenau. The concrete holding the bricks together was sifted and delivered by our own hands. We have forged our own prison.

Roll call in the new blocks is held outside and then we are marched out of the gates to a leather factory, where the laundry has been relocated. Mullenders is our wardress. She is Dutch but speaks German very well. "There are men working in the leather factory," she tells us. "You will not speak with them or have any dealings with them. If I catch any of you carrying on with them you will be punished—severely!" Her cold eyes glare at us so that we catch her meaning.

It is whispered that in Block Eleven they are conducting experiments. Next to us, in Block Five, there are German soldiers known as the Brownshirts hiding in case there is an enemy attack on camp. We can see them through the window of our block when we come back from work.

"They're waiting for the Russians," one of the girls tells me.

A bomb falls in a field, leaving a huge crater, but no one is even remotely injured. The transports keep coming, the gas chambers keep killing, the crematoriums keep burning. The first few days are depressing. We have lost our secret supply of food and miss contact with Stasiu Artista. The men from the kitchen who bring our morning tea do not risk sharing any news with us until the situation can be judged safe. We are lost without our daily routine. We hunger and thirst for news of the war.

The old, all too familiar routine begins again. We wake at four A.M. We rise to harsh reminders, *"Raus! Raus!"*

The tea arrives. I stand in line to get my cup, but when it is my turn the server whispers, "Marek is downstairs waiting for you." He pours my tea and I move on. My head is pounding so hard that my ears ring. Danka watches my flushed face as I hurry into the basement.

He leans against a table in the hallway, opening his arms for an embrace.

"Marek! What are you doing?" I can barely whisper out loud, I am so nervous.

"You wouldn't run away with me, so I have come to you." He pulls me close to him. "I've wanted to hold you for so long."

"I must be losing my senses to be here with you. We could both be shot."

"It'll be worth it if only for one kiss." He lowers his head and kisses me, but I am in no mood to kiss back. "That was lovely." He sits on the table, pulling me onto his lap, holding me tight. I cannot resist the warmth of human comfort, the longing to be held close and dear. I kiss him long and endearingly.

"That was really worth it!" He smiles. "And now you must get upstairs before anyone notices you're missing, and I must get back to serving tea before they notice my absence."

"Please be careful. I'll die if anything happens to you."

"Nothing will happen to me. I've been tortured and beaten by the Gestapo—what more is there?" I do not answer him. Taking his scarred hands, I stroke the places where his fingernails once were.

"When we are free, will you marry me?"

"Marek, how do we know what will be?" We kiss once more before I flee upstairs. Danka and Dina are waiting for me, and together the three of us run out of the block and into our positions for roll call. My face is glowing, my belly is wound up so tight I cannot even eat the portion of bread I saved from last night.

Four A.M.

"Raus! Raus!"

We are woken with orders to line up for roll call, then we are ordered to march. Confused but obedient, we head out of the gates in neat rows of five. Using side glances, we look at one another warily, sending warnings like silent Morse code with our blinking eyes.

Our hearts sink as we approach the electric fences of Birkenau. The band is playing as we march beneath the sign ARBEIT MACHT FREI. The entire women's camp is standing at attention facing a platform.

"Halt!" We stop, turning to face the gallows.

We wait. Camp waits.

Drexler steps up on the platform. "Today we will witness the execution of a prisoner who tried to escape. This is what you all have waiting for you should you even think about escape from Auschwitz!"

Mala is brought up on the platform. She is calm, undisturbed.

Drexler continues talking about how foolish Mala was to think she could escape the Third Reich. "We will rule the world," she reminds us. I remember Wardress Grese telling me about Madagascar. We will always be slaves, there is no hope. There is no reason to fight against them. They are everywhere. Drexler's voice drones on, instilling fear and trepidation into our veins.

Mala is standing there holding her hands gently in front of her, a faint smile on her face. She looks victorious. There is no regret in her eyes. Her dress is extremely dirty. I am sure they tortured her, trying to extract information and the names of the underground who helped them escape. She does not look as if she told them anything, though. She has pride. Her chin is up, her eyes are unwavering.

We have stepped over so many dead bodies that death is something we have become immune to, but this execution disturbs us. Why do we feel so terrible? Why is this so much worse than the suicides on the wire, the selections, the endless murders? But they were dead faces devoid of hope, and here is Mala shining despite the darkness in camp. Her face never falls in despair. Why did it happen? Why can't just one of us stay in the free world and survive?

She is so beautiful. The sun in the sky isn't shining for us, but Mala is. She is our sun. She has tasted freedom and seen heaven in the world outside. There is no hope for us, we may not survive—but Mala, her chin lifted high, has escaped from all this madness. She has been the secret ray of hope, and now they're going to try to snuff our only light out.

They move her toward the noose, but in one adept movement she pulls a razor blade from her sleeve and slits her wrists. Her blood spills across the platform.

Taube tries to stop the bleeding. *"Scheiss-Jude,* you will die by hanging, not by your own hand!" He swears and curses her. She slaps him in the face, digging her fingers into his eyes.

"I'll kill you with my bare hands!" he yells, beating her body unmercifully. "Bring the cart!" he bellows, wiping his hands in disgust. A wheelbarrow flies toward the gallows, and prisoners carry her body to it.

"Take her to the crematorium at once. She is to die in the fire!" Her crumpled body no longer cares where it goes. Her spirit is already hovering over this world. The cart races toward the death chambers; her arm, dangling just outside of the cart, gushes her life's blood upon the soil of Poland.

"Please let her die," we pray. "Please let her die before they put her in the ovens."

Four A.M.
"Raus! Raus!"
It is hard to wake up. The vision of Mala bleeding to death disturbed our sleep and rocked all dreams of freedom we had fostered from her escape. The kettle of tea waits like a cauldron of doom. Then the whisper cascades gently through our ranks, nourishing us with what little courage we have left.

"An SS took mercy on her and shot her before she was put in the oven." Our prayers were answered—by a German, of all things.[4]

It is a warm Sunday. We open the windows to let fresh air into the block. Standing at the windows, we stare at Block Five and the Brownshirts stare back at us.

Silently, we flirt. We are young and so are they; it is only natural. One of them holds a loaf of bread and points at it smiling and nodding. He runs downstairs and places a whole loaf of bread outside, then dashes back inside.

---

4. On September 15, 1944, the executions of Mala Zimetbaum and Edward Galiński are scheduled to take place simultaneously, in the separate men's and women's camps. "Mala succeeds in preventing the execution. While the sentence is being read she slits her wrists and hits SS man Ruitters, who attempts to stop her, in the face with her bleeding hands. The execution was interrupted. Mala Zimetbaum is taken in a cart to the prisoners' infirmary to stop the bleeding so that the execution can proceed" (Czech, 710). Accounts differ on who the actual SS man was that Mala slapped, and on whether she died on the way to the crematorium or was shot before reaching the crematorium.

I run down to retrieve it. He has paused at the doorway and we look at one another from our separate worlds. I smile briefly and mouth *Danke schön* before disappearing back into our block.

"Look, it's a whole loaf of bread!" We can't believe our good fortune. "How many are there of us?" We divide the loaf up into twelve chunks and inhale it hungrily.

BOOM! We jump. Air raid sirens wail across the camps.

"*Raus! Raus!*" our block elder yells. "Follow me! Quickly! Into the basement." We run downstairs. A door opens and we cram ourselves through it, bumping into one another. We try to turn around and move apart, only to step on each other's toes. Turning around to see if there is more room somewhere else, I see an SS officer shut the door. The latch clicks.

"Don't lock us in here!" somebody wails. "Don't forget us!"

The space is suffocating. We are all terrified. What if the building collapses and we're trapped inside? The whole structure is shaking and we are crammed against each other in this small crawlspace. Flashbacks grab my mind—our first night in Auschwitz, the transport from Slovakia.

"Are you afraid?" Danka's voice anchors me back in the present.

"No," I lie to her, controlling the panic that tries to steal my breath. I put my arms around her, pulling her close. My heart is pounding so loudly, though, that I switch sides, holding her against the right side of my chest so she cannot feel it.

I cradle her like a baby in my arms. Her eyes look up at me for assurance as she wraps her arms around my neck. The ground beneath us rumbles. My legs are liquid, struggling to keep us both from collapsing to the floor. Nobody moves. One girl faints, and then another. There is a huge crash outside.

Silence.

What if the building above us has been destroyed and we are buried alive? They will not save us. We are prisoners—refuse. No one will dig us out of this grave.

We lose all track of time and space, trapped as we are. No one speaks. No one can move. Another girl faints, her body hits the floor with a dull thump. My skin creeps eerily under my clothes.

Silence. Time stops.

There are footsteps outside. A key scrapes against the lock. Light sears into our widened pupils, causing them to retreat too quickly. We wince. Dazed and blinded, we struggle out of our cell. Each girl clutches a friend as our weakened knees buckle struggling up the stairs into daylight. There are ambulances and air raid sirens screaming across the complexes. We look out the windows, stunned.

Block Five is gone, flattened beyond recognition. Medical teams run this way and that, carrying stretchers. Frantically, the SS work to free their fellow soldiers from the rubble, but there is no one to save, all of the Brownshirts are dead. I stand at the window avoiding the tears smarting in my eyes. I am sorry that the soldier who brought us the bread is dead. I do not understand how I can feel this way about a German soldier, but I do. I conceal my sorrow. I do not love the Germans. I hate what they have done—are doing—to me, my sister, and my people, but I do not understand why somebody who was nice to us must die. I do not understand why anyone must die. None of it makes any sense at all.

Everyone is dizzy with the bombings; suddenly it seems as if the war might end someday and we are filled with anticipation masked only by our servitude. Jusek, one of the men working in the leather factory, steals a few words with Danka one day as we are passing by. It is innocent, nothing more than what might happen in the free world when people feel hope. We go into the laundry not thinking anything more about it.

Wardress Mullenders stalks in behind us. Her eyes shift slyly. "Your number is up!" She looks directly at Danka and then exits.

Danka's flushed cheeks go white. She leans against the wall, covering her face.

"Maybe she is just threatening to give your number up." I try to comfort my baby sister, but I'm scared. Mullenders has no softness toward us. She is cruel.

"What will happen?" Danka looks at me for direction. "Oh, God, what will happen to me?"

I do not answer. I do not know.

That night we enter the block with our bread and tea; we sit numbly on the bunk, trying to force the food down our tightening throats. There is a bit of commotion on the other side of the room, but we pay no attention. My mind is racing. What can I do to save Danka?

Dina sits down on the bunk and says matter-of-factly, "Danka will not be getting reported."

"I won't?"

"No. Everyone has pitched in with bits of jewelry, somebody even had a watch. We bought Mullenders off."

"What can I do?" I ask.

Dina shakes her head. "Nothing, Rena. It is done." The girls around us smile, their faces shining in the dark with pride and self-esteem. This is how close we are. These girl-women with whom we have worked and lived for almost a year have saved Danka's life.

"Rena, what's wrong with your voice?" Danka looks at me worriedly.

"I don't know."

"I think we need to do something about it."

"It'll go away, you'll see."

"You said that two months ago, and it's only gotten hoarser. Now it's getting cold again. I think this is something serious."

"There's nothing I can do about it, Danka." She's right though, it hasn't gone away. I almost sound like a man now; in another few weeks I may lose the ability to speak all together. Fortunately, there's little reason to speak out loud and no one inspects our throats or voices, but this loss of my voice is reason to be selected should an SS notice it.

"I heard what you were saying," a nurse says to us quietly. "We'll bring you something from the hospital. Saturday, after roll call."

"Thank you." Danka smiles.

It is Saturday night. We chew our bread slowly waiting for the nurses to come. "Thank you for being so concerned," I tell Danka.

"I can't let you get selected," she tells me. "We have an oath." I smile. We do have an oath, but it never occurred to me before that she's just as committed to my survival as I am to hers. "I have to go watch the door." She gets up off the bunk, slipping downstairs to wait. I watch her, amazed. This is my baby sister. When did she grow up?

We are deep into the night when four nurses arrive at my bedside. Silence is imperative; if any of us are caught we will all be shot.

The nurse in charge pulls a needle out of her pocket. "I am going to inject you with strychnine," she whispers. "Give me your arm."[5]

"It'll be okay, Rena." Danka strokes my brow. "You're brave. You can do this." I try to look confident for my sister but cannot muster any feeling but fear. It is her eyes that are full of confidence and courage, and I lean on her strength, fighting the urge to panic.

The needle glimmers. Her firm hand is cool on my skin as she prepares for the injection. The needle penetrates my flesh and immediately there is a burning fire raging through my body. My muscles spasm as I lurch to scream, but their hands hold me down, pressing firmly on my mouth. The pain is excruciating. I try to re-

5. "At one time strychnine was used as a tonic and a central nervous system stimulant, but because of its high toxicity (5 mg/kg is a lethal dose in the rat) and the availability of more effective substances, it no longer has a place in human medicine" (Bartlett, 534).

mind myself to be silent, but there are moans escaping from my body which I have no control over. It is as if pins dance in my veins and puncture my lungs. I pant and heave, but cannot vomit.

"Get cold compresses! Water!" I hear the nurse order her assistants. I can feel something wet on my skin.

Minutes . . . hours . . . I do not know how long I thrash and writhe in agony, incapable of controlling my limbs. The compresses seem to help. I scream when they change them. Danka's face is stained with tears.

In a fugue state I hover just above unconsciousness. The body sleeps fitfully, waking me with its sporadic twitching as the poison does its work. My mind is far away.

The morning light in the block hurts my eyes. "How do you feel?" Danka's voice wakes me.

"Terrible." I can barely mouth the words. She holds her finger up to her mouth, indicating for me to lie quietly.

"Something went wrong, I don't know what, but it was close. The nurse said you'll feel weak today, but tomorrow you'll feel better and in a few days your voice should start to return to normal." She hands me a cup full of water. I gulp it thirstily.

"Thank you." I try to speak again.

"Shhh." Danka smiles. "Rest now."

It takes a few weeks, but slowly my voice does return to normal.

❖   ❖   ❖

There is an explosion outside. We all stop working. It doesn't sound like a bomb, there are no planes going over, but it sounds like it's just a few kilometers away. Mullenders runs to the door. We follow her slowly, glancing at one another carefully. There is smoke billowing up from the direction of Birkenau. We do not smile but our hearts grin. We wait, listening for more explosions and praying, though we do not know what we are praying for.

The next morning the news arrives with our tea. One of the crematoriums was blown up by the Sonderkommando.[6] We have finally struck a blow against our captors. We hope, feebly, that it is the beginning of the end, but the SS catch everyone in the Sonderkommando and kill them. Four girls have been arrested from the gunpowder factory; they helped smuggle the powder out. Those of us who continue to live sit silent shiva for our brave copatriots.

Danka has excruciating pain due to a rotten tooth. On Sunday she and ten other girls finally get permission from the camp commandant to go to the camp dentist in Auschwitz. I stand by the fence watching my sister head out the gates of our camp without me to protect her, guarded by the SS who do not care whether she lives or dies. I am nervous being separated from my sister even though I know where she is going; too much can happen in a second and I am uneasy. I try to tell myself that I am being ridiculous and instead of pacing the block go to the window and look out. It is a bright sunny day, but that brings me no peace. My mind is whirling with alarm and fear. There is a plane. I blink hard, staring into the sky. I cannot see it but I can hear it. The air raid sirens begin to whine.

Maria yells upstairs. *"Raus!* Get to the basement."

"My sister is out there!"

"Rena! Come on!" Dina shouts at me. I run across the room toward the stairs. The windows behind us shatter; glass shards shower down on our heads.

"Danka!" I scream. All is chaos.

In the basement we shiver with fear. I wish that Danka were in my arms like the last time. If I was with her at least I could do

6. October 7, 1944, . . . there is a revolt by the Jewish *Sonderkommando,* with explosives smuggled in by women prisoners. The *Sonderkommando* labor squad was periodically exterminated, the members of this detail planned the revolt knowing they would be killed anyway, whether or not they destroyed the crematoriums. The plan to destroy all of the crematoriums was thwarted by the Germans but the men in the *Sonderkommando* did successfully wreck Crematorium IV before the uprising was crushed. (Source: Rittner and Roth, 31).

something . . . anything. I feel as if I'm going crazy with worry. I will never forgive myself if my sister dies without me. I squeeze my hands until I cannot make fists anymore. My God has abandoned me, left me cold; still I pray but in the same breath I doubt his power. "Please don't let my sister die," I plead. "I cannot live without her . . . ." I try to mask my futility and fear with bravado, but what will I tell Mama if something happens to Danka?

Finally the sirens stop and we are released from our dark and airless cell. I run up the stairs. Smoke is billowing into huge black thunderheads from the direction of Auschwitz. A girl returns through the gate. She is alone except for her guard.

"What happened?" I grab her collar. "Where's my sister?"

"I don't know. It was mayhem. Some people were killed."

"I have to get my sister!" My head pounds as the blood rushes into it; my vision goes black. Blindly, I run toward the gate to find my sister. I don't care about the guards in the towers. I do not care about anything but finding my sister.

"Grab her!" Dina yells. I feel firm hands gripping my arms, pinning me down. Out of my mind with grief, I try to shake them loose.

"I've got her!" Janka yells.

"Let me go!" I scream at them. They are the enemy. They are against me. I struggle to shake them off. I do not know how many girls hold on to prevent me from going through the gates and getting shot.

"Rena. Listen to me. You can't do anything. You have to wait here," Dina says.

Finally Janka's voice sinks through my outburst. "What if she is fine and you get shot trying to leave without permission? What would Danka do without you?"

"Be still. She'll be back," Dina reassures me. "You'll see. Everything will be fine."

"I can't live without my sister." I am vehement.

"You don't know. Wait before you get yourself killed. Get hold of yourself." I gasp for air trying to listen to their cool, calm logic.

"I'm okay," I finally manage to say. "You can let me go. I won't run off, I promise." They move away slowly. Dina and Janka stay close by me as I pace back and forth in front of our block, remembering Block Five, remembering how in Auschwitz people die for no reason.

There are some figures coming toward our complex. I stare and stare at their forms, trying to make out if one of them is Danka through the wire mesh. I think I see her but I could be making it up, I could be crazy and seeing things. I feel Dina's hand squeeze my shoulder.

"Is it her?" I am afraid that I have gone mad.

"That's her," Dina whispers.

"Thank you, God." But I am not sure if it is God's doing that she is alive. It could be simply luck, or a mistake. Chance is the only order in our universe.

They come through the gate and the SS guard leaves them. I hug and kiss my sister over and over, not allowing her time to explain.

"What's wrong?" she asks. "What did you think?"

"I thought you were among the dead! Promise me you'll never leave my side again." I lean exhausted against the block.

"I promise, Rena." She takes my hand, smiling into my worried eyes.

"Line up!" SS Mullenders orders us. It is the middle of the day. We freeze, then move quickly into line.

"March!" she orders. We march out of the leather factory. It is not time to stop working and we do not head toward the new blocks. "I want you to sing German marching songs." We open our mouths but no sound comes out.

"Sing or you will be punished!" She begins to sing, waving her whip at us threateningly. We join, our voices shaking in fear. She makes an unmistakable turn in the road. Birkenau looms before us. Our hearts are in our throats but still she forces us to sing.

We march under the hated sign. We do not know immediately what the purpose of our return to Birkenau is, but we fear it worse than death.

"Line up! Face front!" she orders. "Keep your eyes open and face the gallows."

We line up with sinking hearts. We are, all of us, shaking uncontrollably. The whole of the women's camp is lined up facing a platform with four nooses. I stare and stare at the girl-women trapped in the camp, a sea of conquered spirits. Then I close my mind so that I cannot see anything else.

Ella, Roza, Regina, and Ester walk bravely toward the platform. They have been tortured. I know their names from the men who bring us the tea. I know they were arrested for smuggling the gunpowder out of the factory they worked in so that the Sonderkommando could blow up the crematoriums. I know that they never gave one name or contact of the many people who were involved in the sabotage. I wonder if I would have had the courage to do what they did; I marvel at their strength. I weep inside, where no one can see.

"These traitors to the Third Reich are condemned to die by order of the Führer, for espionage. You will watch these filthy traitors hang until they die, so you will be reminded what happens to enemies of the Reich! All caught closing their eyes will be shot for failing to learn this lesson!" Commandant Hössler yells.[7]

The girls go up on the chairs. The SS put the nooses over their heads. "Long live Israel!" They begin in unison to recite a Hebrew

7. "January 6 [1945]. . . . In the evening four female Jewish prisoners, Ella Gartner, Róza Robota, Regina Safir, and Estera Wajsblum, are hanged in the women's camp of Auschwitz. . . . The reason for the sentence is read by First Protective Custody Commander Hössler in Auschwitz; he screams that all traitors will be destroyed in this manner" (Czech, 775).

prayer. Their voices are cut short as the chairs are pulled out from underneath them. There is no God to save them.

I have to watch, it's the least I can do; it is how I honor them. We stand and wait until the last body has stopped its death dance in the air. They take the bodies down, loading them into a cart and wheeling them to the crematorium.[8]

"One of them is still alive," it is whispered through the rows. "One of them is still breathing." In a civilized world if the condemned survives hanging they are pardoned, but not in Auschwitz-Birkenau. We pray that she will die before she is put in the ovens.

Mullenders makes us march back to our camp singing more German songs. "Louder!" she orders. "Chins up!" We sing in our dry and cracking voices, our spirits trying not to break.

In the morning we wake slowly, depressed by the loss of our comrades. The kettle of tea arrives. We are in mourning for the girls who have died and not eager for news of the war today. One of the kitchen men whispers, "She died on the way to the crematorium." We breathe a sigh of relief. She did not suffer.

I get my tea. A note is slipped into my hand smoothly without a second's falter. It is from Marek: *They're going to march us out of camp. The Russians are very close. You must decide if you want to feign illness and stay in camp or march. I will help you either way and meet you in America. When you get out, go to America and find Charles Boyer. Tell him I sent you, he is a friend of mine from Belgium. He's such a famous actor even little children in New York know his name . . .*

---

8. In November and December of 1944, demolition squads were created who were responsible for dismantling some of the crematoriums. "After the beginning of the demolition of the extermination facilities probably no more selections are conducted among the prisoners. The prisoners die a 'natural death' from starvation, heavy labor, and the inconceivable living, hygiene, and sanitary conditions." In the camp registry 322 women, who died by violent means, were listed as dying because of "special treatment." (Source: Czech; quote, 756.)

I fight back the tears. Children may know who Charles Boyer is, but I don't. America seems like such a far-off place.

We get more and more information that the Russians are coming and we are going to be freed. So we start talking about what we're going to do—should we stay or try to escape?

"They're going to leave all the sick in Birkenau and the rest will have to march to Germany," one of the girls in our block tells us.

"Well, then, we should pretend to be sick."

"I heard that they're planning to set fire on all four sides of the camp, lock the gates, and leave the electric wires on, so everyone will burn inside," one of the scribes tells us.

"So if we pretend to be sick we could burn to death?"

"That's what I heard."

"What should we do?" Danka asks me.

"I don't know. What are you going to do, Aranka? Act sick or march out?"

"I'm going to take a chance and march out. Maybe I can escape on the march."

"Maybe they're going to shoot you."

"It seems like our chances would better of escaping on the march then locked inside a burning camp, though."

"All I know is that I don't want to die here. Let me die anywhere but Auschwitz." The voice is passionate. We all look at Janka. Her seventeen-year-old eyes have seen much in all of her years in the ghetto and camp. She has said what we all feel deep down inside. We will die if we must, but not here, not in the flames.

We continue to work at the laundry every day, but Mullenders is jumpy and ill-tempered. Her regular morning speeches terrify us, but now we glare at her with hatred. We would not have dared to do so a few weeks before, but the songs she forced us to sing are still sticking to our tongues no matter how hard we scrub to rid our mouths of their taste. We know now that she will not have control over us forever and we hate her with a vengeance.

Our work days are not as long and we discuss things more openly than ever before, worrying about what to do. It's not that we speak in front of Mullenders, that would be foolish, but when she moves away from us we whisper. Guesswork and rumors, guesswork and rumors—that is all we know. Nobody knows for sure whether staying or going is safer.[9]

The morning tea arrives. I hold out my bowl, feeling a note slipped into my hand by the server.

"*Jękuje*, thank you for my tea." I say to him in Polish.

"You're welcome." He has kind eyes. What is it about these men in the kitchen that they will risk their lives to bring notes to us? Sometimes I am in such awe of their bravery. They do not know me, they are not blood relations, but they would die before they gave up my number.

I disappear quickly to read the note from Marek. It says, *How many girls do you want supplies for?* I show Danka the note. How many should we try and help?"

"We have to help Dina."

"Yah, for sure. But who else?"

"Janka . . . Mania and Lentzi." I nod. We cannot help everyone, but we can help a few, and these are our friends who have helped us.

Clothes and food for six, I write to Marek. *Thank you.* The men with the kettle are preparing to leave. I slip the note to the one with kind eyes and move away.

The day passes slowly. The weather is worsening. Clouds are everywhere, and it looks as if we'll be in for a snowstorm tomorrow. We hang up the boxer shorts and SS long johns on the lines inside. It suddenly seems so ridiculous, the days we spent watching the laundry in sleet and snow and rain. At least it's warm in the leather factory and the clothes dry quickly. The soup comes at

9. "The last roll call [in Auschwitz-Birkenau] had included 31,894 prisoners—16,577 of them women" (Rittner and Roth, 14). "No. 202499 [is] the last number assigned to a [male] prisoner in Auschwitz" (Czech, 785).

noon. I receive another note: *Watch for the tea tomorrow. Don't forget—America.* I walk to the toilet casually and flush. We fold the underwear that has dried into our baskets and leave what has not dried hanging for the next day—if there is a next day.

❖   ❖   ❖

Morning comes. There is no work today. I get my tea and my instructions: *There is a kettle in the basement. Get everything out of it and leave.* I nod to Mania, who is the biggest and strongest of us. Danka knows to follow in a few minutes with Dina; then Janka and Lentzi will sneak downstairs. We must hide the food and clothes quickly, without anyone noticing. There is a loaf of bread for each of us, four bags of sugar, six pairs of pants, shoes, socks, and sweaters. I divide them up. Mania helps me. We conceal the clothes under our mattresses, hiding them for later.

"You're more robust—being a secretary and working inside— can you carry two bags of sugar?" I ask Mania.

"Sure." She takes the bags under her arms. There is one little package wrapped in a rag that says *Rena* on it. I open it excitedly and find a chrome watch. Marek knows how particular I am. I smile to myself, fastening the band onto my wrist, remembering the last watch I wore. Pulling the sleeve down over my wrist, I return upstairs.

The SS have a lot on their minds, trying to destroy records, gathering things around camp. There are bonfires of paper that remind me of that dreaded night six years ago when the Nazis ignited our holy books outside the temple and shaved Papa's beard and earlocks. The flames are no longer newborn, they are aged and smile wickedly at those of us who have seen evil mature, unhindered. Like Mengele's mask of beauty, no one will believe what this evil has cultivated behind its walls. They destroy the evidence so that there will be no proof, no records, nothing but our memories, if we survive, and they will try to obliterate those, too. I look out the window of our block; the landscape is spotted with puffs of gray smoke and black cinders drifting up over the SS offices. For the first time since the beginning of our horror, the air smells like burning paper rather than burning flesh.

We wait through the day, putting our extra clothes on, changing our boots so that we are ready. This is almost as bad as being in quarantine. We have no clue as to what will happen to us, but at least it will be different. We're going to leave Auschwitz-Birkenau, despite our fear. There is a sense of anticipation for the unknown, but still the dread hangs over us. We do not know when, but we know that soon they will come in and say, March out! We are too tense to sleep. All day we wait. We try to rest. I clean my fingernails eight times.

"What time is it, Rena?" Danka asks from our bunk.

"Two o'clock."

"Where's the soup? They're late."

"They won't feed us today." A voice comes down from the bed above us.

"Why not?"

"They're saving the food for themselves." We're nothing but cover against the Russians, and expendable. They're not going to waste something as precious as food on us. We wait. We rest. It grows dark outside. No one brings our evening bread. Our block elder is agitated; she will have to march with the rest of us. Danka dozes. My eyes grow heavy, then jerk open; I'm afraid I'll miss something. The lights are still on in our block. There is stamping outside.

"Raus! Raus!"

We line up outside the block just as we always have. The SS count us and then give the orders. "March out!"

I look down at my watch. It is exactly one o'clock in the morning. It is January 18, 1945. We step outside the gates.

There are thousands of people before us. Bonfires speckle the landscape. Tramping through the well-packed snow, we march in neat rows of five, orderly to the end, leaving behind us the iron curse ARBEIT MACHT FREI: the words are branded on our souls. It is snowing. The blizzard has arrived. Is this for life or is it for death?

We are the only women on the road, but there are men's bodies scattered across our path. Tramping and tramping, our legs ache with fatigue yet move as if they were mechanical. Stepping over bodies already covered with snow, we march for an hour, maybe two, before we are herded into a barn. Are the Russians near? Is freedom here? We collapse in the straw for a brief respite. Sleep is dark, dreamless.

"*Raus! Raus!*" We get up stiffly. A few do not wake. They are prodded, then shot. The snowdrifts are knee-deep and the wind is picking up; still, we do not have to break the trail as the men before us did. The sun rises in an overcast sky. It is a gray day. Our flesh is gray. Tramp, tramp; we step over three and four bodies at one time. Gunshots come from in front of us and in back of us, in front of us and in back of us. We're so numb to it that the bullets feel as if they're in our own heads. The snow is endless. It does not stall or slow down, it falls in sheets. I have blisters on my feet which would hurt more if my feet weren't so cold. When we stop for rest periods there is no food. We ration what food we brought with us; it is disappearing fast. The bread will be gone tomorrow and the sugar is too low. We eat snow.

"Why don't I take one of the bags of sugar, Mania? So you don't have so much to carry."

"I only have one bag left."

"How can it all be gone?"

"We've eaten it." She dares me to question her. I don't believe her but am too weak to argue. If we starve because of her selfishness, it will be on her head.

We tramp through white and red snow. We lurch over bodies. We stop. In a barn, the six of us divide up the last of our bread and sugar. I'm so tired. It feels as if tomorrow will be the end for me. I wonder if I shouldn't just give up. It is almost as if I am hearing voices in my head while I lean against the thin barn wall. I stop my musing, listening for a familiar sound. Then I hear it—a family speaking Polish in the farmhouse connected to the barn. Their door is ajar. The voices tug at me, drawing me to them. I must go see these people who were my people before this war. The SS guards are outside.

I slip up to the kitchen, my knuckle raps at the door. "I am sorry to bother you," I say in Polish, "but I have a sister and we're both very hungry. We're from Tylicz. If you can spare one potato I'll give her half. If you give me two I'll take one."

I hear the husband say, "We don't have enough to spare!"

"She's from Tylicz!" the wife exclaims. The family discusses this briefly. Not wanting to endanger them, I wait outside, catching bits and pieces of their conversation. The door opens a crack. A ray of warm, golden light drifts across my face. The wife's eyes are moist with worry and fear. "Take these." She hands me two hard-boiled eggs and two cooked potatoes. I hold them in my hands, letting the warmth seep into my skin and the smell waft up to my nostrils.

"*Jękuje. Bóg zapłać.* May God reward you for this favor." I back away from the door. "I will never forget you." That night we eat.

I do not know how long we have been walking, or how far. I cannot remember how many times the sky has grown light and then dark, how many times my watch has done twenty-four revolutions, or how many barns we have collapsed in. We could have been walking for one day or ten. I do not know, I do not care. I am so sick I want to die. I have such terrible diarrhea that I run to the outhouse without asking. The SS must be tired of shooting people, because they haven't shot me yet for leaving the barn without permission. I try to sleep through the night, but we are freezing and my stomach is empty.

"*Raus! Raus!*" I get up and go to the outhouse. I am going to stay there. They have shot girls for trying to hide and escape, but I don't care anymore. I listen to the SS lining everyone up, leaning my head on my hands because I am too weak to hold my head up any longer.

I hear someone outside the door. I am going to be shot. It will be a relief. I wait.

"Rena." I hear Danka's voice outside the door.

I pull my pants up and tie them tight but fall back down on the seat, unable to stand up.

"Rena, what're you doing?" She opens the door.

"Go on without me," I tell her. "I'm staying here."

"No, you're not. You're coming with me."

"I can't walk, Danka . . . save yourself."

"Look at those bodies. Look at all those who are dead, but we're still alive. You're not going to die now. I'm not going to let you! Janka!" I can hear the tremor in her voice. She is so brave. "Come help me." I unlatch the door. I cannot look in my sister's face. I wait for their hands to hoist me up between them. We stumble into formation.

Mustering all the strength and courage in the world, with Danka and Janka supporting my elbows, I tramp through the snow again. We walk forever. The sun comes up cold against the barren landscape. Their hands are firm under my elbows. We walk as if there were nothing wrong with me. It is forever. Then, suddenly, my strength comes back.

"I can stand on my own two feet now." I manage to whisper.

"Are you sure?" I nod. Janka lets go first. I do not stumble. Slowly Danka releases her hold on me. I walk. It is a miracle. I am better.

For hours we tramp over bodies, through snow. Gunshots fell those of us who are too weak to continue and those of us still trying to escape. Do I wish that we had stayed in Auschwitz-Birkenau? Despite the cold, the hunger, no. I am glad that we will not die behind that sign, behind Hades' gates. We could be walking in circles the way the path is strewn with bodies; they all look the same, frozen, desperate. Free.

We arrive at a train depot.

"Get into the coal cars," they order. We can barely get in without help, but there is no help. Everyone is exhausted and too weak to climb into the empty cars. I help Danka in, who helps Dina, and so on; everyone has just enough strength to help one other person. We lean in the corner, finally able to rest. Then we start to shiver. The cold bares its fangs and digs into our flesh. I don't want to sit down because of the soot, but that concern does not last long. Overcome by fatigue, I collapse with the others onto the black, dirty floor.[10]

Air raid sirens begin to wail and planes come swooping overhead as the SS and German people run into the railway station, leaving us outside. We huddle in the cars hoping the bombs will not kill us—hoping this ordeal will end. We pass out despite the sounds of war overhead.

Quiet.

I stir and crawl up the side of the car to look out at the people just starting to return to the platform. A lady holding her infant stands nearby. "Please, can you hand me some clean snow from the ground?" I ask in German. "We are so thirsty and the snow is too dirty up here to eat."

Her eyes register fear as she looks at the SS with their guns. She looks at her baby, shaking her head. I understand. The snow

10. "Columns arrive by foot in Wodzislaw in Silesia. From there they are taken to Sachsenhausen and Flossenbürg [Germany] in open freight cars, which normally are used for transporting coal. Almost half of the prisoners die on the way of hunger, of exhaustion from the long march, and of freezing" (Czech, 789). "Auschwitz was liberated by the Red Army on January 27, 1945. Those troops found about 7,000 sick and exhausted prisoners—4,000 of them women" (Rittner and Roth, 14).

begins to fall again and after a little while I am able to scrape a tiny layer of fresh clean snow off the ridge of the car before it turns black. This we melt in our mouths, trying to quench our thirst.

Finally the train starts. Wind whips our faces with bitter, sub-zero breath. I do not know what time it is. Every time I look at my watch I forget what the hands say and I don't want to raise my cuff and give any reason for the cold air to touch my skin directly. For how long the train races through the night I do not know. We get in and stay there until we are told to get out; it is dark and light somewhere in between.

"*Raus! Raus!*" We are ordered off the train. Our legs are cramped from sitting still and our joints don't bend easily as we leap into the snowdrifts below us. Four feet down.

We march again for a very long time through the dark. It is below zero. The snow is at our knees. No one has come before us to break the trail. There are no footprints to indicate that others have traveled this path; the bodies that strew the landscape are still warm. They are all girl-women. Where are they taking us?

Gunshots rip through the air like swatting flies on a hot summer day; still we march. I look at my watch but the numbers have no meaning. There are lights ahead. We march toward the lights, through the snow toward the gate of another camp, Ravensbrück. The words cackle across the dawn—ARBEIT MACHT FREI. My heart collapses. We are not free.[11]

There is nothing here, no blankets, no bunks; there are lots of girl-women and all the beds are occupied. We are so tired we curl up on cold dirt floors. I am so hungry that I sneak outside to find us food. There was a pile of potatoes we passed on our way through camp. Edging along the blocks, I scour the complex for the shadow I think will fill our bellies. There are no potatoes, only piles of bodies in the dark.

11. "January 24 [1945]. . . . a transport with female prisoners from Auschwitz, including 166 Poles, arrives in Ravensbrück" (Czech, 800).

Four A.M.

"Raus! Raus!"

They wake us with watery tea and a crust of bread. I cannot remember when we ate last, then I recall it was the Polish woman.

Is this for life or is it for death?

NEÜSTADT GLEWE

We are in Ravensbrück for a few days, but there are so many of us and such little food that they decide to divide the camp up. The thumbs choose Danka, Dina, and me; I look around for Janka, Mania, and Lentzi, but they're not in our group. I don't know where they are. Danka, Dina, and I are piled into a flatbed truck, clinging to each other. Are they taking us to the gas? The flatbeds cross out under the gates of Ravensbrück and turn west; they are moving us again. We lean against the wood sides of the truck, jostling into one another. The road is full of potholes and bumps. Danka and I avoid looking at the girl-women riding with us. We are too tired to care where they're taking us or why; we just want to rest and eat.

We arrive at Neüstadt Glewe, get counted, and are handed pieces of bread.[1] At least we don't have to sleep on the floor here. In the morning we stand at roll call and quickly notice that there is no crematorium in this camp. There is a mound of bodies, though, about six feet high. The smell in camp is of decaying rather than burning flesh.

We are marched through the middle of town to work. The townspeople come out of their shops and homes to spit at us as we pass. The hatred in their eyes is dismaying; we are not human beings to them, we are lower than dogs. At the edge of town we are

1. Neüstadt Glewe is approximately 132 kilometers northwest of Ravensbrück.

forced to dig trenches in an effort to stop the Allied forces. One would think the townspeople would be grateful for the work we do to protect them, but they spit at us that evening as well. We get another crust of bread and half a bowl of tea that night; that is all the food we are given. Rations are shrinking before our eyes. The Germans are losing the war.

For a month we are chased out of dreamless sleep and marched through town, and every morning, every night we are spit at as we pass. We wake. We get counted. We march. We dig. We eat. We starve. We wonder if it will ever end.

Four A.M.

"Raus! Raus!" We stand at attention for roll call and are then dismissed.

"It isn't Sunday, is it?"

"I don't think so." Part of the camp continues to work at an airplane factory; the rest of us have nothing to do. Rumors circulate that we won't be working anymore.

"The Allies must be close," our whispers speculate. "Maybe the war is almost over." We hope this is true, but after the death march, we know better than to put any hope in this desire. They could move us again to another prison if they wanted to. They could march us to Madagascar.

The lull of not working and spending all day behind the fences is enough to drive me crazy. I notice that the pile of bodies lying behind the barracks in camp is getting larger and I learn from the other prisoners that many of these women were arrested after the Warsaw Uprising. They are Jews and Poles, left to rot together outside without even a ditch to be buried in.

I go to the camp elder and say, "With no other work in camp to do, I was wondering if you might give us permission to bury the bodies of these few hundred women?"

"Jawohl," she says. "I'll give you a hand wagon. Choose nine

others to help you. You start tomorrow morning. I'll assign two SS men to escort you." I make a note: she has a green triangle on her uniform, she is a murderer.

I ask for volunteers for this leichenkommando. Danka and Dina volunteer, as well as seven other girls. Covering our noses, we take the cart out to the mound of bodies. "We don't have gloves, so we must be careful," I warn the girls. "Only touch the arms and legs, and be very careful of any open wounds. We can't wash our hands before we eat, so we must be very careful so that we don't get sick." I take the arms while another girl takes the legs, and we swing a corpse onto the cart. It sighs as the last air is expelled from its lungs.

We falter. "Come on, *schnell!*" The guards yell. We load the cart as quickly as possible, about fifteen bodies. Then we begin our march to the burial place. Across the road is a men's camp of Italian political prisoners.

"Not much longer! Not much longer!" they shout as we walk by. We do not have a radio in camp; the news of the world has been cut off from us. We stare at these wild-eyed men; they do not look crazy, just desperate for freedom. "Not much longer! Not much longer!" Can they be right? How far away is not much longer?

The SS take us up a hill. The cart is heavy and we strain our muscles to keep it moving. It figures they would choose a burial site that is difficult to reach.

"You will bury them here." The guards stop, pointing to the area where we should dig, then they move away to rest on their rifles.

I thrust my shovel into the soil. It's rock-hard. We try to dig deep, as we're supposed to, but it is impossible. I get in the hole to dig out the bottom. The soil is so unforgiving that it takes hours to dig the graves, though. Thoughts run through my head while I'm in the hole trying to dig a little deeper; the SS could just shoot us and we'd fall in having dug our own graves.

"Help me out," I call to the girls above. A hand reaches over the side; it's my sister pulling me up out of the pit.

"I don't like seeing you in there," she murmurs.

"I don't like being in there." I mean it, too. This is so difficult and we are so weak. But finally we get all the holes dug and the bodies are put to rest in unmarked graves. We stand on the hill, the sun slowly sinking toward the horizon.

"Let's say a prayer for the women we've buried," I whisper. There is a unanimous nod. Over the mounds of fresh dirt we say a prayer. The guards do not notice our stillness, our silence. It is very important to me to give these women who have died some sacred ground in recognition of their lives. The prayer make us feel good, and there is not much that does that. We walk wearily down the hill back toward camp. We have worked hard today and buried only fifteen women, and the mound of bodies still in camp looks no smaller for all our effort. I am sorry that I volunteered us for this job.

"Do you think I could sneak some potatoes from the pile and get something to eat?" I ask Dina one Sunday afternoon. The portions are getting smaller and we can no longer count on getting both soup and bread every day.

"I heard that the camp elder killed a girl for stealing a potato when she went out to get coal; she made the girl empty the bucket and there it was. She kicked the girl until she fell on the ground, threw a board on top of her, and jumped on the board until she was dead," someone tells me.

"Oh my God."

"Don't do anything to make this camp elder mad," another girl-woman adds. "She killed her husband and her in-laws. She's insane."

I shudder but am still enamored by the thought of trying to get two potatoes without getting caught. I am more capable than the girl who is now dead. I know I can do it.

The mound of bodies does not get smaller very quickly. The first week we bury about eighty bodies, but new ones have been added to the top of the heap.

The SS men who take us to the burial site are old and tired and mean. We do not fear them as much as we feared the younger, stronger SS men in Auschwitz-Birkenau, though. "I think we should devise a plan to overcome them. Knock them out," one of the girls from our kommando suggests.

"We could hit them on the head with our shovels and throw them in a really deep grave so they couldn't get out. Then we could escape!"

"Yah!" Their eyes dance with the thought of rebellion.

"I can't kill anyone," I whisper.

"Not kill—we'll just stun them."

"Think about it." I look at their fervored faces. "First of all, think how hard it'd be to make a hole that deep—we'd kill ourselves trying. Second, we're in Germany. There's not one German in this town who would help a Pole, let alone a Jew. Do you think it will be different elsewhere in this country? They hate us. If we were in Poland it would be different, we might be able to count on our own people to help us escape. But we're not. We don't even know where we are. How far is it to the Polish border? Which way should we walk?" No one can answer my questions. "We would be caught and killed by villagers, or by the SS. Besides, my guess is we're far from any borders."

Their faces fall with disappointment.

"Maybe the Italians are right and it won't be long now. Maybe we'll be freed soon."

"Maybe." No one really believes it, though.

We have started putting two or three bodies in each grave. Our strength is failing fast with the lack of food and the terrible conditions in camp. Pushing the cart up the hill is a chore we can barely accomplish. The chance of overpowering the old men is slipping away as quickly as our weight and our hope that liberation will come soon. The lower the pile of bodies gets, the worse it gets for us, because it is spring and the bodies are beginning to decompose. There are fresh bodies on top now, too, so it's hard to tell until you touch one how long it's been lying there. Some of them we have to leave or they will fall apart. We're very careful not to disturb the very old, decaying bodies.

I wake, huddling in our bunk alone. Was it another nightmare that woke me? Rain falls on the roof overhead. The sky above us rumbles and clashes as violently as if God were at war rather than mankind. Where is Danka? She is terrified of thunderstorms. Mama used to light candles and say a prayer during electrical storms in Tylicz. There are no candles here. I stare through the darkness, unable to tell whether she is in the block or not. Other eyes shine in the dark. Finally the storm overhead moves on. I wonder if its rain has fallen on Allied as well German heads. The door creaks open and my sister steps inside. Like a mirage she glimmers in the dark. Her red hair, finally growing back after several months of not being shaved, frames her face.

"Where have you been?" I cannot tell if her cheeks are wet from tears or rain. She shakes her head, silent. "Danka, what were you doing?" I demand.

"Praying," she whispers hoarsely. "I was outside praying that the lightning would strike me dead so I wouldn't be hungry anymore."

We get in late one night, after the bread has been handed out, and there is nothing left for those of us who have worked all day. I volunteer to get a bucket of coals for the block elder to put in the stove. Danka and Dina send me a warning glance. I ignore them both. At the pile of coal I check the vicinity, grab two potatoes, and thrust them under the coal in the bucket. Head forward, eyes down, I walk slowly across the compound.

"Let me see you empty that bucket on the ground." I freeze.

Turning slowly around, I come face to face with the camp elder herself. "Well?"

Trembling, I spill the contents out, hoping the potatoes are covered by enough coal dust to be masked amidst the odd-shaped lumps of coal.

"You stole potatoes!" She hits me in the left eye before I can even think to duck. She throws me on the ground, kicking me, stomping on me with her boots, trying to tear the flesh from my bones with her fingernails. I cannot see anything but the blazing hatred in her face; it is the face of Death itself. She loses her grasp on me for a second. I scramble away, fleeing across camp. "Thief! Thief! *Scheiss-Jude!* Get back here you filthy dog!" Her voice follows my tracks like a bloodhound hot on the trail. I vanish behind the blocks, dodging searchlights and the madwoman's screaming voice. Under the cover of darkness I slip into one of the other blocks.

"I stole a potato and she's going to kill me for sure," I whisper into the dark.

"Come here." I hear a friendly anonymous voice and quickly crawl in between two bodies, hiding under their blanket. We can hear her for at least an hour yelling, "Come out you miserable *mist biene!* Come out here! You can't hide forever. I'm going to get you!" Finally she quiets down. I wait for a little bit longer just to make sure she's not hiding somewhere and then slip out of the bunk I've hidden in. "Thank you for saving my life," I whisper to the girls whose faces I do not know, then creep back across camp so she won't know which block has hidden me. I cannot see out of my left eye at all. Stealthily I thread my way through shadows and along walls until I reach our block. I slip into bed with Danka.

"Oh, Rena. What's going to happen?"

"I don't know." We hold each other all night, sobbing, both of us shaking in terror. This is it. I am done for. That is all I know and all either of us can think about. There is nothing we can do but cling to each other for the last time. I will never survive roll call with this black eye. My teeth chatter from the chill of fear, the fear of death itself. Liberation is so close, and now this. Danka will be alone in the world after the camp elder gets through with me. We do not sleep at all.

"*Raus! Raus!*"

Danka and I line up in the very back of the rows. The camp elder stalks across the front rows, screaming and cursing us.

"Anyone who knows who stole the potatoes last night should turn the prisoner in immediately. If I find out you are withholding information from me I will kill you instead. Who knows who stole the potatoes?" No one moves, no one makes a sound. The SS women walk up and down the rows counting each prisoner, looking for me. Surely the camp elder saw my face and recognized me as the one from the leichenkommando. She'll see me and kill me. I stand in the back trying not to tremble, trying to be brave.

"You'd better turn yourself in! You'd better come out!" the SS yell. No one says a word, no one lets them know where I am. An SS woman comes down our row, counting us, inspecting us, looking for me.

Suddenly I feel very calm and warm. There is the slightest tingle on my cheek as if someone has touched my face. *Mama?*

She is just a few prisoners away. I am warm and comforted. *Remember how you escaped Mengele.* I remember—I told Danka we were invisible and we were. All of my fear drains through the heels of my feet into the earth and I stand confident that I am imperceptible. *Mama is here, standing next to me, holding her hand over my eye.* The SS woman looks at me, counts me, and turns away. Danka sighs.

Protect me through the gate, Mama, I pray. I still have to march out with the bodies, and the camp elder is always standing there, counting the bodies, checking our numbers. I pretend to be rearranging the bodies in the back of the cart, making sure there is an arm obscuring my eye so she can't see my face and won't recognize me.

Every morning I feel a warm tingle on my cheeks as the SS walk right past my black-and-blue, swollen eye. Every morning I fumble with the bodies while we take them out the gate, and every morning I pass unseen under the nose of the camp elder.

How long can this go on? For six days I hide from the murderess, and she never sees my face. They don't see me because they are blinded by prejudice. We all look alike to them. We have the identity of shit—*scheiss-Judes, mist bienes.*

❖   ❖   ❖

May 2, 1945.
Four A.M. We wake up automatically and step into the dawn nervously, wondering what new trick this is that our captors are playing. There is no roll call. There is no one but us in camp, just one lone guard still in the watchtower. Not one SS woman, no wardress, no camp elder anywhere to be seen. We stand on the camp road gazing at the guard in the watchtower, wondering what to do. He is the only thing between us and freedom, and his gun is aimed directly at us. I look at my watch. It's ten o'clock. How long must we wait here when freedom is laughing just on the other side of these gates?

A mother and daughter decide they are hungry enough to brave getting to the pile of potatoes. They run across camp toward the only food left. A gunshot rips through the girl's heart. She collapses. Her mother screams, rending her clothes and cursing God. No one dares to go comfort her. A second shot rips her throat out. Lamentations. Their bodies taint that fatal pile of potatoes. The sweet taste of freedom grows bitter in our mouths.

The SS in the watchtower finally climbs down and disappears. At eleven o'clock the Italians from the prison camp down the road shout outside our fences: "We're free!"

They have rubber gloves and wire cutters. "Come on! Storm the gates!" They sever the wires, breaking the electrical current and leaving a hole big enough for us to tear through. I grab

Danka's hand, dragging her through the fence. We have bloody hands from the barbs we push out of the way. My sweater catches on the wire. I do not stop. It rips. I do not care.

Suddenly we are on the road. We blink, unable to believe our eyes. Soldiers dressed in dark green and olive, Russian and American soldiers are coming toward us.

"We're free!" We hug each other, crying. "We are free!" My heart is a stone in a river of tears.

The girls from camp disperse down the roads. There are girls going this way and that, all in confusion, all lost, trying to decide which way is home. Danka and a small group of girl-women watch me as if I should know what to do.

We walk for a little while until we reach a crossroads. Danka, Dina, and I stop and look down the two paths. One goes east, to the Russians and eventually to Poland; the other goes west, to the Americans. I do not know which way to turn. The sun is gold and brilliant, burning through the layers of obscurity in my mind. My fog begins to lift.

I see Mama's figure in the distance. Her babushka has fallen from her head, her arm is waving more slowly now. Which way should we go, Mama? . . . She is no longer running through the snow; the long winter has melted into spring. Go west, Rena. She pulls her babushka back up around her head and blows me a kiss. Don't go, Mama. Wait for me. I brought you the baby back! . . .

Good-bye, Rena. You are a good daughter. I stand in the middle of the crossroads waving to the vision that has kept me alive. Mama!

She stands there for one brief moment, her arm still in the air. Good-bye. Her image shatters into a thousand shards of light. My eyes wince with pain as the slivers of glass fall from my eyes. The dream is gone. There is no one to go home to anymore.

EPILOGUE

On the "American side of Germany," Dina, Rena, and Danka were
taken to the city of Ludwigslust by an American major. He was so
moved by their ordeal that he took them to a mansion in the occupied town and ordered the housekeeper to treat the girls like royalty,
give them the best rooms, and serve them breakfast in bed. This respite was like a dream, but the real world was not far away; after a
few days they were moved to a refugee camp and then to Holland.
In Holland, they were put in a hospital and almost sent back to Germany because they had no papers. Rena went to the major in
charge and begged him, on her knees, not to send them back to Germany. He took special consideration for their case and sent them to
the Dutch Red Cross, hoping they could find a place for the girls.
(On the morning they were moved, Dina was separated from the
rest of the group.)

John Gelissen, commander of Red Cross Relief Team No. 10,
gave Rena and her sister jobs helping Dutch citizens get home after
being released from forced labor camps in Germany. The girls were
given a room with cots to sleep on and three meals a day. Taking
them under his wing, John acted as friend, psychologist, and care-
taker, gradually coaxing them back from their ordeal. He treated
them like women—not prisoners, not victims, but real women.

"We hoarded bread under our cots until it got moldy," Rena remembers, "and John had to take me aside and say, 'You will never lack for bread again.' Slowly, we began to believe him."

They worked at the Red Cross for several months before joining a Jewish youth group that hoped to emigrate to Israel. Rena and Danka decided to stay in Holland, though, because they had fallen in love with Dutchmen—Rena with the Red Cross commander. On July 29, 1947, two years after the war, Rena Kornreich married John Gelissen.

Rena and John emigrated to the United States in 1954. They have four children, Sylvia, Joseph, Peter, and Robert, and three grandchildren, Shaun, Julia, and Zachary John. They have retired in the Blue Ridge Mountains of North Carolina, which remind Rena of the Carpathian Mountains in Poland.

"I found a good husband and have a good life . . . but I will never forget. Every year on May second John gives me white and red carnations, to celebrate the anniversary of our liberation. *This day is more important than your birthday*, he writes, *because without this day there would be no birthdays to celebrate. Love, John*."

Danka married Elie Brandel in 1948, and emigrated to the United States in 1951. They have two children, Norman and Sara, and five grandchildren—Andrew, Eric, Jamie, Jenna, and Adam. **Gertrude** (Rena's oldest sister) emigrated to the United States in 1921. She married David Shane and had one son, Irvin. All of the family photographs from before the war come from Gertrude, who died in New York in 1994 at the age of eighty-eight. Rena has no idea what fate befell **Zosia** and her children, **Herschel** and **Ester Stuhr**. Despite efforts to locate the children in hopes they had been hidden in a Christian orphanage, Rena was never able to find her niece or nephew. Any information about their fates would be appreciated. It is believed that **Nathan Stuhr**, Zosia's husband, was lost in Siberia.

The fate of **Sara** and **Chaim Kornreich** is unknown. Rena believes that they were among the one and a half million Jews exterminated in the gas chambers of Auschwitz. According to **Alex** (Joseph's son), the Jews forced to leave Tylicz for Florynka—**Joseph**, his family, and the Kornreichs—were transferred to Grybów, Poland. Alex escaped from Grybów and fled to Slovakia where he worked in the resistance. While working for the underground he heard reports that the Jews in Grybów were forced into the Nowy Sacz ghetto or put into vans and gassed. Alex survived the war; he has one son and two daughters and lives in New York City.

Dina was separated from Danka and Rena in a military compound in Holland; she emigrated to France, is married, and has one son. **Erna** and **Fela Drenger** survived Auschwitz and emigrated to Israel. There were twenty-five Jewish families who lived in Tylicz before the war; none lives there now.

Frania Kieblesz, one of Rena's best friends, still lives in Tylicz. She has nine children. What happened to **Tolek**, from Muszynka, Poland, is unknown. After saving Rena and her father, according to the rumor in Tylicz at the time, Officer **Hans Joskch** was transferred to the Russian front.

Because of the coat she found in "Canada," Rena believes that **Jacob** and **Regina Schützer** were exterminated in the gas chambers at Auschwitz. Rena does not know whether their daughter, **Cili Schützer**, escaped from Slovakia and survived the Holocaust. The family Rena was staying with when she turned herself in, the **Silbers**, were able to escape from Slovakia and emigrated to America.

What became of the kapos **Emma** and **Erika** is unknown.

Of the men prisoners who helped Rena and Danka little is known: **Heniek** and **Bolek**, **Stasiu** (Artista), and **Tadziu** (Wisniewski, the water pump operator) were Polish citizens. While Rena does not know if they survived or if they are still alive, she would like to thank them, wherever they are, for helping save her life and her sister's. **Marek Sterenberg** did survive the death march; he never made it to America, though. He stayed in Poland and became a guard over Nazi prisoners, the very men who had tortured and brutalized him. In retaliation he took vengeance on his former captors. Marek was overpowered and disarmed by one of the SS prisoners, and shot to death.

After the death march, **Janka** was separated from Rena and Danka in Ravensbrück. She survived the war and is married and lives in Germany. Rena does not know what happened to **Mania** and **Lentzi**, who were also separated from Rena and Danka in Ravensbrück. It is not known what happened to **Aranka**.

Andrzej Garbera saved many lives, including Rena's; he died a war hero at the age of twenty-three. In 1990, Rena returned to Poland for the first time since the war and was finally able to place flowers on his grave.

Of the SS Rena came into contact with, especially the lesser-ranking SS, little is known. The following information has been compiled for the reader's information from various sources, including two survivors' personal accounts.

"It is estimated that [**Carl Clauberg**] conducted sterilization experiments on about 700 women. In 1948 he was tried in the Soviet Union and sentenced to 25 years in prison. Freed in an amnesty in 1955, he returned to Kiel in the German Federal Republic, boasting of his 'scientific achievements.' Only after the Central Council of Jews denounced him was he arrested, in November 1955; he died in August 1957, shortly before his trial was to begin" (Czech, 810). **Josef Mengele** was "accused of selections, fatal injections (phenol), shootings, beatings, and other forms of deliberate killing" and the suspicion was raised that "he threw newborn infants directly into the crematoriums and into open fires. . . . For over twenty years Mengele was able to evade all extradition attempts; he died in a swimming accident in Brazil in 1979" (Czech, 819).

"**Heinrich Himmler** . . . used terror and force against the opponents of the Third Reich and transformed his fanatical race ideology into concrete politics and organization—like the system of the concentration camps. . . . At the end of the war, Himmler tried to escape capture disguised as an army private; after his discovery and arrest, he committed suicide on May 23, 1945. . . . **Rudolf Höss** (SS Lieutenant Colonel) . . . was named Commandant of Auschwitz in 1940. Characterized as an assiduous, petit bourgeois executive, he organized mass murder with technical and administrative meticulousness. Arrested in 1946, he testified at the Nuremberg Trial . . . and was extradited to Poland in May of that year. In April 1947 he was sentenced to be hanged and was executed on the grounds of the camp [Auschwitz]" (Czech, 814).

"Among the SS supervisors, Mandel, Taube, Drexler, and Hasse distinguished themselves in their savage treatment of women prisoners" (Strezelecka, 396). **Margot Drexler** finished the war in Bergen-Belsen. There is a survivor's account that on the day of liberation female prisoners dragged her into the latrine and held her head under the sewage; this account does not confirm whether she died or not, or if she was ever put on trial for war crimes. **Irma Grese** was put on trial at the Bergen-Belsen war crimes trials and was sentenced to death by hanging for torturing and assaulting prisoners (source: Gutman, 1499). **Maria Mandel** was put on trial for war crimes and sentenced to death by a Polish court. She was executed in December 1947 (source: Rittner and Roth, 29). It is unknown whether her sister, Elisabeth Hasse, was ever held accountable for her actions, or what happened to **Maria Mullenders**.

Of Reporting Officer **Anton Taube** and his cohort **Stibitz**, it is unknown whether or not either of these SS men was ever held accountable for their "calisthenics" and other murderous actions in Auschwitz.

ACKNOWLEDGMENTS

We would like to thank the following people for their belief in us and their support: John, for his calm assurance throughout this project, making sure we took lunch breaks, providing Dutch jokes, and for being the wonderful husband he is; Danka, for surviving and letting us share her part in her sister's story; Karen, for her unconditional love and belief in us—for being a maid when she could have been working on her own art and for encouraging Heather to take this project on; Corrine Johnson, for introducing us; Dr. Annette Allen, for the hours she spent discussing the initial drafts, her insight and help in refining the accepted manuscript, and the beautiful poem she wrote for this book; speed-reader extraordinaire Joanne Pankow, for proofing the manuscript twice in thirty-six hours before it went to our agent, Sarah Jane; Sarah Jane Freymann, for having the courage to believe in a first-time author, representing us, and bringing this story to our publisher; Beacon Press, for publishing this story; our editor, Deb Chasman, for accepting this book in the first place, for seeing its potential and bringing that potential to the surface—it is her talent, empathy, love, and patience that brought this book to fruition; Chris Kochansky, our copy editor; Penny Niven and Gerald Jackson, for answering all those panicky phone calls and explaining the business of writing biography, editing, and getting published.

We would also like to thank Rena's children, Sylvia, Joseph, Peter, and Robert, for their enthusiasm; Carol Engel, Rena's confidant and dearest friend, who heard her story long ago and told her it should be a book; Elaine Grenata, for helping Rena cope with her memories;

Sara Cuneo, for asking Rena to tell her story twenty years ago and encouraging her to let the world know; Heather's mother and her brother, Loch, who read all three of the first versions and helped put the project in perspective; Vincent Bridges, for introducing Heather to Corrine and telling Heather to write; Tamara and the Telberg family, for the attic and everything else; Olivia Vlahos, who was the first person to invite Rena to speak to her students back when no one wanted to listen; Patricia Raskin, for putting us on TV for the first time; Liz Bergstone, for the Mac; the gang at Franklin's Printing, for all those copies! We would also like to thank Dean Patterson, Dr. Clauss, and all of the teachers, office staff, and students at Salem College who welcomed us into their community and gave this story its first public reception.

BIBLIOGRAPHY

Bartlett, Neil, et al., eds. *McGraw-Hill Encyclopedia of Science & Technology.* 7th ed. Vol. 17. New York: McGraw-Hill, 1992.

Czech, Danuta. *Auschwitz Chronicles 1939–1945.* London: I. B. Tauris, 1990.

Gutman, Yisrael, ed. *Encyclopedia of the Holocaust.* 4 vols. New York: Macmillan, 1990.

Hellman, Peter. *The Auschwitz Album.* New York: Random House, 1981.

Langer, Lawrence L. *Holocaust Testimonies: The Ruins of Memory.* New Haven: Yale University Press, 1991.

Posner, Gerald L., and Ware, John. *Mengele: The Complete Story.* New York: McGraw-Hill, 1986.

Rittner, Carol, and Roth, John K., eds. "Prologue: Women and the Holocaust" and "Chronology." *Women and the Holocaust: Different Voices.* New York: Paragon, 1993.

Strezlecka, Irena. "Women." *Anatomy of the Auschwitz Death Camp.* Yisrael Gutman and Michael Berenbaum, eds. Bloomington: Indiana University Press, 1994.

Wyman, David, ed. *Bombing Auschwitz and the Auschwitz Escapees' Report.* Vol. 12, *America and the Holocaust.* New York: Garland, 1990.